The Roman Mithras Cult

Scientific Studies of Religion: Inquiry and Explanation

Series editors: Donald Wiebe, Luther H. Martin and William W. McCorkle

Scientific Studies of Religion: Inquiry and Explanation publishes cutting-edge research in the new and growing field of scientific studies in religion. Its aim is to publish empirical, experimental, historical and ethnographic research on religious thought, behaviour and institutional structures.

The series works with a broad notion of 'scientific' that will include innovative work on understanding religion(s), both past and present. With an emphasis on the cognitive science of religion, the series includes complementary approaches to the study of religion, such as psychology and computer modelling of religious data. Titles seek to provide explanatory accounts for the religious behaviours under review, both past and present.

The Attraction of Religion, edited by D. Jason Slone and James A. Van Slyke
Contemporary Evolutionary Theories of Culture and the Study of Religion, Radek Kundt
Death Anxiety and Religious Belief, Jonathan Jong and Jamin Halberstadt
New Patterns for Comparative Religion, William E. Paden
Religion Explained?, edited by Luther H. Martin and Donald Wiebe
Religion in Science Fiction, Steven Hrotic
The Mind of Mithraists, Luther H. Martin

The Roman Mithras Cult:
A Cognitive Approach

Olympia Panagiotidou with Roger Beck

BLOOMSBURY ACADEMIC
LONDON • NEW YORK • OXFORD • NEW DELHI • SYDNEY

BLOOMSBURY ACADEMIC
Bloomsbury Publishing Plc
50 Bedford Square, London, WC1B 3DP, UK
1385 Broadway, New York, NY 10018, USA

BLOOMSBURY, BLOOMSBURY ACADEMIC and the Diana logo are
trademarks of Bloomsbury Publishing Plc

First published 2017
Paperback edition first published 2019

Copyright © Olympia Panagiotidou with Roger Beck, 2017

Olympia Panagiotidou and Roger Beck have asserted their rights under the
Copyright, Designs and Patents Act, 1988, to be identified as Authors of this work.

Cover image © Shutterstock

All rights reserved. No part of this publication may be reproduced or
transmitted in any form or by any means, electronic or mechanical, including
photocopying, recording, or any information storage or retrieval system,
without prior permission in writing from the publishers.

Bloomsbury Publishing Plc does not have any control over, or responsibility for,
any third-party websites referred to or in this book. All internet addresses given in this
book were correct at the time of going to press. The author and publisher regret
any inconvenience caused if addresses have changed or sites have ceased to
exist, but can accept no responsibility for any such changes.

A catalogue record for this book is available from the British Library.

Library of Congress Cataloging-in-Publication Data
Names: Panagiotidou, Olympia, author.
Title: The Roman Mithras cult : a cognitive approach /Olympia Panagiotidou,
with Roger Beck.
Description: 1 [edition]. | New York : Bloomsbury Academic, 2019. | Series:
Scientific studies of religion: inquiry and explanation | Includes
Bibliographical references and index.
Identifiers: LCCN 2017036764| ISBN 9781472567413 (hardback)| ISBN
9781472567390(nippod)
Subjects: LCSH: Mithraism. | Rome–Religion. | Mysteries, Religious–Rome. |
Mithras(Zoroastrian deity)–Cult.
Classification: LCC BL1585 .P36 2019 | DDC 299/.15–dc23LC record available at https://lccn.
loc.gov/2017036764

ISBN: HB: 978-1-4725-6741-3
PB: 978-1-4725-6739-0
ePDF: 978-1-4725-6738-3
ePub: 978-1-4725-6740-6

Series: Scientific Studies of Religion: Inquiry and Explanation

Typeset by RefineCatch Limited, Bungay, Suffolk

To find out more about our authors and books visit
www.bloomsbury.com and sign up for our newsletters.

For Maria

Contents

List of Figures		viii
Preface		ix
	Introduction	1
1	The World View of the Mithras Cult	17
2	The Self in the Cult of Mithras	31
3	Space and Time in the Mithras Cult	69
4	The Scene of the Tauroctony as a Symbol System	115
5	The Communities of Mithraists: From Personal Self to Social Identity	141
	Conclusion	165
Notes		171
References		199
Index		223

Figures

2.1	Mithraeum of Santa Maria Capua Vetere	44
2.2	Mithraic vessel from the mithraeum of Mainz	45
2.3	Grades and planets	49
2.4	From higher to lower planets and grades	52
2.5	Planets and grades hierarchy	53
3.1	The celestial sphere	93
3.2	Mithraeum at Vulci	100
3.3	Sette Sfere Mithraeum	101
3.4	Plan of the Sette Sfere Mithraeum	102
3.5	Köln vessel	104
4.1	Tauroctony fresco	121
4.2	Tauroctony relief	121
4.3	Marble statue of tauroctony	122

Preface

This book suggests a cognitive approach to the Graeco-Roman cult of Mithras and especially to the ways in which initiates in the Mithraic mysteries would have experienced their initiations – experiences that would have in turn influenced their wider world view. Beginning with my theoretical premise that we (i.e. moderns) and past agents (e.g. Mithraists) are all human – sounds so obvious! – and moved by my desire to better understand those people in the Graeco-Roman world who chose to participate in the Mithras cult, I found in (neuro-)cognitive studies valuable tools that could help me understand Mithraists' perceptions, conceptions, and even thoughts and emotions during their lived experiences of initiation and participation in the cult.

I realize that my approach may generate some controversy among scholars of religion(s), especially classicists or even cognitivists. The application of modern cognitive theories to past religious institutions has raised a debate regarding the extent to which we can use findings from research in the cognition of modern people in order to decode the minds of people who lived in the past. However, though it is impossible for us to come into direct contact with dead people, I believe that we can use insights into the human cognition in order to generate well-educated guesses about the underlying cognitive processes of past agents' cultural expressions and social interactions and would have been anchored on the material remains preserved today (e.g. artefacts, written testimony). In this light, I approached the material remains of the Mithras cult as traces of the Mithraists' mental representations that I attempted to reconstruct based mainly on probabilities and fragmentary evidence. In other words, in this book I do not propose definitive answers to the historical questions pertaining to the Mithras cult. Mainly I suggest statements about what would have been more or less likely to make 'sense' to the initiates and what would fit the facts of the Mithras cult as we know them. Therefore, readers of this book will not find extended explanations of the preserved historical data, not even interpretations of the symbolic systems and visual representations developed in the Mithraic cult context. Rather, readers will find mainly insights into the underlying processes that could have generated multiple interpretations of the cult visual imagery and symbolic representations as well as the attribution of meanings and significance to personal experiences of initiation.

A concurrence of fortunate circumstances and the contributions of certain individuals led to the publication of this research in the Mithraists' world view.

The original idea was conceived on the occasion of two important events that occurred in 2006. The first of these events was a conference that took place in Thessaloniki during which I had my initial contact with cognitive theories through a talk given by Armin W. Geertz, a pioneer in the study of cognition, culture and religion at Aarhus University. The second was the publication of Roger Beck's monograph *The Religion of the Mithras Cult in the Roman Empire: Mysteries of the Unconquered Sun* (Oxford: Oxford University Press, 2006), which introduced a cognitive approach to the Graeco-Roman cult of Mithras focusing on the initiates' apprehension and experience of the Mithraic symbol systems. These two stimulating events gave rise to my interest in the cognitive processes that could have underlain the initiatory experiences of Mithraists, providing them with a new world view, and were followed by the good fortune for me to personally meet and work with the two scholars that greatly influenced my thought and work.

Firstly, I am grateful to Armin W. Geertz for endorsing my idea to apply a cognitive approach to the world view of Mithraists and for illuminating a path for the application of cognitive theories to the Mithras cult. Then and foremost, I was greatly honoured when Roger Beck, a specialist in Mithraism and conversant with the cognitive study of religion (CSR), agreed to be the co-author of the Introduction and of Chapters 1 and 2 of this volume. Although he was actually involved in the writing up to the second chapter, I consider his wider contribution invaluable, since his deep acquaintance with the Mithras cult and his open mindedness enriched my knowledge and inspired me to look for further insights into the Mithraists' cognition, insights that I developed throughout the rest of the book. Wishing to pay tribute to him, I keep using the first-person plural pronoun (we) throughout this book, hoping that my approach will find him favourably disposed.

As it will be apparent to anyone reading this book, I also owe a great debt to Luther H. Martin, whose work constituted for me an endless source of inspiration. Martin, being a pioneer in the application of cognitive theories to Mithraism and of cognitive historiography in general, provided me with great insights into what cognitive sciences can offer to historical studies and how historians can use the findings of research in human cognition in order to enrich their knowledge of past people's minds. I am grateful to him not only for his writings but also for his encouragement and permanent willingness to read my manuscript providing me with valuable comments and suggestions.

I am also deeply indebted to Martin as well as to Donald Wiebe and William W. McCorkle, the editors of Scientific Studies of Religion: Inquiry and Explanation Series by Bloomsbury Academic, for the publication of this book. I am grateful to them for believing in me and supporting my work. For the publication, I would also like to thank Lalle Pursglove, Senior Commissioning Editor, and Lucy Carroll, Editorial Assistant at Bloomsbury, for their cooperation and assistance during the writing and submission of the manuscript.

I also owe special gratitude to my teacher at Aristotle University, Panayotis Pachis. The idea for this book would have not led to publication without his support and encouragement to get involved in cognitive studies and to apply a cognitive approach to Mithraism.

For the preparation of this volume, I would like to thank the Institute for the Advanced Study of Religion, Toronto, for a grant for editorial assistance. For the final version of the book I owe special thanks to Steven Hrotic, who read through my manuscript, polishing the language and providing me with valuable comments and suggestions. Needless to say, all errors and oversights remaining are entirely my own.

Last but not least, this book would have not be written and completed without the support of my family, which has always been my rock and inspiration. I am deeply thankful to my father, Zafeiris, and my brother Vasilis, who always believe in me, tolerate me and inspire me to follow my dreams. My heartfelt thanks I offer to my husband Nikos for standing beside me throughout writing this book, for reading my writings and offering me his insights and unlimited love and support, and for making the drawings of this volume (Figures 3.1 and 3.4). I also thank my little daughter Melia for being quiet when it was necessary and for making me laugh the rest of the day. Foremost, I am especially grateful to my mother Maria, who experienced all of the ups and downs of my research, who always showed me the positive even in the most negative aspects, who motivated me to transcend my fears and limits and to proceed beyond the average. For this and so many other reasons this book is dedicated to her.

Olympia Panagiotidou
Thessaloniki
12 January 2017

Introduction

I.1 Empire and cult

For anyone proposing, as we do, to study the *cognition* of participants in a long-dead enterprise in a long-dead culture, any description or historical narrative must be very tentative. Otherwise, one risks begging the question of what it was that these participants got to know or understand. Nevertheless, a brief sketch of the institution to be studied and its trajectory across space and time is needed at the outset, as source, content and product of these people's cognitive behaviours.

Here, then, is a provisional description of a historical cognitive space – that of the cult of the god Mithras – based on the extant data through which we moderns in our turn can get to understand the enterprise and its participants. This cult flourished in the Roman Empire during the second and third centuries of the common era; although threatened and diminished, it endured through the fourth. Remains of the cult have been found in every part of the Empire, but their distribution is quite uneven, with particular concentrations (1) in the capital city of Rome and its port, Ostia, at the mouth of the Tiber; and (2) in the Empire's European frontier zones along the Rhine and Danube rivers.[1] The Empire's more populous eastern half (Asia Minor, Syria, Egypt) is by contrast under-represented, although to date it is unclear if this reflects lesser appeal of the cult in these areas, or archaeological contingencies such as less accessible sites.

The term 'cult', applied in an ancient context, carries none of the pejorative connotations nor the implications of eccentricity implied when applied to modern religious phenomena. Nor is the modern distinction between a 'cult' and a 'sect' applicable to the period discussed here.[2] 'Cult', in the ancient Graeco-Roman context, means *worship*, the worship of the gods in general or of a particular god or set of gods.[3] Thus, by 'the Mithras cult' we refer to the worship of the god Mithras; and by the 'Roman Mithras cult' we refer specifically to the worship of Mithras in the Roman Empire within the spatio-temporal parameters mentioned above. Further, since worship was always the business of an institution of one sort or another (state, city, voluntary association, kinship group), we also intend by 'the Mithras cult' the worshippers of Mithras collectively. The institutional form(s) taken by the collectivity of Roman Mithras worshippers will be outlined in due course.

Much of the worship of the gods was public business, conducted by priestly officials appointed, regulated, and to a large extent funded by state or city governments. Public worship was focused on temples, structures as conspicuous as the churches and cathedrals of Christendom which replaced them. The principal form of worship was open-air animal sacrifice, frequently supplemented by processions, pageantry, spectacle, and the witness of large crowds.[4] Vice versa, one might say that public 'spectacles' (Latin *spectacula*) such as chariot racing, gladiatorial games, and plays were supplemented by sacrifice and the public worship of the gods. This would be true only in the sense of proportion of time and money expended on particular activities, however: public spectacle was itself fundamentally worship of the gods, explicitly intended as such – as the Christians well understood when they boycotted all its public manifestations.

In contrast, the cult of Mithras was not a public cult. It was not an enterprise in which the governments of the Empire and its cities were formally invested. That is not to say that the authorities had no interest in it, just that they were not committed to ongoing formal relationships. Nor would it be true to say that the Mithraists, qua Mithraists, were unconcerned with the public good. On the contrary, numerous dedications 'for the well-being' (*pro salute*) of the emperors, the sincerity of which it would be absurd to question, attest the cultists' loyalty. Moreover, participation in cult activities and participation in other religious activities, including those of the public cults, were not mutually exclusive. Membership in the Mithras cult was a religious option, not a devotion to a single 'religion'.[5]

The Mithras cult was one of several 'mysteries', cults of *initiation* into a relationship with a deity or deities and thereby into a relationship with fellow initiates. In fact, the word 'mysteries' in Greek (*mystēria*) means 'initiations'.[6] Ancient mysteries may have been, but were not necessarily or essentially, *mysterious* in the modern sense of difficult to comprehend, or not straightforward. Moreover, they were *secretive* only in that they conveyed matters not to be divulged to the uninitiated outside. The Mithras cult is unique in the sense that worship was *only* via the mystery cult; there was no corresponding public cult as there was for Isis, for example. The mysteries of Mithras and the worship of Mithras within the Roman Empire were co-extensive (see Beck 2006a, citing Sfameni Gasparro 1985: 14).

The mystery cults in the Roman Empire are sometimes called the 'oriental' cults,[7] because, more often than not, they had their ultimate origins in non-Graeco-Roman cultures. Isis was worshipped in Egypt long before she was the focus of Graeco-Roman mysteries; likewise Mithras in Persia. Mithraists in the Empire knew of and took pride in their Persian antecedents. In fact, they did not consider them antecedents at all – they considered them their real origins. So, interestingly, did the outside world. That the Mithriaists were in some sense 'Persian' was one of the very few items of public knowledge concerning their cult in the Roman world.[8]

The supposed Persian origin of the mysteries of Mithras is well captured in an essay entitled 'On the cave of the nymphs in the *Odyssey*' by the third-century Neoplatonist Porphyry:

> The Persians [i.e. the Mithraists] perfect their initiate by inducting him into a mystery of the descent of souls and their exit back out again, calling the place a 'cave'. For Eubulus tells us that Zoroaster was the first to dedicate a natural cave in honour of Mithras, the creator and father of all; it was located in the mountains near Persia and had flowers and springs.
>
> *On the Cave* 6[9]

Porphyry's account is myth-as-history of a familiar sort: discover and locate the founder of the institution in question and fix the foundational event. Porphyry has much of real value to say about the mysteries of Mithras, but his myth of their origins can here be put aside. The Mithraists' perception of themselves as 'Persians' will be of interest to us in this study; the historical validity of this belief – how much was actually transmitted from East to West – is less so.[10] In the present study, we do not propose to offer a factual history of the transmission of Mithras-worship from East to West.[11] For us, the historical reality of the Mithras cult's Persian-ness was a matter of *perception and self-perception*. We shall therefore avoid, as unnecessarily ambiguous, the characterization of Mithraism as an 'oriental cult'.[12]

I.2 The cognitive approach to the study of religious phenomena

The formulation and application of cognitive theories has been one of the most promising developments in the study of cultural phenomena and the human minds that produce them. The movement began in the 1950s in the disciplines of linguistics and psychology,[13] and gradually attracted scholars across the humanities.[14] By the end of the twentieth century a study of religion based on cognitive theories developed into an interdisciplinary research enterprise, termed the 'cognitive science of religion' (CSR).[15] Researchers from a wide range of disciplines[16] are co-operating in order to study and better understand the interactions between the mind and its physical and cultural environments, producing studies that explain the apparent diversity of religion in terms of the common structures of the human mind.

In the wider intellectual context, the application of cognitive theories to certain religious phenomena originally attracted anthropologists and ethnographers, who are generally interested in the ways 'people perceive and categorize their social and natural worlds' (A. Geertz 2004a: 352). In the field of cognitive anthropological research, the various religious attitudes and practices are not treated as *sui generis*, as if they would require unique levels of analysis independent of the methods used by the natural and social sciences. Instead, religious phenomena are considered manifestations of human culture, and do not therefore presuppose the existence of dedicated cognitive and psychological processes disconnected with the other cognitive capacities of the human mind. The cognitive equipment shared by humans provides everything necessary to explain the creation, preservation and transmission of religious concepts and culture (see, e.g., Sperber 1996; Boyer 2002: 8; Guthrie 2002: 41–2; A. Geertz 2004a: 361).

From those research projects that employ cognitive theories to multiple religious systems, practices and institutions, there is a 'resounding' omission of historians of religion and theologians. In general, cognitive approaches have not been well received by historians of ancient polytheistic religions, and particularly not by mainstream classicists.[17] However, Luther H. Martin,[18] being a brilliant exception, has pointed out the value of cognitive approaches to past religious traditions, has criticized the field for failing to recognize this value, and outlined the possible ways of conciliation between history and cognitive sciences.[19]

Cognitive science focuses on human cognition: the functions that enable humans to *acquire, store, transform* and *use* knowledge of their surroundings.[20] Cognitive science uses specific methods and principles borrowed from natural sciences, such as evolutionary biology and psychology, neuroscience, neurobiology and brain science, as well as from research in the fields of computer technology, cybernetics and artificial intelligence (Martin 2012a: 43). The application of cognitive theories to anthropological, ethnographic, and even historical data lead to conclusions that are not exclusively based on theoretical

assumptions and interpretations, but supported by empirical evidence derived from experimental research. Cognitive theories focus on the mental devices and micro-processes within the human brain and body interacting with the environment that enable humans to survive, express themselves, and create cultural meanings.

Cognitive approaches to cultural phenomena do not, of course, reject traditional anthropological and historical research. On the contrary, acting in a complementary rather than competitive fashion, cognitive theories shift their interest from the study of *different* cultural systems, intellectual traditions, and social and natural conditions to the question of understanding the *common* cognitive structures and principles that govern human cognition, making possible human adaptation to multiple environments and the production of cultural diversity in the first place (see Martin 2004a: 7–16).

As Martin has repeatedly pointed out, cognitive theories may offer valuable insights into the work of historians and their data. History does not merely consist of accumulated knowledge about the past: it further refers to human affairs and those human actions and interactions that have formed the wider social, political, and economic conditions, as well as cultural expressions in different historical periods (see Whitehouse 2005: 307). As described by Martin (2005: 12), the people who lived and acted in the past constitute the *historical agents*; they created and participated in the *historical facts*, determined the unfolding of the events, and left certain material and written testimonies about their actions. The people who study the past (i.e. the historians) are also historical agents of their own right: they make inferences from the traces that humans of the past left in space and time within their own era, recounted as historical narratives. That is, they are 'historiographical' agents (Martin 2004a: 9, 2005: 12–13; see Gaddis 2002: 9, 33–36).[21]

Traditional approaches to history attempt to describe a past era through investigation of the social, political, cultural, economic etc., variables that constitute its 'ecological constraints' – constraints that shaped the representations of the people who lived in that era (Martin 2005: 13 citing Gaddis 2002: 53).

In this volume, we shall use the term 'representations' inclusively to cover both the private representations of individuals (thoughts, mental images etc.) and the public representations (artefacts, physical structures, texts, rituals etc.) of cultures and groups, especially of course religious groups, within those cultures. A religion may be described as a stream of representations descending in time: private representations that engender and shape public representations, that are in turn perceived by people engendering further private representations in their minds and so on. Streams of representations do not flow in isolation from each other. No thought was nor could ever have been a purely 'Mithraic' thought. Likewise, the characteristic image of Mithras slaying a bull in the so-called 'tauroctony' was not just a 'Mithraic' representation; it belongs too in the stream of icons of theophany and in countless other streams too.[22] Perhaps it would be better to imagine Mithraism – or for that matter any historical enterprise – not as a stream but as a particular current in the great river of human representations, a current that the historian distinguishes from the rest by dropping, as it were, a Mithaism-tagging phosphorescent dye into the river and noting the particular flows and eddies of representations which light up.[23]

Both the formation of any given sociocultural context and the academic study of this context are 'enabled' and constrained by the inherent cognitive abilities of the human species, which underlie human thought, reasoning and imagination. These 'cognitive constraints' are characteristically neglected by those researchers who do not investigate 'beneath the surface' of the historical events, those microprocesses within the human brain and body that mediate these events (Martin 2005: 13; see Gaddis 2002: 7, 33).

In particular, historians, driven by curiosity and the human tendency for imposing narrative causality on sequences of events[24] that extends to recounting the lives of their ancestors, generally attempt to reconstruct history as a linear narrative. Inevitably, this narrative reflects their own biases of systematization, integration, and coherence (Whitehouse 2005: 309–10). Humans' 'narrative minds' tend to organize their experiences, as well as information about events received from their surroundings and from other people, into causal accounts intended to cover or diminish the gaps in their knowledge (p. 312).[25]

Focusing only on the obvious results of the human actions that moved the historical developments and led to the formation of the present, historians often neglect the manifold dimensions of human thoughts, emotions, motivations and biases that caused the particular historical events they attempt to understand.[26] In most cases, the suggested theories transfer modern concepts and values to the historical agents of different periods. Gaps in historical knowledge are either filled or hidden by commonsensical assumptions made by scholars (Martin 2012b: 160).

Bypassing the conventional metaphors, typologies and concepts that enrich common sense shared by people of each era, cognitive approaches offer explanatory models and tested *a priori* assumptions to the historical approaches in order to explain the various historical forms on the basis of the 'common features of human cognition' (Martin 2005: 12). Thus, cognitive approaches offer a 'shared paradigm' to historical research (p. 15) that historians can use in order to suggest well-articulated explanations of various historical facts. These historical explanations can in turn enhance cognitive theories by confirming the applied theoretical models and allowing theoretical predictions about the course and impacts of particular events, beliefs and practices (Martin 2005: 15, 2012b: 167).[27]

A cognitive approach offers a more scientific method (i.e. based in and compatible with the 'natural' or 'physical' sciences) for explaining religious phenomena in particular (Martin 2005: 7). The need for a scientific study of religion, 'free of confessional interests', was first articulated in the late nineteenth century (pp. 7–8, referring to Harrison 1909: 494–5). Religion, as the classicist and scholar of Mithraism Richard Gordon long ago observed,[28] 'seeks to impose specific cognitive grids upon the experience of the believer, and employs specific means to reinforce its categories in so far as these are not already shared much more widely within the society in which it exists' (1976a: 119). In this way, different religious systems constantly generate new meanings, representations, and ideas about reality – variations that produce patterns in the way people around the globe perceive their worlds. However, despite promising historical, comparative and social-scientific approaches to religion, in the mid-twentieth century the promulgation of historical positivism prompted a reaction by scholars who rejected scientific studies as reductionist and favoured an ahistorical approach to religion as a *sui generis* phenomenon (see Martin 2012b: 155–6). With the notable exception of those pursuing cognitive theories in the second half of the century, the study of religion has been largely uninterested in the theories and practices of the sciences (Martin 2005: 8–9).

As explained by Anders Lisdorf (2010: 234), the main objection of traditional historians to the application of CSR is that we are limited to the *indirect* study of historical agents. Simply put, one cannot extract 'data from dead minds' because the brains which were the substrate of the minds are dead too (see Slingerland 2014). However, the material remains and the written testimony, which constitute the main sources for historical research, are in part the products of the particular cognitive abilities and processes that took place in the brains of their long-ago creators. Material artefacts are the results of the motivations and intentions of people who imagined and actualized them, and further were used by other persons who were able to infer their use and meanings. Written histories, historiographies, and other literary works are made possible by the human tendency to suppose causal chains between the external events, to elaborate these events into structured narratives that communicate the authors' internal thoughts to other people. These abilities allowed ancient historiographers to write their historical works. And they allow modern historians to study the historical sources and to make inferences from the information provided about the historical events and the peoples who lived in past periods.

Research on human cognition provides crucial insights into how modern minds work. Such insights provide the ground for understanding how people from another culture who live in another place perceive their surroundings, think, and create cultural expressions. Similarly, since we have no reason to believe there have been fundamental changes in the way humans think over a mere few millennia (a drop in the bucket in geological time), we may make the same inferences about people who lived in the past and generated various cultural patterns in historical periods. Furthermore, since history is not just objective description and publication of the ancient sources, but involves interpretation and inferences made by the historians, cognitive theories offer an appropriate common ground for the researchers' commonsensical assumptions about the individual motivations, social dynamics, cultural expressions, and religious practices of historical agents (see Lisdorf 2010: 235–7).

From this perspective, historical events cannot be conceived as apersonal, independent of the people who participated in them. The actions of historical agents, guided by their minds and taking place in different surroundings, shaped the particular social, political, cultural and religious developments of every historical period. Historians, then, should not neglect the minds of historical people, among other parameters.[29] And the cognitive sciences offer a useful framework for understanding past minds, extant texts and materials, and, by extension, an additional means of illuminating historical events as well as religious phenomena that do not survive today but are known to us through written records and material remains.

I.3 'Images, suggestions, representations' and the apprehension of symbols

A perceptive contemporary student of ancient religion, Plutarch of Chaeronea (pre–50 to post–120 CE), said of the goddess Isis and her mysteries:

> Nor did she allow the contests and struggles which she had undertaken, and her many deeds of wisdom and bravery, to be engulfed in oblivion and silence, *but*

into the most sacred rites she infused images, suggestions and representations of her experiences at that time (alla tais hagiôtatais anamixasa teletais eikonas kai hyponoias kai mimêmata tôn tote pathêmatôn), and so she consecrated at once a pattern (*didagma*) of piety and an encouragement (*paramythion*) to men and women overtaken by similar misfortunes.

On Isis and Osiris 27, trans. Gwyn Griffith; emphasis added

This quotation served as an answer to the question 'What do you mean by "religion"?' which Beck posed to himself at the start of his monograph *The Religion of the Mithras Cult* (2006a: 2):

> I propose to treat the 'religion' or 'mysteries' of the Mithras cult as a system of 'likenesses and underthoughts and imitations' apprehended and realized by the initiate as the gift of Mithras. Just as 'likenesses' include but are not limited to material icons, so 'imitations' include but are not limited to mimetic rituals. As for the 'underthoughts,' 'mental representations' best approximates the sense in which I take the term. My study of the 'religion' of the Mithras cult is thus a study in *cognition*, a study of how the initiate *gets to know* his mysteries in the context of the life and physical environment of the mithraeum, the 'cave' in which he and his cult brothers assembled.

We think that this answer remains cogent, especially for a *cognitive* study such as we attempt here. We need only add that religion manifests itself particularly in *symbols and complexes of symbols* which the initiate *apprehends* in the basic sense of *grasping*, or 'getting it', as one says. 'Apprehension', too, is a key term to be carried forward from the previous study. *Katalambanein* ('to apprehend') would be the corresponding Greek verb, covering more than just mental *comprehension* in the sense of conscious (and self-conscious) understanding.[30]

By a nice coincidence, Lucinda Dirven (2015) recently used the same passage from Plutarch as her guide in an important study of 'ritual performance and emotional involvement' (her article's subtitle) in the mithraeum.[31] Dirven's interpretation of the triad *eikonas kai hyponoias kai mimêmata* is as follows (pp. 26 f.):

> Greek *eikôn* should be taken here in its widest sense, with reference not only to statues, paintings, and other images, but also to symbolic representations that take shape in the architecture of sanctuaries or other objects. In Plato's day, *hyponoia* was the regular word for what later became known as the allegorical interpretation of myth, and it is certainly used here by Plutarch in that sense, whereas *mimêmata* is generally used to describe ritual performance based upon a mythological narrative.[32]

I.4 Cognition, symbols, 'individual appropriation', and 'lived religion'

Dirven's article is part of the inaugural first issue of the journal *Religion in the Roman Empire*, a number entitled 'Individual Appropriation in Lived Ancient Religion'. 'Individual appropriation' and 'lived religion' are indeed key concepts – and key terms – in the approach that the new journal instantiates.

It is not our intention to criticize this approach, which is not, in itself, problematic. Problems do, however, arise with its claims to novelty. Studying 'individual appropriation' and 'lived religion' is broadly what many scholars in the field of 'religion in the Roman Empire' have been doing all along. More narrowly, in the study of Mithraism, this has been true particularly of Luther Martin's work,[33] of Richard Gordon's work (especially in the 1970s and 1980s), and of Beck's *The Religion of the Mithras Cult in the Roman Empire* (2006a). While Dirven's article is for the most part commendably inclusive, the new journal's programmatic article by Rubina Raja and Jörg Rüpke (2015) is disappointingly exclusive. This might be acceptable if there really were a 'new' distinguishable from the 'old'. Since there is not, the distinctions drawn here reek of a party line, in which those outside are, by definition, deemed not to be studying 'individual appropriation in lived ancient religion'. The abstract of Raja's and Rüpke's article is telling (p. 11). Note their final sentence (our emphasis):

> This article presents the concept of 'lived ancient religion' as the methodological perspective underlying the contributions to this issue. For antiquity, the term is employed in order to denote an approach that focusses on the individual appropriation and embodiment of traditions, religious experiences and communication of religion in different social spaces, and the interaction of different levels facilitated by religious specialists. *This approach is intended to replace the dated (and, with regard to Mediterranean antiquity, anachronistic) model of 'state religion' and 'religions'/'cults' in its variants.*

Early studies of Mithraism did indeed, as Dirven states (2015: 23), focus first on the reconstruction of the cult's 'belief system', as something recoverable 'by decoding the symbols of the cult'. Next, 'after [Franz] Cumont [the acknowledged founder of Mithraic studies] was knocked off his pedestal in the 1970s and a Mithraic doctrine was rejected, symbolism reigned in Mithraic studies' (Dirven 2015: n. 14). Then 'astrology set the tone'. 'Recently,' however, Dirven allows, 'historians who take a cognitive approach towards religion have opted for a more individual and emotional approach to the mystery cults' (p. 25).

In recognizing the usefulness of the cognitive approach, Dirven is atypical of the 'individual appropriation'/'lived religion' school. If practitioners of the 'new' approach have a blind spot, it is cognitive science. Fourteen disciplines are named in the Abstract of the 'Editorial' of the journal's first issue (Rüpke et al. 2015: 1), beginning with 'History of Religion' and ending with 'Oriental Languages' (capitalization and quotation marks *sic*). Of the traditional social sciences only 'Anthropology' gets a mention: there is no reference to the sciences that enable us to understand something of the workings of the human mind – the living, embodied, individual human mind.

Returning to the study of Mithraism, our first rejoinder must be that it was not on symbols per se that Beck focused in his 2006 monograph, but on the *apprehension* of symbols by the initiate. That much is surely clear from the preceding section. And although the systems of symbols can be characterized as something objectively 'out there' as the property of the collectivity (held in trust from the deity, if Plutarch is to be believed), it is the individual initiate who apprehends them.

Secondly, it is a limitation of scholarship and imagination alike to treat astrology in ancient cultures in general and Mithraism in particular as an inert system that cannot be 'lived'; astrology, or more precisely, 'star talk' was, as Beck postulated (pp. 7 f.) and demonstrated at some length (pp. 153–89), the 'peculiar *idiom*' of the mysteries of Mithras, a common language, it was supposed, of gods, men and stars – a dead language now, but living in antiquity.

If you are going to understand the 'lived religion' of the mithraeum, if you are going to understand how the initiate apprehended the mithraeum as a 'cave' and thus, according to Porphyry (*On the Cave* 6), as an 'image of the cosmos ... containing in proportionate arrangement symbols of the elements and climates of the cosmos', the function of which was to enable his 'induction into a mystery of the descent of souls and their exit back out again',[34] if you are going to understand all these matters, then you must internalize a little of the language of the astronomy and astrology of the times, as did the Mithraists.

I.5 Studying Mithraism from a cognitive perspective

To a greater extent than any of its contemporaries, the Mithras cult seems to have relied on expressing and transmitting its precepts and ideas through complex systems of symbols. These symbol systems were given expression in and on what are customarily called the 'monuments' of the cult, that is, in the design of its highly idiosyncratic sacred space and sacred furnishings. Together, these created an integrated world view for its participants. It is this characteristically Mithraic world view that we aim to explore, not some set of Mithraic doctrines or theological symbol systems encoded on the monuments, which would in any case be difficult to reconstruct because of the inherently enigmatic nature of sets of symbols in general, as well as the extreme paucity of extant written testimonies to Mithraism in particular.[35]

An integrated set of Mithraic doctrines is moreover a chimaera, the quest for which was once much pursued but has quite recently been largely abandoned.[36] Here, then, we will investigate the ways in which the initiates of Mithras constructed, processed, and transmitted their tradition. We are embarking on a 'beneath the surface' examination of the sort prescribed by anthropologist Harvey Whitehouse (2005: 309–10). In principle, it is a type of investigation applicable to any sociocultural enterprise – past, present or (yes!) future. Our goal is to understand those conscious or unconscious cognitive and psychological processes that enabled individual Mithraists to construct and share an integrated world view. We shall study the particular experiences of initiates in the context of the cult – experiences that not only altered the way in which Mithraists perceived themselves and the world in the context of the cult's mysteries but also formed a new range of ideas and perceptions about the nature of reality and the elements that co-constitute the world.

In a way, our project was adumbrated by Richard Gordon more than twenty-five years ago (Gordon 1988). For example, although in the following passage he was specifically addressing the seven grades of initiation, what he had to say is germane to the construction of the set of Mithraic symbols in its entirety:[37]

> Notwithstanding the wreck of Mithraic theology, we can glimpse something of the techniques employed to satisfy the cognitive demands of seven initiatory grades. We can also glimpse something of the value of certain logical procedures – mild paradox, analogy and metonymy – applied to an inherently complex aspect of the natural world, the heavenly bodies.[38] It was the products of these techniques which effectively created 'mystery'. Protected by the rule of secrecy, these were the procedures necessary for the development of a body of speculation, of 'theology', always open to individual evocation and interpretation, which was sufficiently complex – but also sufficiently interesting – to permit such a religion to pass from the narrow confines of a particular family, place or historical moment (where most such enterprises are born and die) to become an impersonal project of a collective imagination.
>
> Gordon 1988: 59–60

Our goal for this current volume is to explore the integration of traditional Mithras studies with the powerful tools of cognitive sciences. Since there is no single model of cognition that covers the full array of cognitive and psychological processes that result in the conceptualization of a world view, we apply a wide spectrum of complementary approaches.[39] Accordingly, each chapter applies a particular theoretical model to specific features of the cult of Mithras in order to throw light on the major aspects of the Mithraic world view.[40] For our working model we rely on the definition of religion formulated by anthropologist Clifford Geertz (1990: 90) in order to understand the procedures that resulted in the investment of the symbol systems of Mithraism with a sense of actuality, a process that took place in the context of ritual praxis.

Chapter 1 begins with the problem of categorization: the theoretical models that help us understand the way in which the initiates of Mithras would have perceived and conceptualized the basic categories of their world. As a guideline we have adopted the theory of anthropologist Michael Kearney (1984) regarding world views in different historical, social, and cultural contexts. Although Kearney mainly applied the Marxist historical-materialist approach in his own work, he also emphasized the significance of the basic cognitive structures of the human brain as well as the importance of the processes of perception and conception that interact with the specific surroundings in which each individual lives and acts for the formation of specific *images* and *assumptions* about reality. The first chapter therefore not only applies Kearney's world-view model to Mithraism but also extends it by elaborating on the significance he understood cognitive studies to play. In connection with C. Geertz's definition of religion, in this chapter we further examine the basic ritual means used in the Mithraic cult context by which the relevant experiences would have been inscribed in the memory systems of the participants, following the approach of Lawrence Barsalou (2005).

Chapter 2 concerns Mithraism's structures of authority, and the transformations of identity individuals experience through sublimating those structures. In particular, we pay particular attention to the peculiar seven-grade Mithraic hierarchy (Raven to Nymphus to Soldier to Lion to Persian to Sun-Runner to Father), and to the moral life of the initiates as far as the limited evidence allows. We further investigate the way in which the initiates would have experienced a transformation of their identities in the cultic context – a transformation that would have expanded in the framework of their lives and determined new, different ways of acting in the world. We use Mark Johnson's (1993) theory of the narrative dimension of human experience as the theoretical framework for understanding the broader impact of Mithraic initiation on the construction of the initiates' personal and social identities. We also refer briefly to Antonio Damasio's (2000) approach to the cognitive processes that underlie the arising of consciousness, as well as to Jerome Bruner's (2003) theory of 'turning points'. Further, we investigate to what extent conventional metaphorical mappings would have helped the Mithraists conceptualize the initiatory experience in relation to their self-perception. At this point our study draws upon the work of George Lakoff and Mark Johnson (1980, 1999) concerning conceptual metaphors and the specific cognitive processes that affect and transform the sense that people have about their selves and others.

In Chapter 3 we investigate the ways in which Mithraists would have perceived the major categories of space and time as a function of both the neurocognitive underpinnings of perception and their specific cultic context. Especially, we focus on the ways in which the initiates would have perceived their sacred space – which they called the 'cave' and we nowadays refer to as the 'mithraeum'. We give more weight than most current scholarship to the contemporary testimony of Porphyry in his essay 'On the cave of the nymphs in the *Odyssey*' (see above), borne out by much archaeological evidence (particularly in Ostia, Rome, and central Italy) that the Mithraists designed their 'cave' as a 'model of the cosmos' in order to 'induct their initiates into a mystery of the soul's descent and return back out again' and that for this purpose 'the contents, by their proportionate arrangement, provided symbols of the elements and climates of the cosmos' (*On the Cave* 6). We suggest that the (neuro-)cognition of the human perception of space and time may deepen our understanding of how Mithraists would have constructed multiple images, concepts and representations of phenomenal reality in the cult context. In particular, we use Maurice Merleau-Ponty's (2002) approach to perception of space as a theoretical framework to understand how initiates would have perceived and experienced the sacred space of the mithraeum. Particularly, we employ the 'conceptual blending' theory of Gilles Fauconnier and Mark Turner (2002) in order to explore how Mithraists would have perceived the actual space of the mithraeum as the universe during ritual enactment. Finally, we return to the insights of Lakoff and M. Johnson (1999) on metaphor in conventional expressions of time, in order to illustrate via the symbolic structures of the mithraeum how time would have been perceived and conceptualized by the initiates affecting their 'lived experience' within the Mithraic universe.

As already noted, the Mithras cult conveyed its precepts and ideas about the world and the self within the world through *systems of symbols*. The next chapters accordingly investigate the particular functions of the symbol complexes of Mithraic iconography. We suggest that these symbol complexes would have inculcated their meanings into the minds of the initiates by engraving the initiatory and subsequent esoteric experiences on the memory systems of the participants.

In Chapter 4 we focus on the cult's principal icon, the representation of Mithras sacrificing the bull or 'tauroctony' (as it is now called). The tauroctony, executed in frescos, in sculptural relief or self-standing sculpture, was a major structure of every mithraeum in the Empire. A basic condition for the perception and conceptualization of the symbolic structure of the tauroctony, as for any such icon, was the cognitive capacity for symbolic thought, which developed during the evolution of the human species (see, e.g., Hoopes 1991; Sinha 1996; Deacon 1997). Here we apply the theory of signs formulated by Charles Sanders Peirce (1868, 1931–58) in order to understand the hierarchical structure of human thought leading to the formation, use, and reproduction of symbolic representations during communication.

In Chapter 5 we consider the extent to which Mithraism instantiates Harvey Whitehouse's 'two modes' theory (2004), specifically the 'imagistic mode of religiosity'. Taking into account the critiques as well as the updates and revisions of the theoretical premises of the 'modes of religiosity theory' by Whitehouse (2008; Whitehouse and Lanman 2014), we explore whether or not the Mithras cult met the parameters and criteria predicted by the Modes Theory. From this, we conclude that other features of the cult and cognitive processes – beyond emotional arousal and storage of the initiatory experience in the participants' memory systems – would have mediated the dissemination and reinforcement of the Mithraic communities across space and time. Particularly, we argue that secrecy comprised a distinctive feature of initiates' apprehension of the cult symbols and would have greatly contributed to the coherence of major Mithraic symbolic structures as well as to the development of social cohesion among the cult members.

In the Conclusion we summarize the new insights and benefits for historical research that we gain from applying cognitive theories to the Mithras cult. Furthermore, we suggest that cognitive approaches to ancient cults and religious practices can supplement and complement traditional historical methods, while historical studies can pose new questions and provide new evidence that may support, modify, and refine modern theories of human cognition.

1

The World View of the Mithras Cult

The anthropologist Clifford Geertz famously described a religion as

(1) a system of sacred symbols which acts to (2) establish powerful, pervasive, and long lasting moods and motivations in men by (3) formulating conceptions of a general order of existence and (4) clothing these conceptions with such an aura of factuality that (5) the moods and motivations seem uniquely realistic.

1990: 90

This view of a religion as 'a system of sacred symbols' accords well with anthropologist Michael Kearney's world-view model, which can be used as the basis for studying, understanding, and comparing different systems of world view (see also Goodman 1978).

The study of different world views is one of the main concerns of American cultural anthropology. However, most published studies investigate specific world views as they developed within particular social and historical contexts. Unusually, Kearney[1] argued that despite the variations in world-view systems, there is a fundamental categorization of the elements that compose the world and this categorization is determined and constrained by the basic principles of thought and perception that govern the common structures of human cognition. We argue that, especially in ritual, a world view promoted by a religious system is connected with specific 'moods' (e.g. psychological and mental states like high emotional arousal), which generate certain 'motivations' (e.g. tendencies, behaviours, aspirations, values), thereby creating a sense of absolute truth and thus of the validity of the world-view concepts and precepts.

In this chapter we explore how initiation into the mysteries of Mithras provided, through the symbolic system of the cult, a new view of the cosmos that altered the ways in which Mithraists perceived the world. Then, as now, people constructed representations of reality. For those initiated into the mysteries of Mithras, these representations would have acquired new meanings, since in the cult context the perceivable world transcended the limits of the natural and geographical environment in which people live and act, extending to include Hellenistic astronomy and cosmology.[2] Since the Mithras cult was coterminous with its mysteries – there was no form of Mithras-worship beyond his mysteries – initiation, together with associated rituals and explanations, would have constituted the major means by which Mithraism's specific world view was justified and perceived as the actual state of the universe. Further, we suggest that the cognitive predispositions of the human mind and the major categories of thought that, according to Kearney, structure all world-view systems would have mediated the formation of the Mithraic world view.

In the first section we briefly overview the generalized model of world views suggested by Kearney in his 1984 book *World View*. Then we move to discuss the specific world view of the Mithras cult in terms of the universal categories that structure all world-view systems appearing in all cultural and historical contexts. In parallel, we suggest that the Mithras cult, as would any religious system, instantiated its specific representations of the world in its symbolic systems and that these representations were invested with 'an aura of factuality' (C. Geertz 1990: 90) during ritual practices.

1.1 The Kearney model of world view

Kearney defines the 'world view of a people' as 'their way of looking at reality' (Kearney 1984: 41).[3] In particular, the ways in which different people or groups of people think and describe themselves and the wider context in which they live, move, and act, as well as the basic principles according to which these people perceive space and time, comprise an organized system of thought which constitutes their specific *world view*.

This world view is not equivalent to the external world that exists even in the absence of the human perception and is governed by immutable natural laws operating through consecutive and unbroken processes of alternation between material and energy. Neither does a human world view constitute a *comprehensive* account of the principles underlying the objective world – principles that remain unaffected by the agents who interact with their surroundings.

Rather, a world view is a product of human perception, which is itself affected by different historical, cultural and social contexts (pp. 41–2). Perception mediates between individual brains and minds and their external milieu. This connection between the human mind and the material world is achieved through the sensory organs of the human body. Humans continually receive sensory stimuli from their surroundings, whether they are consciously aware of this process or not. However, they do not equally perceive all information available in the environment. Their sensory and nervous systems have certain limits that predetermine human perceptual abilities and constrain the quantity and quality of the signals and information that will finally impinge on individuals' bodies through their senses. In addition to *hard* limitations that ground perceptual abilities, there are further *soft biases* that enable humans to discern and select those bits of the available information that are more useful for the performance of certain tasks and actions, and to ignore nonessential stimuli (pp. 42–4; see also Hrotic 2009: 120–4).

Thus, humans perceive those aspects of reality that are compatible with their own neuroanatomy, neurophysics, and cognitive biases. Information received through the sensory organs of the human body reaches certain regions of the brain, where it is subject to mental processing. In particular, new information tends be recombined and classified into categories that are already established by individuals' previous experiences. These pre-existing categories form certain '*anticipatory schemata*' in the mind 'that determine the selection of new information' and its gradual transformation first into percepts and then into concepts (pp. 44–5). The *schemata* or *frames* constitute a significant kind of organizational knowledge representing spatial, temporal, causal and intentional relations between entities and events that take place in familiar conditions. The contents of these mental structures are continually enriched and transformed by new information available to humans' sensory organs and their experiences within the world, further confirming pre-existing schemata and representations of reality or generating new ones.[4]

Kearney uses the terms '*images*' and '*assumptions*' to describe the mental representations that humans use when they think about the world. The word 'images' literally refers to the mental representations that are the internal constructions of what were originally visual stimuli. However, because of the significance of this process, the meaning of the term is extended and used to define metaphorically the various mental representations that may be formed in the mind of a person through oral communication or other sensory stimuli apart from vision, as for example acoustic or tactile stimuli, and that are associated and organized according to previously constructed schemata (p. 47). In this view, *images* comprise the major representations that humans use to conceive and describe phenomenal reality. These representations are alternatively called 'assumptions' by Kearney in order to describe the images about the reality used by people who share a common world view.[5] Such images and assumptions structure the persons' thoughts, and influence their behaviours, choices, and actions, and the results of this personal activity can in turn alter the external environment (pp. 47–8).

Furthermore, humans are unusual in the degree to which they can communicate their images and assumptions about themselves and their surroundings to the people with whom they interact within multiple social networks. Each social network constitutes a particular system of communication that formulates multiple channels through which information is received and forwarded, and so exchanged between individuals. Information is organized and transmitted in the form of codes and is dependent on conventions shared by all members of a group. Consequently, the members of a social group share certain images and assumptions about phenomenal reality, and so construct a particular world view, which is the product of both human cognition and reality itself (p. 42).

In short, according to Kearney, the development of a specific world-view system is the result of a series of hierarchical processes that start with received information from the external environment and lead to the transformation of the sensory perceptions and impressions into higher mental abstractions shared between two or more individuals (p. 47). These higher mental products comprise people's *images* and *assumptions* about the world, which are generated and continually transformed through continuous interactions with their surroundings. Further, they are widely accepted by the individuals as the *absolute* and *true state of the world* and *their own existence* within this world without any further critical consideration of the cognitive processes which produce their specific concepts (pp. 46–7). In this way, as Kearney aptly argues, world views are the 'products of reality, mind, action and history' (p. 47). They are generated through the interaction between human agents and their surroundings and are determined by the former's perceptual and cognitive abilities as well as by shared representations that may (in a sense) define a historical period.

The human brain and body are the common factors that underlie all world-view systems and are instantiated in several 'world-view universals' that constitute major categories of thought, which contain and organize people's images and assumptions about their surroundings. In particular, Kearney defines five universals that structure every world view throughout human history: the *perception of the self and the other*, the recognition of the multiple *relationships and causalities* between them, the process of *classification*, and the *perceptions of space* and *of time* (pp. 65–108).

In particular, *self-perception* constitutes the first major prerequisite for the establishment of a world-view system, containing the awareness and knowledge that people have about their own selves, which they are able to differentiate from everything that does not coincide with their selves and therefore constitutes the *other* (pp. 68–9). The *relationships* between the self and the other (i.e. the elements making up perceivable reality (pp. 72–8)), as well as the *causality* that governs these relationships (pp. 84–9), are further subject to mental analysis, which organizes scattered knowledge into categories, classes, and taxonomies and integrates every fragment of phenomenal reality into specific schemata (pp. 78–84).

Humans' ability to perceive *space* and *time* gives a spatio-temporal dimension to their experiences as beings situated in certain places and periods of their lives (pp. 89–106). Every human thought and action occurs in a particular place that influences the nature of that experience. The ways in which people perceive space depend on their own perceptual abilities that enable them to form certain spatial images, which they use in order to orient themselves and interact with their surroundings in everyday activities.[6] Perception of space is further affected by the context in which people live and within which certain places are invested with particular significance and symbolic meanings (pp. 92–4).[7]

Time is more difficult to perceive. Unlike space, time is mostly experienced indirectly through the events and objects which exist, unfold, and develop in space (pp. 94–106). Thus, perception of time is based on sensed information and images derived from space. The temporal dimension of physical events, as well as of human activities, depends on metaphorical perceptions of time based on human spatial experiences (pp. 94–5). Time can be perceived as cyclical: 'a sequence of oscillations between polar opposites' (e.g. night and day, winter and summer) during which regular intervals are repeated (p. 99, quoting Leach 1966: 126). Alternatively, time can be perceived as a linear, irreversible sequence of events that happen once in space, so defining the sectors of the past, the present, and the future (pp. 100–2). Different cultures may have more or less abstract notions of time, but in all cases, time is perceived in relation to movement: repetitions or activities in space.[8]

Space and *time* are fundamental dimensions with which we infer *causality* that grants *coherence* to self-perception and perception of the external world, enabling people to construct an autobiographical sense of their selves as well as to detect causal relations and deeper motivations in otherwise unconnected events that acquire a narrative structure. Furthermore, the twinned principles of space and time ensure the logical and structural integration of world-view systems, assuring individuals of the actuality of their shared surroundings (pp. 89–92).

Despite the universality of the major world-view categories, the contents of these universals – that is the images and assumptions that govern the thoughts and behaviours of the members of a social and cultural group – may vary significantly from culture to culture, since they are formed mainly through humans' interactions with each other and with their surroundings, and of course both social contexts and natural surroundings vary from group to group (42, 48, 65–7). A major part of the images and assumptions being formed in certain contexts is subliminally embedded by individuals who may not be able to access (i.e. be aware of them consciously) and express (i.e. communicate) them explicitly. However, some images and assumptions are transformed into explicit beliefs that people are consciously aware of and can transmit to others. These beliefs constitute a kind of folk knowledge that gives expression to the contents of the world-view universals in different cultural forms (p. 48).

Cultural diversity thus partly derives from the great variety of the contents of the world-view universals that attribute 'logico-structural integration' to each world-view system in accordance with its particular context.[9] Consequently, certain practices and behaviour patterns develop that reflect similarities in the way people perceive and conceive their world and its major components. In this way, the images and assumptions promoted by each world-view system are accepted by individuals as the actual form and nature of the world, thus grounding people's ordinary behaviour and governing multiple aspects of their lives. Over and above the determination of the everyday thought and activity of the members of a group, specific cultural institutions develop, such as religion, ritual and ethics, which express more or less coherently, and justify, the group's world view (pp. 52–3).

In practice, then, a world view operates as a means of communicating perceptions and conceptions of the world among the persons who live and act in the same settings. The contents of the world-view universals are adjusted and influenced by, and in turn affect, the wider natural and social context in which they were formed. In this way, even individual world views comprise integrated systems of thought that provide people with a sense of totality and coherence of the world, which is perceived as actually 'existing in space and time' (p. 66); individuals perceive their selves as parts of this cosmic entity (pp. 68–72). In every moment humans strive, consciously or unconsciously, to conceptualize this relationship between themselves and the cosmic whole, as well as the deeper causality that governs the system, of which they are an integral part (pp. 72–4, 84–8).

1.2 The Mithraic world view

Kearney's valuable insights into the nature of 'world view', not least the relationship between individual experience and shared, transpersonal world views, can illuminate the ways in which various religious systems (similarly to other cultural systems) construct coherent, integrated world views containing specific images and assumptions about the surrounding environment, the individual, and the society in which these systems develop. Seen from a cognitive perspective, Kearney's work indicates that mundane knowledge shared by people about objects, events, and other humans creates clusters of representations, which people later activate in order to communicate specifically beyond their physical and temporal presence, perpetuating these world views between separated individuals.[10] Mundane knowledge, which is contained in every type of experience, enters into specific religious beliefs and practices, which appear in different physical, social, and cultural contexts, and provides the basis for all kinds of religious knowledge. In turn, religious knowledge generates specific representations of the self, the individual body, and the environment, as well as the relationships between them (Barsalou et al. 2005: 15, 18). In this light, a religion is a particular cultural system, which constructs a coherent, integrated world view containing specific images and assumptions about the surrounding environment, the individual, and the society in which it has developed.

Within the broader Graeco-Roman world, the cult of Mithras produced and provided to its initiates such an integrated world view: a system of precepts and ideas about the world, and their own place within it. In particular, initiation into the Mithraic mysteries led initiates to a new and integrated view of the elements that composed the universe and the cosmic order. The deity Mithras was the maintainer and guarantor of this order, revealing to his followers the sympathetic relationship that linked the human microcosm to the universal macrocosm.[11] This revelation would have provided a deeper explanation of and justification for the changes and transitions occurring in initiates' lives as well as a sense of cohesion and coherence both internal (i.e. their personal self-perception) and external (i.e. between their self and the universe).

By participating in the Mithraic mysteries, the initiates would have acquired a new awareness of themselves and further modified their relationships with fellow initiates and non-initiates living in the same surroundings.[12] In particular, through the initiatory rituals the Mithraists would have formed a special community in the service of the god, thereby enjoying his divine favour, guidance, and protection. The members of the Mithraic community were connected with each other in terms of their special relationship with the deity. As one of their *symbola* or sacred slogans declares, each was an 'initiate of the cattle theft' (*mysta booklopiês*) and a 'right-hand-grasper of a/the glorious Father' (*syndexie patros agauou*).[13] Note that the Mithraist is initiated into what amounts to a criminal conspiracy: Mithras *steals* the bull, which he subsequently kills. His initiates become co-conspirators, fellow brigands meeting (where else?) in that archetypal thieves' den, a cave. The fact that this is apprehended as sacred, make-believe thievery – Mithraists aren't cattle-rustlers in 'real life' – does not in any way weaken their sense of bonding with Mithras, their 'Father', with the human 'Father' of their local cult community, and with those who are now by esoteric definition their cult brothers. The sharing of esoteric knowledge would also have served to differentiate the initiates from the uninitiated outside. Moreover, the amount of such knowledge that an initiate had acquired would have partly determined his status within the cult. For example, the *sophistes* ('man of wisdom') acclaimed in a graffito in the Dura Mithraeum was probably of the second highest grade of initiation, the Heliodromus.[14]

The self-awareness that Mithraists formed as members of their community and the ways in which they perceived the world and their roles and positions therein would have been much influenced by their perception of space and time within the sacred space of the mithraeum. The universal macrocosm – an organic part of which is the earth, where humans are born, live, and expire – was instantiated in the microcosm of the mithraeum, which was designed and constructed as an exact image of the universe, as Porphyry tells us in section 6 of his essay *On the Cave*:

> Zoroaster was the first to dedicate a natural cave in honour of Mithras, the creator and father of all ... This cave bore for him [i.e. Zoroaster] the image of the cosmos which Mithras had created, and the things which the cave contained, by their proportionate arrangement, provided him with symbols of the elements and climates of the cosmos.[15]

Here in the mithraeum, time and space are manifestly related in that it is the movement of the celestial bodies in the space of the cosmos that *defines* time.[16] Moreover, the mithraeum would have been apprehended not so much as everyday *geographic* space,[17] but as the *cosmic* space of the celestial firmament.

As we shall see in subsequent chapters, this celestial firmament is related not only to the concept of space but also to the sacred hierarchy within Mithraism: the esoteric grades of initiation were keyed to the major celestial bodies, the seven planets, thus binding 'space' – and through 'space', 'time' – to 'authority'. The best expressions of this linkage are the floor mosaic of the Felicissimus Mithraeum in Ostia[18] in which symbols of the seven grades and their tutelary planets run in panels up the aisle (V299), and the painted acclamations in the Santa Prisca Mithraeum in Rome[19] in the formula 'Hail to the [grade name] under the care of [planet name]' (V480), for example, *Nama Militibus tutela Martis*. Tellingly, the Fathers' spatio-temporal authority was described as coterminous with the earth and with the day: *Nama Patribus ab oriente ad occidentem tutela Saturni* ('Hail to the Fathers from orient to occident under the care of Saturn').[20]

The internal design of the mithraea and the iconographic representations displayed in the 'caves' would have been invested with special meanings comprising the wider symbolic system of Mithraism, which would have been perceived, accepted, and recognized by the members of the cult community.[21] These symbols and symbolic complexes, which occupied a prominent position in the mysteries both in the literal sense that they were physically present and visible in the mithraeum and on its monuments and also in the sense that they were endowed with meaning by the initiates in apprehension and in ritual performance,[22] would have constituted the primary mode of conveying the Mithraic images and assumptions (in Kearney's technical sense of the words – see above) about the initiates' selves, the environment, and the universe, as well as the relationships between these elements and the causality governing these relations.

The capacity for symbolic cognition and communication, which would have allowed Mithraists to share perceptions about a 'general order of existence' (C. Geertz 1990: 90), manifested in their symbolic systems, is grounded in the cognitive ability for symbolic thought selected through the course of human evolution.[23] Symbolic competence permits ascription of specific meanings and significances to objects and events beyond their superficial sensory properties, creating a highly structured version of the subjective world (Deeley 2004: 248).

The symbols of the Mithras cult, thus, would have constituted, in Clifford Geertz's words (1990: 91), 'tangible formulations of notions, abstractions from experience fixed in perceptible forms, concrete embodiments of ideas, attitudes, judgments, longings, and beliefs' that operated as extrinsic sources of information and gave 'objective conceptual form to social and psychological reality' (p. 93) in the cult context. In this way, the symbolic complexes of Mithraism would have constructed a 'model of' the world and a 'model for' the world,[24] and would have indicated an appropriate mode of living within this world.

Presumably, the conviction that the Mithraic images and assumptions about both the cosmic order and human existence – as they were instantiated in the symbolic system of the cult – were actually real was most strongly confirmed during rituals. Unfortunately, the surviving evidence for Mithraic rituals is neither copious nor straightforward.[25] Ancient second-hand literary sources and even the physical culture left by the Mithraists themselves provide only fragmentary data as to the cult's specific ritual practices, as indeed one should expect. The literary sources are mainly Christian and polemical, and although they might include accurate details – such as the refusal of a crown by the members of the third initiatory grade of Milites with the words 'Mithras is my crown' (Tertullian, *On the Crown* 15) – objectivity was not a significant concern! As for the cult's own monuments, rituals of initiation are depicted, most notably in a series of frescos in the Capua Mithraeum (V187-95, Vermaseren 1971: Plates XXI-XXVIII), but such representations give us only a sense of possible rituals that could have taken place in the mithraea.[26] It is our contention, however, that Mithraic ritual performances constructed and expressed Mithraic symbol systems embedded in and expressing their specific world view, integrating that world view with an *ethos* indistinguishable from the cult itself. Within this framework, the symbols would have been transformed from representations of an ideal universe to representations of the supposedly actual universe, so defining the position and appropriate behaviour of humans therein. This transformation would have required specific cognitive and emotional states, in which the initiates' minds would have been made receptive to the impressions and emotions aroused by the ritual representation of 'reality.' This sense of the 'actual real' would have been enforced by particular moods, motivations, and metaphysical conceptions constituting the initiate's mental state (cf. C. Geertz 1990: 112).

The fusion of world view and ethos during ritual practice would have informed the consciousness of the initiates, who would have perceived the ritual as a realization of their ideas, confirming their truth and propriety. The transformation of the way in which people perceived both their existence and the broader actuality of the world would not have been limited to the context of their communal life and 'worship' (however that word is to be understood) within the confines of the mithraeum, but would also have affected their cognition and behaviour in the quotidian world beyond.[27]

According to the psychologist and cognitive scientist Lawrence Barsalou, there are three encoding factors which are immanent in rituals and could be important in terms of persons' ability to retain the memory of their participation in such practices as well as their associated mental and emotional states affecting their world view out of the ritual contexts (Barsalou et al. 2005: 44–6). The first is the '*subject performed task (SPT) benefit*', which refers to the enhancement of the memory of an event at a later time through actions performed by a subject. The second is the '*location benefit*', which refers to the association of an event to the specific place where it took place and was experienced by a subject, an association that is kept in memory and can be recalled. The third is the '*concreteness benefit*', which is generated by tangible, concrete means of conveying the religious ideas perceived and conceived by a subject through this particular experience.

What data we can extract about the Mithraic rituals gives us some idea of how the techniques for memory enhancement described by Barsalou may have been exploited. Bodily action in rituals would have enhanced the mnemonic strength of these practices and have facilitated the transmission of their meanings. Further, the performance of the rituals exclusively in the sacred place of the mithraeum would have been of great importance, since, according to Barsalou's 'location benefit' (above), the reception of information in unique places 'helps insulate it from competing pieces of information' associated with different or broader contexts and 'stored elsewhere in memory' (Barsalou et al. 2005: 45).[28] Furthermore, participation in the rituals taking place in the mithraeum would have been associated with specific mental states and emotions, which could be activated again when the person was once more in the same place or when he remembered his presence there.[29] Also, the symbolic structure of the mithraeum and its distinctive furniture together with the cult's iconography, especially the dominating image of Mithras's bull-killing, would have functioned as a visible and tangible expression of the ideas and perceptions of the Mysteries: these concrete monumental and iconographic representations of the ideas and precepts of the cult would thus acquire what Barsalou referred to as a 'concreteness benefit' aiding perception, conceptualization, and recall.

The communication of religious precepts could also be aided by the mechanism of a strong, memorable narrative that people can remember more easily than isolated, fragmented, and abstract ideas (Barsalou et al. 2005: 45–6) Curiously, unlike the previous examples, this particular technique seems not to have been fundamental to the Mithraic skill set. Ancient testimonies have not preserved a specific Mithras myth embedding the major precepts and ideas of the cult to make them more easily perceivable and contagious. What we find instead in the external sources are references only to single episodes within such a narrative, such as Firmicus Maternus's allusion (*De. Err.* 5.2) to Mithras stealing the bull; further, on the cult's own monuments, there appears to be *no canonical order* in representations of numerous incidents in a Mithras myth.[30]

Martin (2004b) doubts the existence of an explicit, coherent, and comprehensive cult myth. *Symbola* or sacred slogans, such as those discussed above, could have conveyed some precepts in a memorable way but did not compose a coherent narrative.³¹ In any case, the existence of an explicit, coherent, and comprehensive narrative of Mithras does not seem to have been necessary for the transmission of the ideas and concepts of his cult, since these were embedded in the symbolic structures and representations of the mithraeum, and would be readily perceivable and conceivable by the cult members.

Lucinda Dirven put forward the hypothesis that episodes of the Mithras myth were re-enacted as ritual *tableaux vivants* in the mithraeum (Dirven 2015). We find that unlikely: apart from the special case of the cult meal, which certainly does re-enact the feast of Mithras and Sol on the hide of the newly slain bull (pp. 41 f.), there is scant evidence to substantiate this hypothesis. Yes, a large ritual vessel recovered fairly recently from a mithraeum in Mainz (Horn 1994) does indicate that there at least the episode of Mithras shooting from a bow at a rock face to elicit water was adapted into a ritual of initiation in which the community Father takes aim at a cringing person whom one assumes is an initiate (Beck 2000: 149–54), and it is not unreasonable to conjecture that what was ritualized at Mainz was ritualized in other Mithraic communities too. But we have no solid evidence that other episodes were actually re-enacted in mithraea, merely possibilities – more or less plausible – that they might have been. For example, it may well be that joining right hands (*iunctio dextrarum*) in a mithraeum would have put the initiate in mind of the compact of Mithras and Sol, an event in the myth which is represented iconographically (scene 'W' in Gordon 1980b: 216). But that there was a ritual of 'right-hand joining,' the intent of which was to replicate the compact of the two gods, is improbable. If Firmicus (*De. Err.* 5.2) is to be believed, joining hands with your cult Father in a mithraeum had a very different meaning. The initiate is greeted as follows: 'initiate of the cattle theft, right-hand-grasper of a/the glorious Father' (see above, n. 13). That is, rather than symbolize an agreement between gods, shaking hands actually signalled your complicity in a make-believe cattle-stealing conspiracy!

Although primary, ritual would not have been the only activity that took place within the mithraea and in which the world view of the Mithraists would have been entrained. Much might have been social or simply fun. Therefore, it is probably unwise to collapse the cult meal entirely into the category of ritual or to expand 'ritual' to include everything that transpired within a mithraeum. Obviously the Mithraic world view was not, as it were, switched off or inactive during the physical eating and drinking, the giving and receiving of informal instruction, the simple socializing or, in common parlance, just 'hanging out' together.

On the opposite tack, one must keep in mind the likelihood that Mithraism was a religion with many incentives to join and persist in membership and few, if any, disincentives – until the 'triumph' of Christianity, when cult membership became neither a smart career move nor socially reputable. It may be that depth of commitment is not an issue when considering the Mithraists' world view. However, if it is, then we should acknowledge that some of them – it is impossible to say how many, let alone to judge individual cases – belonged primarily for reasons of sociability or secular advancement. Of course, secular and 'religious' motivations are not mutually exclusive, nor can they be cleanly disentangled, and it would be naïve to suppose that our cult carried no 'free riders' – that is, individuals whose loyalty extended only to acquiring the benefits of membership without reciprocity.[32] Our question is rather, to what extent and in what contexts do depth and quality of commitment matter in assessing the world view of the Mithraists – or of any other religious group for that matter?

Subject to these provisos, it is fair to say that the world view of Mithraism would have determined the major principles according to which the initiates perceived their selves in relation to other people, both within and beyond the cult, and their surroundings in the wider framework of their lives. In Kearney's words (1984), the initiates' thoughts and behaviours would have been formed in large measure by the major images and assumptions about the world that comprised the specific contents of the universal categories that structure all world-view systems. Participation in the Mithraic rituals and perception of its symbolic complexes in the cult context would have justified the 'factuality' of the cult world view (cf. C. Geertz 1990: 90) affecting the ways in which persons experienced, constructed, and perceived reality not only in the religious context, but in their everyday interaction with their surroundings as well. As a final caveat, just as the external surroundings of the local Mithraic communities varied widely, so the interior world view of the members of these communities could vary from group to group or even from individual to individual. Such variations would have been facilitated by the absence of concrete narratives which would explicitly determine the Mithraic images and assumptions about the world. Therefore, we are speaking about a world view *typical* of the members of the Mithras cult, not of a 'standard issue' world view. The following chapters will examine the contents of the world view universals as they were shaped in the cult context as well as their grounds in human cognition and bodily situatedness in the world.

2

The Self in the Cult of Mithras

Initiation into the Mithraic mysteries would have revealed a new world view, and re-determined the essential principles according to which the initiates perceived themselves, and their relationships with others and their surroundings. Therefore, participation in the cult of Mithras would have transformed the ways in which the initiates constructed their identities. These identities would not have been limited to the cultic context, but would have expanded into the wider framework of the initiates' lives and determined new, different lines of action.[1]

In order to understand how the initiates would have conceived initiation not as an isolated sequence of actions but as a meaningful coherent event that affected their self-perception and long-term identities, in this chapter we examine the cognitive underpinnings of the narrative construction of the human experiences that compose individuals' wider life-stories. In this framework, we briefly present the cognitive processes that give rise to human consciousness and the autobiographical self, as these processes were described by the neuroscientist Antonio Damasio (2000).

Consciousness is the major cognitive mechanism that enables us to have a long-lasting sense of ourselves as distinct entities and to organize our varied experiences into coherent life-stories. Further imaginative cognitive devices underlie the narrative construction of our individual experiences. The theory of conceptual metaphors, articulated by George Lakoff and Mark Johnson (1999), sheds light on the ways in which we conceive of our subjective experiences and reason about abstract notions and precepts. In particular, we suggest that conceptual metaphors would have mediated the conception of the initiatory experiences as metaphorical journeys that took place in the universal microcosm of the mithraeum.

The Mithraists would have conceived the experiences of initiations as narratives that unfolded within the Mithraic caves. Referring to M. Johnson's (1993) theoretical insights into the narrative construction of human lives, we further suggest that the distinct narratives of initiations would have been integrated in the participants' wider stories of their lives as significant episodes – 'turning points', using Jerome Bruner's term (2003) – that affected the ways in which they perceived themselves and forged their long-term identities.

In what follows, we first briefly present the cognitive processes that underlie the narrative construction of human life and then proceed to examine how these processes may throw light on the conception of the initiatory rituals and their impacts on the initiates' self-perception and social identities.

2.1 The narrative construction of human life

We conceive our varied experiences as narratives and we perceive ourselves as being the protagonists of our coherent life-stories. According to Damasio (2000: 168–9), consciousness is the vital mechanism that enables us to have awareness of our own selves and our surroundings that is not constrained to the present but is extended in time and shapes our long-term identities. The internal cognitive processes through which we acquire a sense of ourselves, distinguishable from everything other, develop in three stages during which consciousness arises as we perceive, act, and interact with the external world (pp. 171–6).

In the first stage, a non-conscious, 'interconnected and temporarily coherent collection of neural patterns' is continually engendered and instantaneously represents the dimensions of the organism's state 'at multiple levels of the brain' (p. 174). Thus the organism forms a 'proto-self', by mapping itself as a unit distinct from the environment within the brain structures. As people interact with their surroundings, the objects encountered are also mapped within the sensorimotor structures of the brain. These mappings of both the organism and the objects as neural patterns constitute the *first-order maps* that can then become images (pp. 153–60).

In the second stage, the first order maps of both the organism and the objects are combined to engender *second-order neural maps* that represent the organism–object relationship. These maps are continually modified, as the organism interacts with external objects. As Damasio pointed out, in this stage the organism and the object are represented in the brain as two players who participate in a proto-narrative with 'a beginning, a middle, and an end': 'The beginning corresponds to the initial state of the organism. The middle is the arrival of the object. The end is made up of reactions that result in a modified state of the organism' (p. 168). This plot is continually reiterated every time an organism/object relationship is perceived and the organism's state is modified as a result. The awareness arising in the second-order maps makes the organism 'conscious' of the situations and of themselves (pp. 168–70). This is the moment at which the 'core self' is coming to the fore, and consciousness begins to rise. However, the core self is constrained to the present, since it lasts only as long as the interaction between the self and an object unfolds. Therefore, in the second stage the awareness of our existence lasts only for fleeting moments (pp. 170–3).

It is in the third stage that we acquire a more lasting sense of ourselves as single entities that seemingly remain stable over time and construct specific concepts about our identities and personalities. 'The abundant flow of nonverbal narratives' from core consciousness (p. 176) do not remain isolated events happening in space and time. They are recorded in autobiographical memory as concrete facts of a unified narrative that accumulate knowledge about ourselves and the world. This knowledge is further enriched by the feedback that we receive both from others and our own behaviours, filtered through culturally constructed categories. In this way we formulate our autobiographical selves, which enable us to be conscious of ourselves throughout our lives and to narrate our life-stories (pp. 172–9).

Once consciousness is in play, we should consider how it operates in order to attribute coherent structure to sequences of events and personal experiences. Lakoff and M. Johnson (1999) described how crucial 'conceptual metaphors' are for this process of an individual's imaginative synthesizing activity (p. 45). As we participate in the world, in addition to our perceptions of our sensorimotor experiences, we have rich subjective experiences (such as desire, likes, dislikes, and fulfilment). Conceptual metaphors make it possible for 'conventional mental imagery from sensorimotor domains' to be transferred to human subjective experiences and to formulate concepts, judgements, and *reasons* about abstract notions (such as significance, similarity, and morality) (pp. 45, 56).

Lakoff and M. Johnson (1999: 46) referred to Christopher Johnson's theory of conflation (1999)[2] and Srini Narayanan's[3] (1997) research on the neurological underpinnings of this conflation in order to show how the transfer of mental imagery from one domain of experience to the other develops engendering conceptual metaphors. As C. Johnson (1999) pointed out, infants originally cannot distinguish their subjective experiences from simultaneous sensorimotor experiences. During this early period of life, these two domains are conflated, creating associations that are preserved when later the children develop the ability to distinguish between different kinds of experiences. From a neural perspective, as Narayanan (1997) showed, the co-occurrence of sensorimotor and subjective experiences in the stage of conflation activates simultaneously parts of the brain that are associated with the two different kinds of experiences, engendering lasting cross-domain neural connections. These connections comprise the basis of conceptual metaphors that constitute the means of conceptualizing subjective experiences. In particular, 'cross-domain mappings' between the sensorimotor domain and the domain of subjective experience engender 'primary metaphors'. During this process, the sensorimotor neural system that has more inferential connections operates as a *source domain* from which inferences flow via the neural connections to the mental systems of subjective experiences that comprise the *target* domains of subjective experience. During *source-to-target activations* primary metaphors are constructed unconsciously, and imbue the way in which we conceptualize our subjective experiences (pp. 55–8).

The significance and function of primary metaphors are further enhanced as they are combined with each other in order to fabricate even more complex metaphors. According to Gilles Fauconnier's and Mark Turner's (1998, 2002, 2003)[4] as well as Joe Grady's theory (1997),[5] an imaginative cognitive process of conceptual blending has as a result a number of primary metaphors to fit together and to be co-activated, establishing 'long-term connections' that constitute complex metaphorical mappings (Lakoff and M. Johnson 1999: 47, 49).

Such complex metaphorical mappings are formalized, entrenched, and stabilized over time, and comprise a store of conventional conceptual metaphors that are available in particular historical, social, and cultural contexts. Complex metaphors that are established in specific cultures and traditions structure a major part of people's conceptual systems, and provide the means for perceptions, conceptions, and reasoning about the world as well as about individual subjective experiences, actions, choices, goals and projects (Lakoff and M. Johnson 1999: 60; M. Johnson 1993: 165–6).

Perception of human actions and conceptualizations of subjective experiences through the use of complex metaphors in concrete day-to-day situations are further integrated into wider narrative contexts. According to M. Johnson (1993), narrative provides the most coherent means to interweave personal goals and actions in a temporal sequence in which past, present, and future are integrated 'into more or less meaningful patterns' (p. 174). This narrative is not just storytelling, but is experienced in concrete situations as responses to particular conditions that demand from us that we define our identities and reason about our choices, actions, and the consequences thereof (p. 174).

As M. Johnson noted, a specific 'conceptual network of action', which he called the '*proto*narrative dimension of experience', evolves and modulates the synthetic base of human experience 'out of which narrative structure emerges' (p. 174). Even the most ordinary and trivial human actions have specific motivations and goals,[6] and are perceived as belonging to a person who is the agent of the action. Every action is embedded into 'an experiential web that develops over time' (p. 174) and is part of a wider life-story that attributes a sense of unity to individual actions. These actions are integrated into wider scripts that unfold in particular contexts, which involve social networks, symbolic systems and common practices, and which ascribe various meanings to individual actions. We develop our identity (or identities) in and through our actions, and we are perceived as responsible for these actions and their results, which may affect both ourselves and others. This sense of responsibility entails our capacity to reason about our intentions, motives and actions, as well as the experienced events (p. 174).

Particularly shaking events may radically transform our identities. Bruner (2003) called these events 'turning points' which prompt us to clarify our self-concepts and redefine our social identities and roles. Such 'turning points' are inscribed as vivid autobiographical events in episodic memory, and are flagged as significant narratives which revealed new directions and ways of action in our wider life-stories (pp. 42, 50).

In this perspective, as M. Johnson (1993) put it, life-stories are tasks that we accomplish in order to give synthetic form to our lives and to perceive ourselves as we move and act in our specific physical, historical, and cultural environments. As we modulate narratives that shape our experiences, the surrounding world is gradually imbued with a projection of those narratives and seems more reasonable (p. 178). Thus, the world comprises the wider contexts for the perception of self and the construction of self-identity, and provides variable motivations for behaviour (p. 159).

Simultaneously, the external contexts draw the limits in which we may evolve our selves-in-process, and develop our identities over time. Particular cultural systems (i.e. social conventions, religious traditions, symbolic systems, ethics and institutions) impose specific roles and commitments on us, influencing perceptions of self and forming social identities. We may choose to transcend these imposed commitments, and to inhabit new roles. But the pre-existing social, cultural and religious backgrounds of our lives continue to be part of our life-stories, thus constraining our options. In this way, the situatedness of the human brain and body within their distinctive worlds allow a modest freedom to form our identities. Identities *continuously* transform, and may in turn shape, the pre-existing structures, roles and meanings of their external world (pp. 150–62).

Therefore, we perceive ourselves in different ways while we continually interact with others in various social and cultural contexts, as a result shaping multiple identities. These identities undergo continual processing (entities-in-process), and are affected by individual actions, choices, purposes and goals, as well as by the wider contexts in which we are situated (pp. 164–5). It is in and through the narrative construction of our experiences that we acquire a long-lasting sense of ourselves, as we try to make our surroundings and our actions more meaningful and manageable. Even the most 'idealized cognitive models' for various situations and institutions (such as initiation and rituals) are embedded in narrative frameworks, and their synchronic perception is only a part of their more essential diachronic synthesis at a narrative level in which people perceive themselves in their activity (M. Johnson 1993: 176).

2.2 The Mithriast's self in society and in the cult

The theoretical insights into the narrative construction of the human life provided in the previous section may illuminate how initiation into the Mithras cult was integrated into the wider life-stories of the initiates as significant episodes that affected their self-perception and reformed their social identities.[7] Since participation in the Mithras cult was not prescribed by any other religious tradition, it was a matter of personal choice. Like all such 'personal choices', context and personal and social conditioning predetermined the likelihood of an individual making this particular choice.

By 'initiation into' we mean not only the *ritual(s)* of initiation, but also the more complex process of *joining* the cult, of moving from outside to inside, that affected the initiate's self-perception. Inevitably, the conception of initiation was conditioned by the wider religious, social, and political contexts in which it took place. Being a *Graeco-Roman* cult, there were broader social constraints on Mithraic concepts; limitations on what actions and identities could be easily entertained. Politically the Graeco-Roman world was an oligarchy: power ultimately resided with the emperor, but was delegated down through provincial governors. This is not to say that the Empire's subjects did not enjoy a dynamic political life, with considerable local powers, centred on the cities. The historical record tells us the most about the populous Greek-speaking cities of the eastern Empire. Though life in rural areas remains relatively obscure – we rely on indirect accounts – we have a fairly reliable understanding of the political power of urban craftsmen and labourers: the urban proletariat may have been far removed from imperial power, but they were not entirely impotent – rioting was always an option.

Ironically, it is precisely in these eastern cities of the Empire that the presence of Mithraism is least attested. Accidents of preservation and loss of evidence over the subsequent centuries may explain some but not all of this huge absence. One can say, then, with some confidence that these culturally vibrant cities were not Mithraism's catchment area. A result of great importance is that the language of the Mithras cult was preponderantly Latin, not Greek, as can be easily confirmed by perusing the two volumes of M. J. Vermaseren's catalogue of Mithraic inscriptions and monuments (1956–60). If you are what you speak, then the Mithraists were self-identified Romans – or wannabe Romans.[8]

Who, then, were the 'typical' Mithraists of the Latin-speaking Europeans and North Africans west of the Empire? In very broad strokes, Mithriasts were 'in-between' people:[9] not of the highest urban socio-political strata,[10] nor the lowest, nor of the rural masses. Rather, they were educated freedmen, soldiers and veterans, members of the municipal elite, or of the upper echelon of slaves (i.e. bureaucrats or members of important households).[11]

How did these people perceive themselves and their positions within the world? Specifically, what sense of himself as a pious and law-abiding denizen of the Roman order would a Mithraist have had? As a research question this may seem almost absurdly ambitious, but this kind of question is precisely what a cognitive approach makes possible, by allowing us to make inferences about what thoughts and schemas are most likely. There is, moreover, an even larger question. What sense of himself as a denizen of the universe articulated by Hellenistic cosmology would a Mithraist have had? But why should we be concerned with such questions in the first place? What do we hope to gain by hypothesizing the cosmological identity of, for example, a soldier serving on Hadrian's Wall? Let us take this last question first.

The distinction between a learned elite (members of which can *comprehend* and can therefore fully participate in a religion), and unlettered common people (Horace's *profanum vulgus* (*Odes* 3.1.1), who cannot) is too often present in more traditional studies of ancient religion. The cognitive science of religion (CSR), however, could (and ought to) highlight the flaw in this dichotomy.

First, let us be clear: questioning this distinction is not to deny the overall control of religion by the elite or the differentiation of roles in religious performance according to status. Nor of course do we overlook differences in education and intellectual pursuits, the lower orders for the most part having none of either. Rather, the supposed dichotomy concerns *comprehension*, the ability to 'get it' (to use the colloquial expression), and severely underestimates the ability of those drawn from 'in-between' people.[12] In the crudest form, the distinction between the wisdom of the elite and the ignorance of the 'vulgar' has been used to dictate to scholars what Mithraism could and could not have been, based on a social profile of its adherents. As one scholar put it, if Mithraism was 'a rude fraternal cult of soldiers on the frontier, many of them adolescents, and perhaps of ancient veterans back in Rome and Ostia', then maybe it was 'nothing much, and perhaps not a serious [!] religion after all' (Swerdlow 1991: 62). Interestingly, the scholar in question, an eminent historian of ancient astronomy, deployed this argument to show that Mithraism did not and *could* not have incorporated things astronomical, astronomy being a quintessentially 'learned' pastime practised by serious – the Greek adjective *spoudaios* comes to mind – and leisured persons.

This imagined dichotomy between the 'wise' and the 'vulgar' originated in antiquity. It was a part of the panoply of self-serving propaganda by which the elite distanced themselves from the lower orders. As a *cognitive* claim, however, it is bogus. Beck challenged it at some length in an earlier study (2006a: Chapters 4 and 6). But not just modern, post hoc analysts challenge this view. Lucian's descriptions offer a vivid counter-example: in his essay 'On the Dance', concerning mass audience reaction to the hugely popular but demanding art form of the pantomime, he provides a vivid demonstration that the common people were – and are – just as capable of 'getting it' as their betters (see Beck 2006a: 99–101).

Unfortunately, the assumption that there are certain things (e.g. astrology) that specialists are interested in and ordinary folk are not underlies the treatment of Mithraism in the recent study of 'Initiation into the Mysteries of the Ancient World' by the distinguished academic Jan Bremmer (2014). Bremmer declared (p. 130):

> Modern scholars have paid much attention to the astrological and cosmological speculations of ancient Mithraists [Beck 2004 and 2006a are here cited in a note] but, just as most modern Protestants have not ploughed through the 13 volumes of Karl Barthes's *Kirkliche Dogmatik* and most Catholics were not terribly interested in the latest dogmatic insights of Pope Benedict XVI, we need not suppose that most Mithras worshippers followed or were interested in these highly complicated speculations.

The analogy is highly tendentious. Contemporary astronomy, astrology and cosmology did not furnish anything similar to a body of Mithraic *doctrine* (Beck 2006a: 41–64). Rather, as Beck argued (pp. 102–52), astronomy, astrology and cosmology provided the substrate for the design and furnishing of the mithraeum 'as an image of the universe ... equipped with symbols of the elements and climates of the universe in proportionate arrangement' (Porphyry, *On the Cave* 6). The mithraeum, says Porphyry, was so designed and furnished in order to 'perfect the initiate by inducting him into a mystery of the descent of souls and their exit back out again' (*houtô kai Persai tên eis katô kathodon kai palin exodon mystagôgountes telousi ton mystên, eponomasantes spêlaion ton topon*). The elite of course would have the education and opportunity to further elaborate, but all Mithraists would have equivalent cognitive capacities and possibly even personal interests to participate in the mystery of the souls' journey. Whether Beck was right or wrong to follow Porphyry is not at issue here; rather, it is the obligation to confront another scholar's actual ideas rather than a straw man of one's own invention. If Bremmer had wanted a germane analogy, he might have done worse than consider the popular uptake of Christian theological controversies in late antiquity. But then the question might not have yielded a pre-determined answer.

The mysteries of Mithras entered a world of wide cognitive horizons. The Empire was known and experienced as a vast physical and political space, especially by the very people who typically joined the cult. Consider the soldiers. Granted, in quiet times the military was largely sedentary. But even those who travelled little knew themselves as members of an organization co-extensive with the civilized world (except perhaps to the east), serving rulers who made similarly grandiose claims.

Vaster still was the cosmos beyond and above the globe of earth. Not the least element in the 'genius of Mithraism' – to borrow the title of A. D. Nock's 1937 article – was to make the heavens familiar territory to its initiates as part of their 'cognized environment'[13] (Beck 2006a: 141–52). As we have already noted – but have yet to demonstrate at length – the cult designed and built its distinctive meeting place as an 'image of the cosmos (*eikona kosmou*) which Mithras had created' (Porphyry, *On the Cave* 6), furnishing it with 'symbols of the elements and climates of the cosmos in proportionate arrangement'.

Becoming a Mithraist would have *added* features to the initiate's cognized environment. It would *not* have erased the old landscape, which would have remained, in Keith Hopkins's memorable phrase, 'a world full of gods' (2000). The phrase is in fact adapted from Petronius's *Satyrica* 17: 'This locality of ours is so crowded with the presence of divinities that it's easier to find a god here than a man' (trans. Walsh). For access to the mindscapes of the people of the times, there are no better sources than the ancient novels, particularly the two great Latin novels of Apuleius: the *Satyrica* and the *Metamorphoses* (or *The Golden*

Ass). These fictional worlds are populated by gods big and little, powerful and limited, benevolent and malevolent, noble and louche – the god to whom the speaker quoted above will introduce the novel's heroes is the ithyphallic Priapus, whose priestess she is and whose rites ... enough said! – and the forces, both personal and impersonal, of magic and of fate.

To this chaotic mind-world Mithras would have brought a sense of order and control. As guarantor of the universe, Mithras is *invictus* ('Unconquered'). He is the ultimate 'winner' – and so therefore are his initiates. More philosophically, he is 'the creator and father of all' and the 'master of genesis', i.e. of coming into being (Porphyry, *On the Cave* 6 18). Through initiation into his mysteries, individuals come under his guidance and protection, forming a personal relationship with him and reaching a different view of the world in which their existence acquires new meaning.

On initiation, the identity of cult members would have been defined by sharing the knowledge that put them in the service of Mithras. This secret knowledge,[14] to which only the initiates had access,[15] would have forged strong relationships between them, regardless of their social status, although of course their sense of external status differences would have been modified and to some extent even reinforced, not obliterated. Mithraists were affiliated with each other by claims of fictive kinship,[16] and constituted closely bonded, exclusivistic communities which defined new specific roles and moral principles for their members (Martin 1997 = 2014: ch. 8, 2004b: 196).[17] One must, however, remember that the Mithraists were not exclusive in the way that monastic communities were and are. A Mithraist would have had, and thus have seen himself as having, a rich exterior life and set of relationships beyond his Mithraic community.

Initiation was constrained by major biological, social, and economic factors which limit the choices that people have at their disposal.[18] The major biological constraint was sex, since women were completely excluded from participating in the Mithras cult.[19] This exclusion is indicated first and foremost by the absence of women from all records of membership.[20] Furthermore, the names of the initiatory grades (*Pater* = Father, *Heliodromus* = Sun-Runner, *Perses* = Persian, *Leo* = Lion, *Miles* = Soldier, *Nymphus* = 'Male Bride' [!], *Corax* = Raven) reveal a preference, to put it mildly, for the male and the masculine over the female and the feminine.[21]

Mithras himself was born not of a woman or a goddess but of a rock, and so the cult images represent him, emerging from the waist up (Gordon 1980a: 54–5; Bremmer 2014: 131, n. 120.).[22] A paradox of fertility in sterility is asserted in the ancient labelling of the image as *Petra Genetrix* ('the Rock that gives birth') or similar phrase. In another story (Ps.-Plutarch, *De fluviis* 23.4),

Mithras wished to have a son, but detested the race of women, and so he ejaculated on to a rock (*petrâi tini*). The stone (*ho lithos*) became pregnant and after the proper time gave up a new-born called Diorphos.

However, we do not know if this story was current in the cult since it is not represented monumentally or otherwise alluded to.

As to the low esteem in which Mithraists held women, a passage from Porphyry's *On Abstinence* 4.16, drawing on Pallas, mentions that they called women 'hyenas':

> There, in order to demonstrate our kinship with animals allegorically, they are accustomed to image us by means of animals. Thus they call those who are full participants (*sc.* in their rites) 'lions', women 'hyenas', and the underlings 'ravens'.[23]

Such hostile symbolic representations of women and the denial of actual procreative processes probably reflect the fantasies of paternalistic communities for a more congenial world where the female would be transmuted and marginalized (Gordon 1988: 70). However, the exclusion of women was limited to cult life and did not affect the initiates' everyday life.[24]

The personal decision of initiation would have been affected by the previous experience and continuing roles that people had in the wider cultural and social context. That context in turn would have constrained how Mithraism's specific ideas and precepts evolved. Given the provenance of so many Mithraists from the military and the bureaucracy, it is not surprising that Mithraism shared the basic principles and values of these social groups and embedded them in its own system of thought, in particular the values of submission and conformity and the acceptance of authority (Merkelbach 1984: 153–88; Clauss 2000: 40–1, 2012: 46–7).[25] These values, however, acquired a new meaning in the cult context. The Mithras cult mirrored the Roman social and hierarchical structures and integrated them into a new world view. In the cult context, initiates would have felt, on the one hand, called upon to put themselves in the service of Mithras and, on the other, to labour for the preservation not only of the Roman Empire but of the whole universal order (Martin 2003: 314).

2.2.1 The 'lived experience' of initiation

Initiation into the Mithraic mysteries, as in most secret or semi-secret societies, was marked by specific institutional acts. It was thus embedded in the context of a prototypical life story that unfolded in a certain place and time.[26] Initiation would have been experienced as a 'turning point' by the initiates in the wider narrative structure of their lives.[27] As Beck observed in an earlier study (2000: 146, n. 10),[28] 'Mithraic ritual seems to be characterized by strangeness, violence, and the extreme.'

Especially with regard to visual representations of Mithraic initiations, the question arises: does this scene have to do with entry into the cult or entry into one of the seven grades in the hierarchy outlined above? It should be emphasized that there was no general or standard ritual of initiation into the mysteries of Mithras. Had there been, it is fair to say that we would have known about it or at least that it had existed. Here, absence of evidence is indeed evidence of absence. Below (section 2.2.2.1) we will examine the grade hierarchy in more detail, but here our focus is on the *lived experience* of Mithraic initiation regardless of grade context.

The historical record indicates that this *lived experience* was intense.[29] A few references, mainly in Christian sources, mention extreme rituals that the candidates had to undergo in order to be initiated into the cult (Clauss 2000: 102–5, 2012: 98–102).[30] In particular, the source known as Ambrosiaster (*Quaest. vet. et nov. test.* 113.11) gives a sense of what *might* have gone on in Mithraic initiations – though allowance must be made for hostile external biases:

> their eyes are blindfolded ... others beat their wings together as birds do, imitating the call of ravens, and others roar like lions; and yet others are pushed across ditches filled with water, their hands tied with chicken intestines; and then somebody comes up and cuts these intestines – he calls himself their 'liberator.'

Although the actuality of such extreme rites in the Mithras cult has been questioned, the distress of novices through processes of humiliation, pain, or even injuries is common in initiatory rituals in the historical and ethnographic record. Excruciating experiences like these would have shaken the foundations of the initiates' personality and rendered them more amenable to new cult identities (Burkert 1987: 102).

As we have already noted, Firmicus Maternus (*De. Err.* 5.2) tells us that a Mithraist was acclaimed as an 'initiate of the cattle theft, right-hand-grasper of the glorious Father' (*Mysta boöklopiês, syndexie Patros agauou*). The 'Father', as we shall see, was the surrogate of Mithras in the cult's hierarchy. The acclamation, then, asserts a father–son relationship between the initiate and both Mithras and the head(s) of the local Mithraic community, a relationship that, presumably, was internalized. This particular acclamation may or may not have been widely current, but there is no reason to doubt its underlying sentiments.

The first part of the acclamation tells us something less trite, namely that what the initiate was inducted into was a mystery of 'cattle theft'. Further, Firmicus

(*De. Err.* 5.2) reveals that the original thief was Mithras himself, whom he characterizes sarcastically as 'the gentleman who drove off cattle' (*virum abactorem bovum*). What are we to make of this? Firmicus's own opinion is predictable: what else would you expect of a god and his followers who shun the light of day and transact their business in a 'cave', the archetypal brigands' lair?

Unlike Firmicus, modern scholars have no axes to grind. Our impression of the Mithraists is that they were the most respectable and law-abiding of people: prior to Christian calumny no taint of scandal marred their record. We must conclude that this aura of criminality was but make-believe. Mithraists in their 'caves' on occasion *played at* being robbers, converting their righteous deity into a Mercury and themselves into co-conspirators. Why they would do this is another matter. But topsy-turvy carnivals and inversions are features of many religions and of the cultures in which they sit (e.g. Mardi Gras, the Saturnalia), so perhaps we should look no further than an occasional release from the high moral seriousness which was Mithraism's norm.[31]

Very few visual representations of Mithraic initiations convey the same extreme ethos as the written testimonies. Paradoxically, these images have the advantage of being a more reliable source of initiates' experiences – how they interpreted and recalled these experiences, what they *felt* – than the specific procedures used to stimulate them. Indisputably, they are internal to the cult. It follows that they record, if not what actually transpired, at least what was thought to have transpired or what ideally ought to have transpired.

One example is a set of frescos on the front of the side-benches in the mithraeum at Capua (V187–97; Figure 2.1), the subject of a monograph by M. J. Vermaseren (1971)[32] and most recently of an important article by Richard Gordon (2009). Typically, the scenes show three figures: (a) an initiand, small, naked, vulnerable, kneeling or prostrate, often blindfolded, humiliated; (b) an initiator, clad in white, who stands behind and physically controls the initiand; and (c) another initiator who manipulates various props in front of the initiand:[33] for example, in one scene (V188),[34] wearing a helmet or Phrygian cap and clad in red, he confronts the initiand who is kneeling and blindfolded, with a torch held close to the latter's head.[35] The scenes have perhaps been over-interpreted for the exact significances of their details.[36] What matters is the ethos of the whole and the manifest relationships between the players. Paradoxically, what they are *feeling* – or more precisely, *how their experiences are individually constructed* – is more obvious than precisely what they are *doing*. Perceptively, Gordon (2009: 304–10) spotlights the emergence of a new

Figure 2.1 Mithraeum of Santa Maria Capua Vetere
Source: Carole Raddato from Frankfurt. Mithraeum (mitreo), Ancient Capua (Flickr)

virtue of endurance in suffering and humiliation, not dissimilar to that of the Christian martyr, as the experience is imprinted on the body of the initiand/martyr.

One representation in the Capua mithraeum merits special attention. This relief sculpture (V186) shows Cupid with a torch conducting the winged Psyche. The motif is commonplace in Roman culture worlds, but *not within Mithraism*. And that is the point: some Capuan Mithraist has introduced into his mithraeum a representation of the story of Love leading the Soul (either commissioning it himself or acquiring it ready-made) and has *re-represented* the story as an allegory of induction into life as a Mithraist.[37] So the interpretive world of Mithraism creatively reshaped a previously known narrative, projecting new significances. Some have seen it as an initiation into a particular grade: Reinhold Merkelbach (1984: 92) argued that Psyche's unusually manly physique suggested this image was meant to indicate initiation into the second grade, the Nymphus: the single feminine stage in an otherwise masculine esoteric career. More important is the high level of allegorical thinking revealed by the monument, and the fact that it is the product of a local initiative, not of some universal Mithraic doctrine (Martin 2009: 117, 145 n. 11).[38]

Figure 2.2 Mithraic vessel from the mithraeum of Mainz
Source: Csaba Szabó

Another visual representation of Mithraic initiation is found in a scene composed of three human figures moulded on to the shoulder of one side of a large ritual vessel recovered fairly recently from a mithraeum in Mainz (Horn 1994; Figure 2.2) (a second set of four figures, moulded on to the other side, will be discussed in due course). In an article devoted to the Mainz Vessel and the significance of its scenes,[39] Beck described this scene as follows (2000: 149; see Plate XIV between pp. 174 and 175):

[The figure] on the left is seated (he is the only one of the seven on the cup so posed). He wears a Persian cap with ear-flaps. He is in the act of drawing a bow. He aims his arrow straight at the figure in front of him, the middle of the three in the scene. This second figure is smaller than the other two and naked. He is shown advancing towards the seated bowman, whom he faces. His arms are crossed in front of him in a gesture of subordination, though they are raised to the level of his head as if to ward off the threat of the drawn bow. Behind him (thus on the right of the scene), the third figure likewise advances leftwards. He gazes upwards, with open mouth as if speaking; his right arm is extended and raised, the hand gesturing with thumb and two fingers (index and middle) extended.

Beck titled this scene 'The Archery of the Father'. As is obvious from similarities with the Capua scenes – the naked, threatened, and humiliated subject; the two agents (one in front, one behind); the use of props – the scene represents an initiation. The enthroned figure is the community's Father, the surrogate of Mithras himself, and he initiates by feigned archery. But why? As Beck argued (2000: 149–54), the Father's action is a mimesis of an act of Mithras himself in the cycle of myth which we know as the 'water miracle', in which Mithras elicits water from a rock by shooting at it.[40] The Father's *deed* is replicated by the mystagogue's *word*, for 'speech' is what the gesture of the figure behind the initiand signifies (pp. 149–54).

The mimetic dimension of this act of initiation is of huge importance. What the Father *does*, what the initiand *suffers*, and what the mystagogue *orates* occur simultaneously on two planes: the immediate plane on which one admits or is admitted into a community in the here and now, and an immanent plane on which one participates in the deeds of the god. Bear in mind too that, whether or not the scene is an idealized representation, these are episodes both in the life stories, actual or imagined, of the three persons involved and in the history of the community. Quintessentially, this is 'lived religion'! We will encounter this duality of planes and the mimesis that joins them again and again, most notably in section 2.2.3 below, which focuses on the cult meal.

2.2.2 The grade hierarchy

Beck (2006a: 11) proposed that 'the [Mithraic] initiate apprehends the symbol complexes' at the core of his mysteries on three '*structured sites*':

1. The physical structure of the mithraeum.
2. The physical structure of the icon of the tauroctony.
3. The organizational structure of the seven grades.

The first two structures were ubiquitous, in the sense that (1) all or virtually all mithraea were designed and constructed with two 'side-benches', for reclining as at a feast, facing each other across a central aisle, and (2) these mithraea were furnished with representations of Mithras killing a bull ('tauroctonies' in modern scholarly parlance), executed in sculpture (usually low relief) or (more rarely) fresco, according to a standard composition permitting few variants, and normally located at the opposite end of the aisle from the entrance.

The third structure, that of the seven grades, differs from the other two distinctive structures in two fundamental ways. First, it was not ubiquitous. To the best of our knowledge, it was not a feature of every Mithraic community, with passage through all or even some of the seven grades everywhere required. In most mithraea, in fact, the presence of grade-holders is not attested at all, and there is no reason to suppose either that epigraphic grade records were widely made but subsequently lost or that for whatever reason there was some bias against recording them. In other words, what we still have is not the tip of a hidden iceberg of grade activity. The grade hierarchy was distinctive but not normative. Secondly, and ultimately of more importance, the grade hierarchy was an organizational structure, *which one ascended over time*, not a physical structure which one *entered and moved around in* (the mithraeum) or *apprehended as an object in space* (the tauroctony).

Seven grades of initiation are recorded.[41] In order of seniority, from lowest to highest, they were: Raven (*Corax*), *Nymphus*,[42] Soldier (*Miles*), Lion (*Leo*), Persian (*Perses*), Sun-Runner (*Heliodromus*), Father (*Pater*). Where the hierarchy existed and was emphasized, initiation into successive grades would have largely defined the identities of the cult members, their behaviour in ritual and in cult life more generally, and the extent to which they would have had access to sacred knowledge (Gordon 1972: 101).[43] This was surely so in the Mithraic communities (1) at Dura–Europos on the Euphrates, (2) in Rome at the Santa Prisca Mithraeum, and (3) in Ostia at the Felicissimus Mithraeum:

(1) The presence and centrality of the grades are richly attested at Dura in the form of graffiti and dipinti – that is drawings and painted inscriptions on the walls – a number of examples of which take the form of *Nama*-acclamations (V54–69).[44] Attributes are sometimes assigned to each grade, suggesting qualities exemplified, at least ideally, in the actual grade-holders. A Soldier, for example, is called 'pure' (*akeraios*).[45] At Dura, too, there is explicit evidence of some specifics of promotion within the grade structure (Francis 1975: 440–5). We hear of a Marinus who is *melloleôn* ('about-to-be Lion') and a Marinus who is *neos leôn* ('new Lion'). Are they the same person progressing through the grades? Posing

the same question of identity, there is also a Marinus who is *petitôr* ('candidate') and one who is *antipatros* ('counter [but in what sense?] Father').

(2) At Santa Prisca,[46] a fresco on the right (south) side of the aisle (V480)[47] shows representatives of the first six grades in proper order, led by a Sun-Runner, approaching a seated Father, whom the composition places closest to the cult-niche. Dipinti (V480)[48] identify each grade-holder and the planetary god who is his patron, with a recurring formula, such as: 'Hail to the Lions, under the protection of Jupiter' (*Nama leonibus tutela Iovis*). The Father is distinguished by a more elaborate text: 'Hail to the Fathers from orient to occident, under Saturn's protection' (*Nama patribus ab oriente ad occidentem tutela Saturni*).[49]

At Santa Prisca particular attention is paid to the Lions: frescoes on either side of the aisle are devoted to them (V481–2).[50] They too are processing with offerings, and they are individually acclaimed in the form (e.g. Nama Gelasio Leoni).[51] Lions are initiates of the median grade in the hierarchy and, as we shall see, the first true 'participants' in the mysteries.

(3) In contrast, from the Felicissimus Mithraeum in Ostia (V299), no acclamations of named grade-holders or even mention of them (as such) have been recovered. All that remains is the none-the-less hugely informative sequence of mosaic panels running up the aisle, each of which contains symbols of both grade and tutelary planet, from the Raven and Mercury at the entrance end to the Father and Saturn at the cult-niche end.[52] The Felicissimus Mithraeum confirms *by spatial arrangement* the matter of seniority: the higher up the aisle, the higher the grade.

2.2.2.1 Grades and planets

At Santa Prisca and Felicissimus, as we have just seen, each grade is paired with a planet, and at Santa Prisca the grade-holders are said to be 'under the protection of' (*tutela*) that planet. The number of grades was not arbitrary. The seven grades were linked one-to-one with the seven planets. In other words, the Mithraists created seven grades and not eight or six *because* in the world view of classical astronomy there were seven planets and not eight or six.

The 'planets' included the two luminaries, i.e. the Sun and Moon, as well as the five planets visible to the naked eye: Mercury, Venus, Mars, Jupiter and Saturn. Grades and planets were paired as shown in Figure 2.3.

The Santa Prisca dipinti imply that the planets were apprehended, at this location at least, as guardians of the initiate as he passes through successive stages in a journey of some sort. In the Felicissimus Mithraeum, rather, the

Grade	Planet
Father *(Pater)*	Saturn
Sun-Runner *(Heliodromus)*	Sun
Persian *(Perses)*	Moon
Lion *(Leo)*	Jupiter
Soldier *(Miles)*	Mars
Nymphus	Venus
Raven *(Corax)*	Mercury

Figure 2.3 Grades and planets

planets are apprehended as the stages themselves in sequence along the aisle of the mithraeum, from the entrance to the cult-niche, implying a *temporal* progression: one is a Raven *before* one is a Nymphus, a Nymphus *before* one becomes a Miles, and so on. Going *up* the aisle from entrance to cult-niche tracks progress through the grades as one moves through life. Going down the aisle is, in this regard, meaningless. In the Santa Prisca fresco, in contrast, time is represented as a single ideal moment when the representatives of the first six grades in proper order, led by the Heliodromus, appear before the seated Father.

The assumption that the system of tutelary planets was part and parcel of the grade system has been challenged by Robert Turcan, who argued (1999) that it was confined to the area in which we have specific iconography, that is, to Rome and Ostia. In the sense that this linkage of grades to planets was formally and systematically developed to the greatest degree in this area, Turcan is probably right. However, it is not a question of all or nothing. We would argue that in a cult that was demonstrably obsessed with the stars and the visible heavens (Beck 1988, 2006a) seven grades would be inevitably associated with the seven planets.

2.2.2.2 What does one mean by 'up' and 'higher'? Conceptual metaphors at work in the Mithraeum

In discussing the Felicissimus Mithraeum we spoke of a 'sequence of mosaic panels running *up* the aisle': 'up' means from lower to higher in a literal, physical sense. But at Felicissimus the cult-niche end of the aisle is no higher physically than the entrance end; and this is the case in most mithraea, although at the cult-niche itself one may climb a final step or two. 'Up', then, is here metaphorical, indicating a sort of sacred ascent from a lowlier area of the mithraeum to one less lowly. Likewise, 'higher' is metaphorical when applied to the grades or the grade-holders in a comparison. Thus, metaphorically, the Lion is 'higher' or 'above' the Soldier: he has progressed farther 'up' the hierarchy.

Disentangling talk of physical realities from metaphorical usages piggybacking on that real-world talk is no easy matter. For historians the most serious difficulty is that the 'real world' of our subjects both *is* and *is not* our own contemporary 'real word' – 'is' in that people now and then share some commonalities of perceiving and experiencing their surroundings; 'is not' in that we and they construct/constructed widely differing representations of the 'real world'.[53] So let us simply speak of two 'cognized environments', theirs and ours: the environment as the ancients constructed, understood, and imagined it in many variant forms; and the environment as we moderns construct, understand, and imagine it in many variant forms. (Speaking of 'cognized environments' here is much the same as speaking of 'world views' à la Michael Kearney; see Chapter 1.) Although historians may be aware of the 'our vs. their world' problems of interpretation, they are relatively unsophisticated in exploring this distinction.[54]

A second problem arises in that our distinction between talking in metaphors and talking directly about the 'real world' (whatever that is) does not necessarily – or even at all – correspond to theirs, that is to distinctions drawn by our historical or anthropological subjects. Consider, as an example both vivid and highly germane here, the 'events' of the Resurrection and Ascension in the Christian narrative, as set out in the so-called 'Apostles' Creed:'

> He descended into hell. On the third day he rose again. He ascended into heaven (*descendit ad ínferos [katelthonta eis ta katôtatô], tertia die resurrexit [anastanta] a mortuis, ascendit ad caelos [anelthonta eis tous ouranous]*).

Literal? Metaphorical? Both? And for whom, when? Here, the questions need only be posed, not answered.

Failure to penetrate far into the languages and cultures of different times and different places is a shortcoming of the otherwise most helpful theory of 'conceptual metaphors' advanced by George Lakoff and Mark Johnson (1980, 1999: 45–73). In what follows we shall make considerable use of this approach. Before we start to do so, we emphasize that these are not abstract language games. The titles alone (1980's *Metaphors We Live By*, 1999's *Philosophy in the Flesh*) indicate otherwise. In the same spirit, we maintain that adopting this approach is an essential part of re-accessing religion *as lived* in the mithraeum.

Returning to UP/DOWN and ABOVE/BELOW in the context of the mithraeum,[55] the language of superiority/inferiority (LOWEST-TO-HIGHEST) when applied to the grade hierarchy is obviously metaphorical: e.g. THE FATHER IS ABOVE THE SUN-RUNNER WHO IS ABOVE THE PERSIAN and so on.[56] However, there is a complication when we turn to the analogy of the tutelary planets. One would expect – and the ancient candidate for initiation into the Mithraic mysteries (at least where the grade hierarchy was known) would most certainly have expected – the order of the tutelary planets to relate to the perceived order of the planets in physical space familiar to the culture of the times as an important aspect of the cognized physical macrocosm. (The objection that this was the macrocosm of only a learned elite we have encountered earlier in the present chapter and we shall encounter again in the following chapters.)

One might expect, then, that the order LOWEST-TO-HIGHEST that we find in the Mithraic grades would reflect a LOWEST-TO-HIGHEST order in their tutelary planets. Interestingly, this is not the case. In fact, as Beck showed in his monograph *Planetary Gods and Planetary Orders in the Mysteries of Mithras* (1988: 1–11), the order of the tutelary planets in the Mithraic mysteries is unique. It is based on, but does not follow precisely, the classic ancient astronomical ordering of the planets by distance from the earth at the centre outwards to the sphere of the fixed stars at the universe's edge.[57] As described in Cicero's famous 'Dream of Scipio':[58]

> The whole universe is comprised of nine circles, or rather spheres. The outermost of these is the celestial sphere, embracing all the rest, itself the supreme god, confining and containing all the other spheres. In it are fixed the eternally revolving movements of the stars. BENEATH it are the seven UNDERLYING spheres, which revolve in an opposite direction to that of the celestial sphere. One of these spheres belongs to that planet which on earth we call Saturn. BELOW it is that brilliant orb, propitious and helpful to the human race, called Jupiter. Next comes the ruddy one, which you call Mars, dreaded on earth. Next and occupying the middle region, comes the sun, leader, chief, and regulator of the other lights, mind and moderator of the universe, of such magnitude that it fills all with its radiance. The sun's companions, so to speak, each in its own sphere, follow – the one Venus, the other Mercury – and in the LOWEST sphere the moon, kindled by the rays of the sun, revolves. BELOW the moon all is mortal and transitory, with the exception of the souls bestowed upon the human race by the benevolence of the gods. ABOVE the moon all things are eternal. Now in the center, the ninth of the spheres, is the earth, never moving and AT THE BOTTOM.

The words above in small capitals are those that convey the order of the planets in the metaphors of DOWN/UP, HIGHER/LOWER, ABOVE/BELOW. That this language is indeed metaphorical follows from the fact that no planet is *literally* higher than any other. It is 'higher' or 'lower' by the equation of literal distance from the earth with *height*: the more distant the planet the HIGHER it is, the closer to earth the LOWER.[59] It is this metaphor that gives us the technical term 'superior' for those planets that are beyond the sun (Mars, Jupiter, Saturn) and 'inferior' for those deemed nearer to the earth than the sun (Venus, Mercury, Moon). From being metaphorically HIGHER or LOWER the planets acquire a SUPERIORITY OR INFERIORITY OF STATUS. And so, esoterically, the HIGHER a planet, the HIGHER the Mithraic grade under its tutelage – at least for the five planets proper (i.e. excluding the two luminaries):

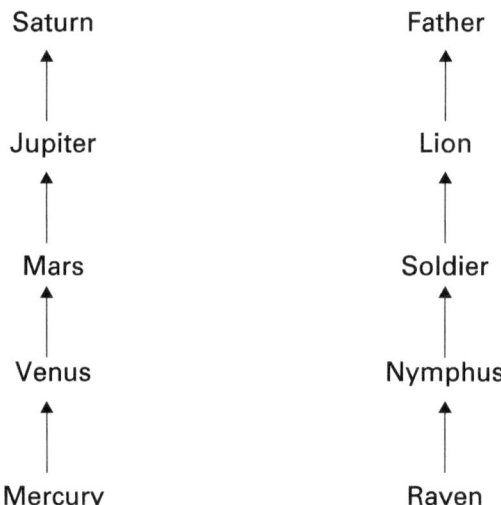

Figure 2.4 From higher to lower planets and grades

Had the order of the planets by distance from Earth been strictly followed, the Persian, under the moon's protection, would have been the first and lowest grade, and the Sun-Runner, would have been the median grade in order and dignity alike. Understandably, however, these two grades have been promoted or, to retain our metaphor, ELEVATED. They merit a HIGHER position in the hierarchy. So the Persian is placed ABOVE the Lion and the Sun-Runner ABOVE the Persian and INFERIOR only to the Father. Tracking what we might call the 'master metaphor' (HEIGHT) enables us to understand 'what's going on here' – and why:

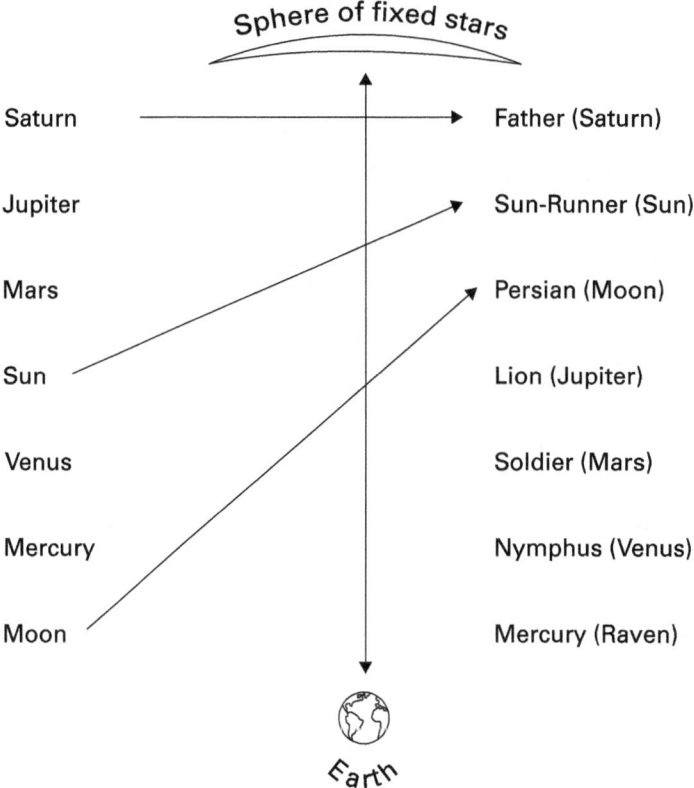

Figure 2.5 Planets and grades hierarchy

For the Sun-Runner, the elevation is not all gain. He loses his planet's literal centrality in the spatial order (three planets one side, three the other). Metaphorically, then, he loses the AUTHORITY that comes with CENTRALITY ('leader, chief, and regulator', as Cicero puts it) but does not acquire that of the SUMMIT or TOP. He is the 'second-in-command'. There is something of a paradox here. Mithraism was a solar cult. Its god was named Deus Sol Invictus Mithras. Yet the sun *as planet* is not supreme – Saturn is. This leads to a second paradox. In representations of the cult myth, Sol, the sun, appears as a separate character who interacts with Mithras. For example, he feasts with Mithras on the hide of the bull that Mithras has just killed. In the end, it will not be our business to try to 'resolve' either of these two paradoxes. They should be apprehended – and allowed to stand. But it is worth pointing out that the Father in the cult's economy is the surrogate of Mithras, as we noted above in discussing the 'Archery of the Father' scene on the Mainz ritual vessel. It is therefore only fitting that he should be ABOVE the grade-holder whose tutelary planet is the sun.

As we conclude this section, let us emphasize again that neither the modern reader – nor we, as the historians – can comprehend the cognitive processes of a Mithraic grade-holder unless we are prepared to enter empathetically the Mithraist's cognized environment. To do that, one must not only 'appropriate' – to use the fashionable term of 'lived ancient religion' scholarship – the macrocosm of Scipio's Dream but also re-imagine the Mithraist's own *largely unselfconscious* appropriation of the sort of details, frequently paradoxical or even contradictory, that we have set out in the last few pages and will continue to present in the section which follows. Above all, do not imagine some sort of Mithraic design team negotiating the details, all of which are on the table at a modern workshop on the grade hierarchy.

Panagiotidou (2016a, 2016b), in her study of the Asclepius cult, suggests that cognitive approaches to ancient evidence provide historians with the means of releasing themselves from their own common-sense understanding of the world in order to comprehend more deeply the world view of past people. In particular, she has examined the likely reception of the healing inscriptions found at the asclepieia, which record narratives of treatments performed by Asclepius. Some of these treatments have been characterized as miraculous, extraordinary, or even inconceivable by historians in terms of the implicit theoretical premise that they would have violated intuitive expectations of the 'real world' shared by Asclepius's supplicants,[60] since they more or less violate our modern common-sense perception of reality (Panagiotidou 2016b). However, these paradoxical or incomprehensible narratives mediated the development of the Asclepius cult into one of the most popular healing alternatives available in the 'cognized environment' of the Graeco-Roman era.

Cognitive theories[61] provide crucial insights into the impacts and processes of transmission of the healing narratives of Asclepius, throwing light on the ways in which historical agents would have 'lived' the phenomenal reality, experienced the infliction of an illness or a disease, sought relief and survival in adverse conditions, appropriated the available cultural practices, and internalized seemingly irrational beliefs in response to their current exigencies. Consequently, a new and continually growing set of evidence on human cognition may enrich historical explanations of religious transmission by taking into consideration the involvement of personal needs, goals, uncertainties, emotional and mental states, as well as of the processes of social interaction and cultural learning in the historical agents' decision-making and appropriation of the available religious alternatives (Panagiotidou 2014). Similarly, in the study of the Mithras cult, the primary challenge for historians is not to resolve the phenomenal paradoxes of the cult and to assess conceivability of its specific symbolic systems and precepts and their plausibility in reference to the wider historical contexts, but to explore the processes of internalization of the Mithraic symbolic systems, the impacts those systems would have had on the initiates' mental and bodily states, the ways the initiands experienced their entry into the mysteries, and how Mithraists' choices and actions influenced both their self-perception and world view.

2.2.2.3 *Progress* UP *the grade hierarchy and the metaphor of the* JOURNEY

As described earlier in this chapter, Porphyry (*On Abstinence* 4.16) reported that an earlier writer, Pallas, claimed that Mithraists call women 'hyenas', those who are participants (*metechontes*) 'lions', and the UNDERLINGS (HYPÊRETOUNTES) 'ravens'. This is best construed as meaning that initiates of the Lion grade and ABOVE were full participants in the mysteries, while those BELOW (HYP-), starting with the initial grade of Raven, served them (Gordon 1980a: 32–3). From a structural point of view, it is worth noting that the TOP three grades, i.e. the *metechontes* ABOVE Leo, have as their tutelary planets in sequence the LOWEST of the planets (the moon with the Persian), the MEDIAN planet (the sun with the Sun-Runner), and HIGHEST of the planets (Saturn with the Father). The TOP three grades thus replicate the first, middle, and final stages of a true planetary ASCENT.

We may now look at the individual grades in turn from LOWEST (Raven) to HIGHEST (Father), asking what it means to *be*, esoterically, first a Raven, then a Nymphus, then a Soldier, and so on UP. We have seen already that it means undertaking a peculiar – in the strict sense of that word – planetary journey. As our route map, we shall for the most part rely on Richard Gordon's classic article 'Reality evocation, and boundary in the Mysteries of Mithras' (1980a).[62] Following Gordon, for us, will itself be a JOURNEY; so, at least for some Mithraists, was PROGRESS through the grades. The path, as Gordon (1980a: 23) rightly stresses, winds through make-believe and pretence; roles are taken up, played with, and discarded; one *is by pretending to be*.

In the quotation which follows Gordon conflates two of Mithraism's esoteric journeys: the JOURNEY of celestial ASCENT, which we shall discuss more fully in the next chapter, and the JOURNEY UP the grade hierarchy. It is the latter that concerns us now.

> The journey is thus (1) a 'journey' which one can in truth only perform in spirit[63] (2) a 'journey' which purports to be vertical but which is in fact horizontal (3) a 'journey' which takes place entirely within a room which is called the 'cosmos' (4) a 'journey' which can be known only by its internal markings in the cult, the grades, through which one climbs simply by fulfilling the overt ritual and moral requirements. Pretended (if actual) acts-in-the-world take one along an improbable path to an absurd goal – and all without one's having to move at all. Real acts, that only change the real world, could never achieve such things; but, by pretended acts, you can 'do' anything.
> Gordon 1980a: 39

Symbols of the planets are depicted on each of the mosaic panels UP the aisle of the Felicissimus Mithraeum (V299) along with additional symbols that are associated with each grade:[64]

(1) The Felicissimus symbols of the Raven, the first and LOWEST of the grades, whose panel is closest to the entrance and farthest from the cult-niche, are (a) a raven, (b) the caduceus of Mercury, the messenger of the gods and the Mithraic Raven's tutelary planet, and (c) a small one-handled cup.

Self-evidently, the Raven is the 'gofer' grade, in the slang sense of one 'who performs minor or menial tasks such as running errands' (*Webster's*, 'from being asked to *go for* whatever is needed'). The Raven's function follows from and is indicated by the errand-running function of his tutelary god. Also, we should keep in mind Pallas's testimony (via Porphyry, *On Abstinence* 4.16) mentioned above, that the Mithraists' 'ravens' are the UNDERLINGS (HYPÊRETOUNTES). Whatever else this passage implies about the hierarchy, it shows that the Ravens were at the BOTTOM of the pecking order (pun intended).

'UNDERLINGS' typically 'wait table', and there are four representations of persons with ravens' heads doing precisely that for the banquet of Mithras and Sol: (a) V42.13 (a fresco from Dura),[65] (b) V397 (reverse of a fragmentary relief from Rome), (c) V483 (the Santa Prisca fresco discussed above, section 2.2.2), (d) V1896 (reverse of a relief from Konjic, Dalmatia).[66] So it is easy enough to imagine the initiate appropriating the Raven's basic role of service at the outset of his sacred career. Of the evocations of the Felicissimus symbol of a cup, serving a drink would be the most straightforward.

As Gordon demonstrated (1980a: 25–32), the raven has a special niche in the animal lore of the ancient world.[67] He is a go-between who conveys signs from gods to men, and is uniquely able to comprehend the import of the signs he brings.⁶⁸ But as an errand-boy he is unreliable,⁶⁹ and although there is no proven incident of out-and-out theft on his ancient mythological record, he is not entirely 'of good character'. That, however, might not have been to the disadvantage of his namesakes in a cult whose members, as we saw (above, section 2.2.1), prided themselves on being 'initiates of the cattle-theft'.

(2) The Felicissimus symbols of the Nymphus, the second grade, are lost except for a diadem and a lamp together on the right in what remains of the physically damaged panel. Both symbols denote the tutelary planet, Venus. The lamp alludes to the planet Venus as Phosphorus, the 'Light-Bearer', the Morning Star who rises before the Sun to announce the coming dawn (Gordon 1980a: 49–51). As every Mithraist and most of their contemporaries would have known, she was also the Evening Star, becoming visible above the western horizon after the sun has set.⁷⁰

There is no clearer illustration of the difference between what the ancients, Mithraists included, 'had in mind' and what most of us moderns 'have in mind' – in other words between their cognized environment and ours. Ask almost anyone today the identity of 'that brilliant star over there', while indicating Venus, and the likelihood of their responding correctly is minimal.⁷¹ Asking the same question of an ancient would have got you a pitying or withering look.

The Nymphus, like his tutelary planet, is new light brought to the community, as a greeting preserved by Firmicus Maternus (*De. Err.* 19.1) attests: 'Behold Nymphus! Hail Nymphus! Hail New Light!'⁷² Neither this nor any other testimony indicates how precisely the Nymphus instantiates the community's 'new light'.

The term 'Nymphus' is a Mithraic coinage, intentionally paradoxical, in that it denotes a socio-cultural impossibility in the ancient world: a person who is both male (the masculine ending *–us*) and a 'bride' (*nymph-*). The Nymphus is thus a recognition of sorts of the female within an exclusively male cult within a patriarchal culture. But the recognition is scarcely complimentary. Let us recall Pallas's statement that the Mithraists called women 'hyenas' (Porphyry *On Abstinence* 4.16). As Gordon demonstrated (1980a: 58–61), the hyena in the ancient encyclopedia instantiated many sinister and alarming traits, not the least of which was its ability to change its sex. One can imagine few endowments more unsettling to a sense of rightful male superiority and control. One wonders, then, why the Mysteries thought it desirable for their initiates, where the full sevenfold grade sequence was in place, to include a 'male bride' at all.⁷³ The answer must surely be that, while one might choose to erase women in certain contexts, no such option was possible for the planet Venus. Of whom or what could she be the tutelary planet? The Nymphus was the rather clumsy compromise solution.

(3) The third grade, that of Soldier (*Miles*), used to seem as straightforward as the second seemed problematic. Many Mithraists were soldiers or veterans and most people throughout the Empire knew what a soldier did and, more importantly, what he was *obliged* to do. So, it seemed, one probably would not have required the same level of cognitive training to be a Mithraic 'Soldier' as was required for a Mithraic 'Raven' or 'Nymphus'. Two of the Felicissimus symbols of the Soldier, those on the right side of the panel, are likewise straightforward: a spear above a helmet. They allude, obviously, to a soldier's function and accoutrement, and also to the grade's tutelary planet, Mars.

The third symbol seemed unproblematic too ... at least for as long as the common-sense identification of the object as a *sarcina* ('military bag' V299.7) went largely unchallenged.[74] Recently, however, A. Chalupa and T. Glomb (2013) have convincingly argued this symbol represented not a bag, but a joint of meat, specifically a bull's hindquarter.[75] Gordon (2013: 37) fits this new identification into a larger scheme of *community service functions* for a set of the Felicissimus symbols:

> the cup in the *Corax* panel evokes serving at the feast, a role that is explicit in several representations of the mythical feast; the lamp in the *Nymphus* panel evokes the role of light in the cult, and specifically lighting lamps; the fire-shovel in the Leo panel evokes their role in the tending of fire. By implication, the severed hind-quarter in the *Miles* panel evokes the role of this grade in Mithraic sacrificial practice namely butchery of the animals required for the communal meal.

As Gordon has also demonstrated (1980a: 53) the soldier was a rather marginal figure, barred from contracting full civil marriage, one of the key rights (and obligations) of a socially engaged citizen.

Tertullian, in his treatise *De Corona Militis*, 15 3–4,[76] describes a ritual of initiation into the grade of Soldier:

> You should be ashamed now, fellow soldier [sc. of Christ], not of being judged by him but by some soldier of Mithras. When he is initiated in the cave, in the real camp of darkness, he is offered a crown on a sword point, a sort of mockery of martyrdom, which is then fitted on his head, but he is instructed to remove it with his hand from his head and to transfer it, if possible, to his shoulders, saying that Mithras is his crown. And from then on he never wears a crown, and has that as mark of his initiation, whenever he is put to the test at the oath-taking, and is immediately recognized as a soldier of Mithras, if he rejects the crown, if he says that in his god he has his crown.
>
> trans. Beard, North, and Price 1998: vol. 2, 312

Remarkable is the Mithraic Soldier's renunciation of any distinction other than Mithras himself.

(4) The Lions (*Leones*) constituted the middle grade: half way UP, three grades BELOW, three ABOVE. We have already noted the testimony of Pallas recorded by Porphyry (*On Abstinence* 4.16), the Lions were called participants (*metechontes*); and we have observed that the testimony is best construed as meaning that initiates of the Lion grade and ABOVE were full participants in the Mysteries, while those BELOW, starting with the initial grade of Raven, served them (Gordon 1980a: 32-3). Promotion to Lion thus indicates a significant shift from the preparatory state of the first three grades, which were in the service of their SUPERIORS, to full participation in the Mysteries.

After the Fathers (100 identified individuals, mentioned 122 times), the Lions constitute the most frequently attested of the grades: 41 individuals mentioned the same number of times (Clauss 1990: 185).[77] We have already noticed their presence and importance at the Santa Prisca Mithraeum: they have their own special procession with individual *nama*-acclamations. In the so-called 'Mithraic Catechism from Egypt' (Brashear 1992) they even have their own space, a *leonteion* (line 8 recto). Indeed, the 'catechism', which takes the form of alternating questions and responses, may well be a ritual of initiation into the Lion grade. Line 14 verso reads (trans. Brashear):

> did you become a Leo (*leôn*)?' Say: 'By the ... of the father.'[78]

The Felicissimus symbols for the Lions are (left to right) a fire shovel, a sistrum, and a thunderbolt. The intent of the last of these is straightforward: it signifies Jupiter, the grade's tutelary planet. The fact that Jupiter is the supreme god of the Roman state further enhances the grade's importance, its CENTRALITY in more ways than one.

When one has stated the obvious, that the fire shovel signifies fire, the important question becomes: what, in the context of Mithraic Lions, does fire signify? Literally, as the quotation from Gordon's article above suggests (2013: 37), tending fires, for whatever purposes, appears to have been the Lions' role in the domestic economy of Mithraic communities. But, more generally, fire purifies by burning away impurities, and there is unusually ample evidence that it was precisely this higher function in the cult's sacred economy that was served by the Lions. Water, of course, serves and symbolizes the same end of purification – think 'ablution', 'washing away sins', and so on – but it was the medium of fire that the Mithraists employed, entrusting the task to their Lions.[79]

If a fiery liquid is required for ablution, honey meets the need,[80] as Porphyry records, speaking specifically about Mithraic Lions (*On the Cave* 15):

> So in the Lion mysteries, when honey is poured instead of water for purification on the hands of the initiates, they are exhorted to keep them pure from everything distressing, harmful and loathsome; and since he is an initiate of fire, which has a cathartic effect, they use on him a liquid related to fire, rejecting water as inimical to it.
>
> trans. Arethusa ed.

The Lions, at Santa Prisca at least, were the 'incense burners,' through whom the community 'gave incense', as the following dipinto intimates (V485):

> *Accipe thuricremos, pater, accipe sancte Leones*
> *per quos thuradamus, per quos consumimur ipsi.*
> Father, receive those who burn incense, holy one, receive the Lions,
> through whom we offer incense, through whom we ourselves are consumed.

Incense, self-evidently, is another fiery substance.[81] Its offering here by the Lions is a radical act of dedication and purification, which in some sense 'consumes' the Mithraic community (the 'we' of *consumimur*).[82]

As Gordon showed (1980a: 33–7), the animal lore of antiquity depicted lions, at least the males,[83] as moral creatures 'capable of discerning moral faults in human beings' and with 'an uncanny capacity to remember those who had helped or harmed [them]' (p. 33, with n. 21).[84] The leonine virtue of courage with overtones of nobility and generosity, still encapsulated in the epithet 'lion-hearted', is perennial. Presumably, Mithraic Lions can be expected to be no different.

In Egypt, Aelian tells us (*On the Nature of Animals* 12.7) that lions in some places were cared for and entertained like humans and even 'shared a measure of respect due the gods'. Hence, perhaps, the Lions' Felicissimus symbol of the sistrum, the distinctive rattle of Egyptian religious ritual and procession (Gordon 1980a: 35 f.).

To grasp fully the fiery ethos of lions one must look to the heavens and to the constellation and zodiacal sign of Leo. Leo is the astrological 'house' of the Sun, as the Sun is 'at home' there in high summer. 'There,' said Aratus (*Phaenomena* 149), 'are the Sun's hottest pathways.' The fire of the celestial Lion, however, in contrast to the righteous and purifying fire of Mithraic lions and the lions in Egyptian culture mentioned above, is mostly destructive and predatory.[85]

(5) Much less is known about the grade of Persian which, as can be assumed from its name, referred to the cult's supposed Iranian origins and thus to its

putative founder Zoroaster. The grade's primary associations, however, are with vegetation, agriculture, and crops. Porphyry refers to this in *On the Cave* 16 (trans. Arethusa ed.): 'when, on the other hand, they offer honey to the Persian as the preserver of fruits, it is its preservative powers that they treat symbolically.' The contrast here ('on the other hand') is with the use of honey as a paradoxically fiery liquid to purify Lions (see above).

We are now in a position to explicate the grade's four Felicissimus symbols. On the left is the harpê, which is *both* a sickle for reaping *and* the sword with which Perseus, the eponymous ancestor of the Persian race, decapitated Medusa.[86] To its right, one above the other, are (a) a crescent moon, (b) a star, and (c) a plough.[87] Self-evidently, the lunar crescent represents the grade's tutelary planet. The moon, in the circumambient culture, governed agricultural operations, some being appropriate to the waxing moon, others to the waning moon (Lunais 1979). Lastly, the star, we suggest, is not mere celestial decoration. Rather it alludes to the imagined etymology of that archetypal Persian Zoroaster's name. *Aster-* is Greek for 'star', and that for some was warrant enough to turn him into a star-worshipper (Beck 1991: 523).

(6) The sixth grade of initiation had the name Heliodromus ('Sun-Runner'). The term itself was of Mithraic coinage. The grade's associations are entirely with the sun, as exemplified by its Felicissimus symbols: (l. to r.) a raised torch, such as we find carried by Cautes, who symbolizes sunrise and the sun ascending from the midwinter to the midsummer solstice; a seven-rayed bonnet with tied strings for fastening beneath the chin; and the whip with which the Sun drives his four-horse team. The solar bonnet is manifestly a stage prop – wisely so, for a proper radiate crown might intimate aspirations beyond mere role-playing.

Inside the mithraeum, the lived relationship between the Sun-Runner and the TOPMOST grade of Father would have taught the initiates, by observed precedence in ritual and physical placement, that of the two aspects of *Deus* **Sol** *Invictus* **Mithras**, the former is secondary within the Mysteries, the latter primary.

As described in an earlier section (2.2.2.2) of this chapter, the scene represented on one side of the Mainz Vessel portrays a cult Father drawing a bow at an initiand in a ritual act of initiation. The other side is described by Beck as 'the Procession of the Sun-Runner' (2000: 154–67, with Plate XIV):

> The other side of the vessel shows a processional scene with four figures moving in file to the left (Plate XIV [between pp. 174 and 175]). The first figure wears a breastplate and is the only one on the vessel so clad. The second and the fourth carry rods, held in front of them in the right hand, but in strikingly different and

contrasted positions: no. 2 downwards as one might hold a walking stick, no. 4 upwards almost vertically. They are further differentiated in that no. 2 wears a Persian cap (like the Father in scene A), while no 4. is bareheaded. The figure between them, no. 3 in the procession, brandishes a whip [154].

The first, breast-plated figure is arguably an initiate of the Soldier grade, the second and fourth with their raised and lowered rods imitate Cautes and Cautopates,[88] while the third is a Sun-Runner himself. The intent of the procession, Beck argued, is to represent and so celebrate the sun's annual journey around the heavens, by replicating it in the mithraeum qua 'image of the universe'.[89] Role-playing – or watching your colleagues play roles – thus reinforces identity, even when that identity is pure make-believe: to seem to be is to be.[90]

(7) Finally, at the TOP of the hierarchy was the grade of Father, the goal of the JOURNEY for those initiates taking all seven stages of this COURSE. The Father's Felicissimus symbols are (l. to r.) a *patera* or plate for pouring libations, a staff, a Persian cap, and a sickle. The sickle alludes to the grade's tutelary planet, Saturn, in his Latin and Roman persona as an agricultural deity. The Persian cap identifies him as the surrogate of Mithras himself in the cult's sacred economy. The staff or sceptre confirms his authority and right to rule. Likewise the *patera* confirms his sacred authority: he is the licensed intermediary between his community and the gods. The extent of his authority is emphasized at Santa Prisca where the phrase 'from orient to occident' is added to his *nama*-acclamation – and to his only (see above, section 2.2.3).

We also saw above (section 2.2.2) how, in the community at Mainz, it was the Father who conducted an initiation. We may generalize from this that the Father was in charge of admission to the community. *A priori*, this is more likely than not: if not the Father, then who? And we have already discussed Firmicus Maternus's information that the cult member, to become an 'initiate of the cattle theft' and so to identify with Mithras and his doings, enters into a special relationship with the Father by becoming the latter's 'right-hand-grasper' (*syndexios*).[91]

2.2.3 Feasting and fellowship on the divine and human planes: the cult meal

As the surrogate of Mithras, the Father presides over the cult meal.[92] This we see most clearly in the representation of the banquet of Mithras and Sol from Konjic in Dalmatia (V1896).[93] Not that Mithras himself is here represented in an obvious way as a cult Father, nor, for that matter, Sol as a Sun-Runner. Rather, because two of the servitors who are represented as lesser grade-holders (one with the head of a lion and the other with the head of a raven[94]), we may infer that the cult meal of the initiates is understood to replicate the banquet of the two gods. The same holds true for the banquet scene at Santa Prisca (V483: see above, section 2.2.2.3),[95] where too there is a raven-headed servitor. Actually, the Konjic relief and the Santa Prisca fresco merely confirm, in a vivid way, what we should have assumed all along: that in the apprehension of the initiates, the boundary between feast of the gods and human cult meal is quite permeable, although a particular representation may tend to emphasize one aspect over the other. The Konjic relief, for example, emphasizes the human by alluding explicitly to the grades of Raven and Lion, which, as we saw in the preceding section, are identities assumed by initiates.

A raven-headed servitor, as we noted above, is represented also in a fresco from Dura (V42.13) and on the reverse of a fragmentary relief from Rome (V397). Here it is important to keep in mind what the initiate apprehends at the deepest level on viewing such bizarre representations: not a detail in a narrative about the two gods ('they were attended by raven-headed servants' – although maybe the story was sometimes told that way); not a detail in an actual prescribed ritual ('our Ravens put on full-head raven outfits when serving at our cult meal' – although maybe they sometimes did); but a blending of the two, cult myth and cult meal, at this point into a single whole. The initiate's personal take-away? *Et in Arcadia ego*: I too belong in this fused world. It is the genius of the Santa Prisca Mithraeum frescos, where the banquet scene on the left (north) wall merges with the procession of Lions leading up to it, to represent this fused world of gods and humans.

As one might expect, the Mithraists were not alone in the fusion of two realities at an association's meal. Philip Harland (2003: 55–88) has shown that, despite earlier scholars' insistence on the separation of the eating and drinking from more esoteric religious components, the two were actually inseparable. The fusion is best exemplified in the convivialities of the association of the Iobacchoi at Athens (pp. 81–3), whose regulations include protocols for keeping the merry-making within reasonable bounds. For Mithraism, recent excavations, with a more sophisticated study of the animal remains from the sites in the north-west of the Empire,[96] have led us to appreciate just how ample and varied was the meat consumed by the feasting initiates.

In the mithraeum, the cult meal was celebrated on the two side benches facing each other across the central aisle, at the top of which stood the icon of the bull-killing Mithras. This means that, as Manfred Clauss succinctly concludes (2012: 108), '*der Gott is somit selbst der Gastgeber*'.[97] This point is brought home by representing the banquet scene on the reverse of the tauroctony in the Konjic relief and three reliefs from Germany: V1083 (Hedderheim I), 1137 (Rückingen), 1247 (Dieburg).[98] The three reliefs from Germany had pivots for changing the scene on display to the initiates as appropriate to the liturgical context.

2.2.4 Long-term purposeful activities are journeys

The rituals of initiation into the Mithras cult would have had an underlying narrative structure that embedded coherent sequences of actions with specific starting points, certain courses, and final culminations. These sequences of actions would have been conceptualized as literal or mental movements along certain paths by the initiates via the SOURCE–PATH–GOAL schema. The SOURCE–PATH–GOAL schema provides the prototypical narrative structure for all human physical movements. Every human action takes place in space and time, and presupposes that the subjects move along various pathways towards goal destinations (M. Johnson 1993: 168–9). During real physical journeys stories unfold as the travellers move from a specific starting-point, along a road to a particular location. Humans can metaphorically represent the same process as they evolve from the beginning to the end, and they can further perceive every purposeful activity as a natural or mental movement toward the realization of a goal. In this light, the SOURCE–PATH–GOAL schema pertains to all kinds of spatial actions and temporal processes. According to M. Johnson, 'the SOURCE–PATH–GOAL schema, by means of various metaphorical mappings, relates patterns in domains of experience as diverse as physical travel, long-term purposeful activity, following the connection of episodes, and grasping the character's intentional states and actions' (p. 168). Thereby, this cognitive pattern provides an isomorphism for the conceptual metaphors humans construct during their everyday interactions with the world.

Initiation into the Mithraic mysteries is itself a prototypical story of a journey, which would have been conceptualized by the initiates on the basis of the complex LONG-TERM PURPOSEFUL ACTIVITIES ARE JOURNEYS metaphor (M. Johnson 1993: 16; Lakoff and M. Johnson 1999: 60–1). From a neural perspective, the LONG-TERM PURPOSEFUL ACTIVITIES ARE JOURNEYS metaphor is generated by parallel activation of neural connections that forge a mapping between other primary metaphors, and in particular between the PURPOSES ARE DESTINATIONS and ACTION IS MOTION metaphors – a combination that further formulates the notion of a journey as a long route through a sequence of destinations (Lakoff and M. Johnson 1999: 62).

For *some* Mithraists, as we have seen (section 2.2.2.3), the JOURNEY led THROUGH and UP a hierarchy of grades. Each grade could be regarded as a STAGE in the JOURNEY. As we also saw, each grade was under the protection of one of the seven planets, but the tutelary planets were not so assigned that one passed through the grades in the sequence corresponding to what the ancients supposed were the planets' actual physical arrangement in space (section 2.2.2.1). This is of crucial importance, for there was another sense in which the initiates were thought to pass through the planets – or, strictly speaking, through their spheres.

The Mithraists, we are told in a passage from Porphyry's *On the Cave* (6) already mentioned, 'induct[ed] their initiate into a mystery of the descent of souls and their exit back out again (*tên eis katô kathodon kai palin exodon mystagôgountes telousi ton mystên*)'. What is transmitted in this mystery is not a metaphorical journey (as, for example, John Bunyan's *Pilgrim's Progress* is a metaphor for the trials and tribulations of a Christian life). No, 'the descent of souls and their exit back out again' was or was supposed to be an actual journey down to Earth from a gate in the sphere of the fixed stars via the seven spheres of the planets and back up and out of another gate in the celestial sphere via those same planetary spheres in the reverse order. Our main goal here is to emphasize that, to the Mithraist, what may seem to be a metaphorical journey was, to them, factual. Granted, the journey – not to mention the postulated travellers – is preposterous from a modern point of view, but it is not merely metaphorical.

Porphyry's account is supported and amplified by a quotation from the anti-Christian polemicist Celsus, preserved in Origen's rebuttal (*Against Celsus* 6.22):

> These things [i.e. the celestial ascent of souls] the teaching (*logos*) of the Persians and their Mithraic initiation (*hê tou Mithrou teletê*) intimate. For there is in that initiation a symbol (*symbolon*) of the two celestial revolutions (*periodôn*), that of the fixed stars and that assigned to the planets, and of the route of the soul through and out (*diexodou*) of them. Such is the symbol: a seven-gated ladder and an eighth [sc. gate] on top (*klimax heptapylos, epi de autêi ogdoê*).

Here there is indeed a metaphor, but it is not the *diexodos*, the 'route through and out'. Rather, it is something both material and visually apprehended: it is the ladder with eight 'gates' or, as we would say, 'rungs' – seven for the spheres of the planets and one for the sphere of the fixed stars.[99]

In the metaphorical ITINERARY of progress THROUGH the grades, each grade signified a mediated station THROUGH which the initiate should pass in order to arrive at the destination, which, whether reached or not, was presumably the status of Father, the embodiment of wisdom and authority. As we saw above (section 2.2.2), however, it is improbable in the extreme that passage through the grades was required of, or even available to, every initiate in every community. Nevertheless, some sort of esoteric NURTURE, to switch metaphors, was surely available to those not choosing or unable to choose the grade option. Initiation into a serious enterprise is seldom a one-off event. The cult would have provided both sorts of initiate with the essential intellectual, psychological, constitutional, and material resources for their JOURNEYS.

2.2.5 A purposeful life is a journey

As we saw in the previous section, the imaginative function of the LONG-TERM PURPOSEFUL ACTIVITIES ARE JOURNEYS metaphor would have underlined the inner synthetic structure of the experience of the initiation. Initiation into the mysteries of Mithras, however, would not have been just a sequence of coherent actions and experiences that took place during the ritual practices with no connection to the initiates' wider life-stories. On the contrary, initiations would have been experienced as significant events that would have signalled important transitions in life and would have affected the ways in which initiates perceived themselves and their world, shaped their long-term identities, and planned their actions.

In particular, initiation into the Mithraic mysteries provided a new purpose to the initiates' lives, which would have been conceptualized according to the complex A PURPOSEFUL LIFE IS A JOURNEY metaphor (Lakoff and M. Johnson 1999: 61–2). Mithraists, largely deriving from characteristically mobile social ranks (for example, the army and imperial bureaucracy) – or at least by the potential for mobility – within the vast Roman Empire, would have perceived their lives not as an ordinary peregrination, but as a specific journey which defined their wider life-plans. Initiation into the Mithraic mysteries provided to them a new strategy of existence. In the cultic context, the world was perceived as integrated logically and structurally, and initiates acquired a specific orientation and position within it. Through their initiation, they had been placed in the service of Mithras, and their mission was to strive for the preservation of the cosmic order for which the god stood and, as we shall see in the next chapter, their final destiny was the ascent of their souls to the sphere of the fixed stars and immortality.

2.3 The narrative of initiation and the initiates' life-stories

As M. Johnson aptly noted, 'stories are lived before they are told' (M. Johnson 1993: 177) and the initiatory rituals to the Mithras cult comprised such kinds of stories that unfolded within the mithraea. In this chapter we have illuminated how the conceptualization of the initiations as meaningful narratives would have been grounded on imaginative cognitive devices common to humans, such as conceptual metaphors. Complex conceptual metaphors, as well as other resources that were available in the historical, social, and cultural contexts of the Graeco-Roman world (such as myths, folk stories, encyclopaedia, established exemplars), would have organized the initiates' lived experiences within the mithraea into coherent narrative schemas that affected their self-perception and formed their cult identities. These identities would have lasted more than the initiatory rituals affecting the initiates' long-term self-perception, since the initiations would have been integrated as significant episodes in their wider life-stories that embraced the temporality and the intentional organization of the lived initiatory experiences at a more general level (M. Johnson 1993: 170–1).

After initiation, new directions, new motives and meanings would have been revealed to the initiates, affecting their future actions and choices. The wider narrative structure of their lives would have embodied the behavioural principles and precepts that inspired the initiates in the Mithraic context, and could provide them with the means to trace potential actions within concrete day-to-day situations that would be in line with these principles (cf. pp. 175–6).

3

Space and Time in the Mithras Cult

Initiations into the Mithraic mysteries were carried out in specific places (i.e. the mithraea), and were high points in the process of integrating members into their communities. The metaphorical conception of the mithraeum constituted one of the major symbolic structures that represented, expressed and justified the Mithraic world view. In Chapter 2, we outlined the conceptual metaphor theory of Lakoff and M. Johnson (1999), which provides insights into the neural underpinnings of metaphorical thought and may illuminate how the initiates would have conceptualized the lived experience of initiation into the cult, and how this lived experience would have affected their self-perception and long-term identities. As mentioned in the previous chapter, initiatory rituals would have been stored in the initiates' episodic memory as significant personal experiences, which would have subsequently affected the ways in which they perceived themselves and their role and position in the world.

In this chapter, the conceptual metaphor theory may throw some light on the Mithraists' metaphorical perception of space as well as in the ways they would have conceptualized time in terms of inferences that derived from their embodied perception of space. Initiations into the Mithraic mysteries of course took place in space and time, but in addition to their naturally occurring spatial and temporal dimensions,[1] the rituals were invested with complex metaphorical meanings and concepts that would have altered the initiate's perception of universal space and time as fundamental categories of the world.[2] Supplementary to Lakoff and M. Johnson's theory, we will refer to the conceptual blending (or integration) theory suggested by Fauconnier and Turner (2002) in order to explore how more complex conceptual metaphors of space and time would have mediated perception of the mithraeum as the universe.

But before we proceed to explore the metaphorical perception of space and time in the Mithras cult, we will briefly describe the cognitive processes through which spatial and temporal metaphors emerge. Beginning from the theoretical premise that Mithraists would have shared with us the same basic cognitive functions and abilities, a brief look at the neurological underpinnings of the embodied cognition may illuminate the ways in which the multiple stimuli of the Mithras cult would have been processed by the Mithraists' cognitive systems and would have mediated the conception of space and time within the mithraeum in both literal and metaphorical terms. Our goal may seem trivial: arguing that the initiates had 'human minds' may sound self-evident. However, emphasizing the ordinary cognitive mechanisms shared by humans may support our commonsensical historical assumptions about how the initiates would have perceived and conceived the spatio-temporal dimensions of the world – both terrestrial and celestial – offering some deeper insights into their lived experiences within the Mithraic microcosm.

In particular, cognitive science has gained a great deal of insight about the embodied perceptions and metaphorical conceptions of space and time in general – insights that we briefly outline in the first two sections (3.1–3.2) before moving to an application of it to our fragmentary knowledge of Mithraic concepts and practices with the intent of shedding some light on the ways in which Mithraists would have perceived the spatial and temporal dimensions of their initiatory experiences (3.3).

3.1 Embodied cognition and perception of space

In the middle of the twentieth century, the French philosopher Maurice Merleau-Ponty challenged the Cartesian idea that the world is simply an extension of the human mind and thought (2002: x–xii, 429–75). In his *Phenomenology of Perception* (2002, first published in 1945) he suggested a phenomenological approach according to which 'the world is always "already there" before reflection begins' (2002: vii) and explored how objective reality is subjectively experienced by humans. Transcending the separation between mind and body,[3] Merleau-Ponty argued that the 'lived body' is the locus of the human situatedness in the world and the 'medium' through which we *view* and *feel* the world, and reach knowledge and expression of what we *view* and *feel* (Tilley 2004: 2–3; see Merleau-Ponty 2002: 95, 120, 169). In this respect the body is an 'object', a 'being-in-itself' (Tilley 2004: 3) that, among other material objects comprising the world, situates us – and other lived organisms – in space and time through its corporeal existence. However, we cannot experience our bodies 'from the outside' as material objects (p. 3). We identify with our bodies and live through them. Therefore the body is also a 'subject', a 'being-for-itself'. The *embodied perception* is the portal which connects the 'lived bodies' with their surroundings and mediates self-awareness of the embodied subjects as unique entities (p. 3).

Although Merleau-Ponty (2002: ix) criticized scientific explanations of human existence, his approach contributed to the turn of cognitive sciences to the study of the close connection between the body, the brain and the world, and gave rise to the notion of *embodied cognition* (see, e.g., Varela et al. 1991; Damasio 1994; Clark 1997, 2008; Jeannerod 2006; A. Geertz 2010; Shapiro 2011; Kimmel 2013). Research on human cognition from the mid-twentieth century onwards seems to confirm the inextricable connections between body and mind and provides insights into how embodied cognition determines which aspects of the world are perceptible, thereby engendering phenomenal reality. In this light, 'embodiment' is not just a philosophical argument, but rather the roots of cognition are fundamentally concerned with maintaining communication within and outside the body; as such functions aren't localized, but rather are distributed throughout the system.

3.1.1 Neural underpinnings of embodied perception

Modern research on human cognition illuminates the complexity of our brain systems that are inextricably connected to and communicate with our whole body through which varied stimuli cross the boundaries of our perception. The central nervous system (CNS), defined as the brain and the spinal cord, appears to coordinate the whole activity of the human body and to process the information received from both the internal bodily milieu and the external world (see, e.g., Nieuwenhuys et al. 2008 [1976]; Augustine 2008; Brodal 2010). The limbic system, located in deeper parts of the brain (including the cingulate gyrus, thalamus, hypothalamus, hippocampus, septal nuclei, amygdala, and the olfactory bulb), is the centre of emotions, which generates feelings and emotional reactions triggered by external or internal stimuli, like smells and images, thoughts, and memories.[4] The executive functions and higher order cognitive processing take place in the prefrontal cortex and the anterior cingulate cortex, which connects the emotional and cognitive processes, and enables self-awareness, reasoning, decision-making, task-solving, abstract thought and execution.[5] The complex subsystems of the CNS are closely associated with each other and are further connected with the whole body through the peripheral nervous system (PNS). The PNS comprises nerves and ganglia throughout the body and continually supplies the brain with data and information from the other bodily parts and internal organs, as well as from the external world (see, e.g., Ashwell and Waite 2004: 94–110). The autonomic (or visceral) system,[6] which includes the sympathetic (SNS) and the parasympathetic subsystems (PSNS) is the part of the PNS that, closely associated with the CNS, regulates the unconscious bodily actions and ensures homeostasis.[7] A complex interoceptive somatosensory system connects bodily tissues with the brain and continually sends and receives information from within the body about the physiological state of the organism. This interoceptive information is meta-represented in the right anterior insula cortex, so that the organism as a 'feeling self' is aware of its internal conditions and needs (hunger, thirst, internal sensations and so on (Craig 2003: 501, 503–4)). Simultaneously, the exteroceptive sensory system[8] connects the human body with its external surroundings, determines the receptive field, and sends data for perception to specific regions of the brain: ophthalmoception takes place in the visual cortex, audioception in the auditory cortex, gustaoception in the gustatory cortex, olfacoception in the olfactory bulb, and tactioception, including the kinesthetic sense (proprioception),[9] temperature (thermoreception), pain (nociception) and discriminative touch (mechanoreception), in the parietal lobe (see, e.g., May 2007; Harris 2014).

In this light, perception is not a single mental process, but is engendered through the operation of multiple brain systems that process different information received both from within the human body and from the external world. Most perceptual processes take place below the threshold of consciousness without being the object of explicit mental processing and thinking. Our perceptual abilities, however, ensure our survival, and ground our situatedness in the world and the experiences of our surroundings.

3.1.2 Memory organization of embodied percepts

Multiple stimuli and information deriving from both our bodies and the external world and represented in our brains are encoded, stored, and organized by complex memory systems that mediate both short-term awareness and long-term reasoning about our spatio-temporal experiences. The distinction between *short-term* and *long-term memory* constitutes a general model (e.g., Atkinson and Shiffrin 1968) for defining those mechanisms that process transient information and retrieve stored knowledge. Short-term memory plays a crucial role in real-time perception, holding a limited amount of information for a few seconds[10] – when processes of rehearsal (mental repetition of the received information)[11] or chunking (combination and grouping of scattered received information in more meaningful patterns)[12] are not involved – after which the retained information may gradually decay (e.g., A. Miller 1956; Baddeley et al. 1975; Broadbent 1975; Cowan 2001).

However, certain stimuli and information are *encoded* in *long-term memory* that stores and accumulates information for longer periods of time enabling their future *retrieval* and *recall*. Some information are unconsciously stored in *long-term non-declarative/implicit memory* that mediates the acquisition of motor skills, the performance of sensorimotor and other everyday activities, and registers primary emotional experiences without being consciously processed (e.g. Mancia 2006). Stimuli and information that reach consciousness are stored in *long-term declarative/explicit memory* that is further divided to *semantic* and *episodic memory*. *Semantic memory*, on the one hand, contains knowledge and information encoded, stored and recalled during embodied experiences and interactions while one can't consciously recall the encoding event, or the circumstances under which it was learned (Binder and Desai 2011; Yee et al. 2013). Episodic memory, on the other hand, associates explicit information and knowledge with the events (episodes) in which this information and knowledge were acquired, and these events comprise our autobiographical stories and knowledge of ourselves (e.g. Tulving 1972, 1983, 2002). Information being processed in short-term memory or retrieved from long-term memory is continually retrieved and activated in *working memory* that mediates online thought, reasoning, decision making and behaviour (e.g. Baddeley and Hitch 1974; Cowan 2001; Diamond 2013).

Our memory systems are vital to the embodied perception of ourselves, and of the world that enables transient interactions with our surroundings and accumulation of knowledge and information that affects current conceptions and behaviours. In particular, memory plays a crucial role in perception of space and time and provides the components for the establishment of more stable spatio-temporal percepts and concepts, cultural notions, and metaphorical mappings of space and time.

3.1.3 Perception of the body and egocentric point of view

Our bodies are 'lived objects' that situate us in our recent spatial settings, as the bodies of the Mithraists would have situated them in the mithraeum, being encircled by other things – other people, natural landscapes, material representations, and spatial constructions – constantly transmitting multiple sensory stimuli from all directions (Tilley 2004: 3). Simultaneously, our bodies are 'lived subjects' in the sense that we cannot – and presumably Mithraists could not either – experience our own bodies from the outside – from an external point of view (p. 3). We sense our own bodies, positions, and movements through our proprioceptive system that, along with the other sensory modalities, generates an intrinsic cognitive mapping of our bodies and enables us to navigate ourselves in space. This mapping is continually updated as we interact with extrinsic objects in order to determine how our body is situated in our surroundings (Iriki 2014: 439). Such perception comprises an intrinsic egocentric axis of spatial orientation, which we use as a primary reference system for cognitively mapping the external world with ourselves at the centre (see, e.g., Klatzky 1998: 5; Yamamoto and Shelton 2005: 141; Evans 2010: 39).

These cognitive spatial mappings, however, do not constitute the complete image and structure of the objective reality.[13] The external world – terrestrial and celestial, natural and artificial – consists of a mixture of sound waves and electromagnetic fields interrelated and governed by strict natural laws, only some of which are perceptible. The visual system determines which part of the electromagnetic spectrum we can detect (the 'visual field' comprising only wavelengths ranging between 400 and 700 nm; see, e.g., Simos 2002: 27; Foley and Matlin 2015 [1991]: 44–6). Visible light is transformed into neural information, which is processed in the visual cortex enabling us to perceive textures and shapes, to perceive depth, height and breadth (stereoscopic vision), and to discern three-dimensional scenes (binocular vision)[14] comprising distinct objects, surfaces and grounds, and thus to produce an egocentric model of our surroundings (figure–ground perception; see Evans 2010: 29–39; cf. Rubin 1915, 1958; Pind 2012).

This egocentric angle of vision is supplemented by the vestibular system, which, along with the cochlea located in the ears, enables us to maintain our bodily balance in upright positions. In addition, the vestibular system plays a crucial role in vision, coordinating the movements of the body and the head, and the relative motion of the eyes, which are thereby able to maintain a clear vision and to detect motion in the external world (vestibuo-couclar reflex; Evans 2010: 26–7). Thereby, while we horizontally or vertically move in space, we retain a stable vision and monitor the position and movements of external objects with reference to our bodies and from our own embodied perspective.

Therefore, perception of space is egocentric, deeply grounded in our bodily presence in the world, and gives rise to spatial dimensions specifically in reference to our bodies. This short-term embodied perception of space provides the ground for the emergence of more lasting spatial percepts that engender long-term spatial concepts and enable further metaphorical conceptualization of specific spatial dimensions and structures that are expressed in varied cultural contexts.

3.1.4 From percepts to image-schemas and the rise of concepts

As shown above, the experience of our bodies and our embodied perception of the world generates rudimentary spatial percepts that attribute essential spatial dimensions to our surroundings and enable our current movements in space and our interactions with external objects. Some constantly emerging spatial percepts are stored in non-declarative/implicit memory and combined to form elementary 'image-schemas'[15] that originate in our bodies and give further shape to our surroundings (see M. Turner 1987; M. Johnson 1987, 2007, Lakoff 1990; Cervel 2003).

In particular, the image-schema of CONTAINER[16] emerges from the primary perception of the body, which includes the internal bodily organs and has certain boundaries which separate it from its external surroundings (Lakoff and M. Johnson 1999: 31–2, 266). The same image-schema is projected to conceive any external object and entity which is perceived as having an interior, boundaries and an exterior. From the image-schema of CONTAINER the percepts of 'in' and 'out' of a restricted area become meaningful concepts.

As embodied subjects move from one location to another, the function of movement is associated with spatial displays from the point of departure to the point of destination and such recurrent spatial experiences give rise to the more complex image-schema of PATH.[17] As we interact with our surroundings, we identify further recurrent patterns and generate durable image-schemas – such as CONTACT, BALANCE, VERTICALITY, CENTRE–PERIPHERY, FORCE–COUNTERFORCE – which provide the ground for more complex conceptual structures.

In this way, multimodal percepts generated from the embodied experience are stabilized in our mnemonic systems and provide an inventory for categorizing future perceptions of reality in terms of recurrent image-schemas that are further transformed into concepts which schematize the external world (Burgess 2006: 557; Evans 2010: 39–40).

3.1.5 The body-schema and short-term egocentric maps

Major spatial dimensions, originating in the perception of our own body image-schema, mediate our instantaneous navigation in space and generate more stable spatial concepts. Merleau-Ponty suggested that humans perceive six major spatial dimensions in reference to their bodily coordinates. He formulates these dimensions as three contrasting pairs that define what is perceived to be 'ABOVE' and 'BELOW', 'IN FRONT OF' and 'BEHIND', and 'TO THE LEFT' and 'TO THE RIGHT' (Tilley 2004: 4; cf. Franklin and Tversky 1990; Bryant and Tversky 1999). These spatial representations are instantiated into the human body and form the intrinsic cognitive mapping of the bodily space ('body-schema'; see Iriki 2014: 439). Thus we are proprioceptively aware of our bodily parts, which are unconsciously perceived as being BELOW (like the feet) or ABOVE (like the head), IN FRONT (like the breast) or BEHIND (like the back), while the bilateral bodily symmetry determines the 'RIGHT' and the 'LEFT' sides of the body (a hand, a foot, an ear, an eye, etc. in each side of the body).

Therefore, the concepts of 'UP' vs 'DOWN', 'IN FRONT OF' vs 'BEHIND', and 'TO THE LEFT' vs 'TO THE RIGHT' are not objective dimensions of the real world. They primarily originate in the body-schema, which is the frame of *relative* reference for determining the location of external components of the world (see Iriki 2014: 439–40). During locomotion we can perceive and then conceive something as being 'UP' when we need to look upwards in order to see it or to move upwards in order to reach it. Similarly, we can perceive an object as being 'DOWN' when we need to turn our heads downwards in order to make visual contact, when we need to stoop in order to interact with it or when the object is perceived as being on a lower level in relation to our bodily position (see Tilley 2004: 5–6).

Embodied subjects move mainly on the horizontal axis, which appears more mutable than the vertical axis. The perception of what lies IN FRONT OF or BEHIND the lived body is directly dependent on human vision,[18] which is localized in the front part of the body and which determines the visual field – what people can see and interact with (egocentric front; see Sholl and Nolin 1997: 1497). We mostly move, act and manipulate objects which are in front of us. Everything that is out of the individual's visual field is considered to be behind (Lakoff and M. Johnson 1999: 34; Tilley 2004: 6; see Franklin and Tversky 1990: 74). As we move forward along the horizontal plane, the egocentric perception of FRONT and BEHIND is fluid, since the objects which were in front of us appear to flow behind us. Such phenomenal movement of the external objects is perceived to be faster the shorter the distance between the perceiver and perceived object, while entities that are at a greater distance seem to move more slowly or even to remain stationary in reference to the moving body (cf. 'optic flow patterns', Evans 2010: 37; see Gibson 1950; Royden and Moore 2012). The bilateral symmetry of the human body mediates the perception of what lies TO THE LEFT or TO THE RIGHT but these dimensions are always perceived in reference to the front and alter with bodily rotation (Franklin and Tversky 1990: 74; Tilley 2004: 6).

The three-fold spatial dualisms mentioned above mediate embodied experiences of space and derive from constant spatial correlations between the perceiver's bodily positions and the locations of the external objects (self-to-object spatial relations; cf. Easton and Sholl 1995; Sholl and Nolin 1997; Sholl 2001; Sholl and Bartels 2002; Mou et al. 2004: 34). These dualisms are relative and dependent upon the alterations of the egocentric viewpoint angles (Merleau-Ponty 2002: 236–7; Tilley 2004: 5; cf. alignment effects, Burgess 2006: 551, 554), which rapidly change as the embodied subject slightly alters its direction (spatial updating; Burgess 2006: 552). Therefore, such egocentric perceptions of space that create online flowing multimodal spatial mappings in the parietal lobe tend to be largely episodic, lasting and being altered as long as the spatial experience endures (Burgess 2006: 551; Evans 2010: 22).

3.1.6 Long-term allocentric maps

The egocentric spatial mappings arising from our embodied perception of the world enable us to continually orient ourselves in space and interact with the external world. Even slight movements entail immediate alterations of the egocentric points of view and a remapping of the self-to-objects relations.

Such mappings do not, however, provide any stable frame for spatial orientation and navigation over time. In parallel with the momentary perceptions of the external world, humans combine the immediate perceptual stimuli to generate more enduring offline cognitive maps (see Burgess 2006). Such spatial mapping, taking place in the hippocampus and parahippocampal regions of the brain, enables us to have a lasting sense of space even when we no longer receive immediate sensory inputs from our surroundings (e.g. O'Keefe and Nadel 1978; Nadel and MacDonald 1980; O'Keefe 1991; Frank et al. 2000; Burgess et al. 2001; Parslow et al. 2004; Kumaran and Maguire 2005; Byrne et al. 2007; Suthana et al. 2009). Contrary to the egocentric frame of reference, these spatial maps are allocentric in the sense that they are independent of the perceiver's own bodily presence and current position (O'Keefe and Nadel 1978; Klatzky 1998: 3; Evans 2010: 39–40). Such cognitive processing combines image-schemas and egocentric spatial percepts (e.g. Burgess 2006; Waller and Hodgson 2006), which have been encoded and retained in long-term memory, and enable us to discern geographical places and locations, and to recognize connections between them, such as distances and directions, without experiencing these spatial dimensions bodily. As we experience landscapes from closer distances and from an egocentric perspective, we can discern more details. Paying attention to objects and structures in our visual field, we recognize the spatial positions and relations between these perceived entities, which can also be kept in memory, updating, thereby, the allocentric spatial maps with further material cues and mental representations (object-to-object spatial relations).[19]

We constantly create egocentric and allocentric spatial maps through which we comprehend physical space and orient ourselves in our spatial surroundings (e.g. Burgess 2006: 3-4; Xiao et al. 2009). The transient egocentric mapping allows us, as 'moving subjects', to manoeuvre our movements in response to environmental conditions (e.g. slippery ground, water surface, puddles, pits) and to material objects confronted during locomotion (e.g. doors, stairs, obstacles).[20] The enduring allocentric mappings enable us to keep the places, objects, and entities we meet in memory and to be aware that these entities are still there even when they are not included in the receptive field. In allocentric representations, movements of the subject entail an alteration of their self-location in relation to more stable surroundings (Burgess 2006: 4).

As we interact with familiar surroundings and are called upon to explore novel environments, we switch between egocentric and allocentric representations in order to orient ourselves in space (e.g. Holmes and Sholl 2005; Burgess 2006; Xiao et al. 2009). These two distinct processes for comprehending physical space originate in the perception of our body that is projected onto the external world and provides the ground for more complex metaphorical conceptions of terrestrial and universal space.

3.1.7 From embodied perception to metaphorical conception of the universe

So far we have provided some insights into how repeated fleeting egocentric perceptions engender lasting image-schemas that compose the allocentric maps. Particularly, the image-schemas of our bodily dimensions, as described by Merleau-Ponty, are projected onto the external world mediating our embodied perception of external entities and generating the concepts of spatial dimensions.

The vertical axis of the human body standing in an upright posture is extended onto the extrinsic objects, which are perceived as comprising upper and lower parts (Franklin and Tversky 1990: 74). The coincidence of human vision with the front is also projected onto other lived subjects and material objects in order to determine their front and back sides.[21] Much more effort is demanded in order to conceive of the left and right parts of other objects which are also bilaterally symmetrical, since correspondences are needed to be identified between the front and behind parts from which the left and right parts of the perceived objects are deduced (p. 74).

When the egocentric vertical axis, which determines 'up and down' with respect to the human body, extends to the universal cosmos, the earth, which lies below the feet, is separated from the celestial sphere, which extends above the head, and determines the locations of lived bodies in reference to the wider cosmic space. The line of the horizon marks the limit which separates the 'above and below' halves of the universal space (Tilley 2004: 5–6; cf. O'Keefe and Nadel 1978: 2; Evans 2010: 40). Similarly, the horizontal axis – sourced into the body and then extended in the extrinsic objects – is projected onto the universe and mediates a more stable allocentric mapping of both the terrestrial and the celestial domains.

Given that egocentric mapping is transient during locomotion and that the more stable allocentric spatial maps of the earthly space are updated as long as new geographical surfaces and objects are perceived, spatial cognitive mappings pertaining to the horizontal terrestrial axis cannot provide an absolute reference frame for spatial orientation. Contrary to the phenomenal fluidity and diversity of the terrestrial domain, the celestial space appears to be more steady and reliable. The great distance between the earth and the celestial realm entails a slow optic flow that gives the sense that the image of the heavens remains more or less stationary and only slowly and slightly changes independently of the human bodily movements (see Evans 2010: 37).

The phenomenal motions of the sun, the planets, and the stars seem to be independent of the lived subjects' movements on the earth. In our culture, and as we will see in due course in the Mithraic cosmology as well, we extend our bodily symmetry to the heavens; we conventionally consider that the sun rises in the east (that we identify with the RIGHT) and sets in the west (that we identify with the LEFT). When we align our right and left parts to the celestial right (east) and left (west), we have the north IN FRONT OF us and the south BEHIND. Thereby, embodied experience with reference to the heavens entails the transformation of the image-schemas of elementary spatial dimensions (UP and DOWN, FRONT and BEHIND, RIGHT and LEFT) into primary metaphorical concepts of spatial orientation ('celestial up', 'terrestrial down', east, west, north, south) and provides the most absolute frame of navigation for the terrestrial level (cf. Burgess 2006: 6–7).

The same image-schemas and primary metaphors are associated with further aspects of the sensorimotor experiences generating, thereby, more complex metaphorical mappings pertaining to subjective experiences (cf. Lakoff and

M. Johnson 1999: 47, 49, 55–8). Thus, experiencing gravity and multiplicity on earth and the brightness and uniformity of the heavens, in the Mithras cult[22] the 'terrestrial down' was associated with the human domain, genesis, mortality and death, while the 'celestial up' was connected with the divine realm, apogenesis and immortality. As we will see later in this chapter, even more complex conceptual metaphors were instantiated within the mithraeum signifying the association of the sunrise in the east with light, warmth, growth and prosperity, and of the sunset in the west with darkness, cold, decline and decay.[23] Setting out from here, one may explore the metaphorical connotations of the Mithraic space. But first, let's take a look at the cognitive processes that could have mediated the metaphorical conception of the mithraeum as the universe.

3.1.8 Blended mental spaces and material anchors of spatial orientation

In the previous chapter, we employed the conceptual metaphor theory suggested by Lakoff and M. Johnson (1999) to throw some light on the metaphorical conception of the initiatory experiences in the Mithraic mysteries. In particular, we showed how neural connections between our ordinary sensorimotor and subjective experiences enable the flow of inferences from the former domain to the latter generating metaphorical conceptualizations of our subjective experiences. Supplementary (see, e.g., Grady et al. 1999; Mierzwińska-Hajnos 2009) to conceptual metaphor theory, the conceptual blending (or integration) theory suggested by Fauconnier and Turner (2002) investigates the metaphorical mappings between different conceptual domains.

In particular, Fauconnier and Turner (1998, 2002) explored the conceptual processes through which image-schemas that, as noted above, arise from our embodied perception of both ourselves and the world acquire further conceptual meanings and are transformed into primary concepts. They defined the mental representations of these primary concepts as 'mental spaces' stored in long-term memory and comprising our *offline* conceptual inventory for conceptualizing our experiences. As we interact with the world, perceiving and experiencing new things, we continually *blend* new perceptions and experiences with previously stored *mental spaces* generating ever more complex metaphorical conceptions of our online experiences. Some of these complex conceptual representations – *blended mental spaces* – can be stabilized and stored in memory mediating the metaphorical conception and interpretation of the perceived reality and the construction of certain world views.

As Fauconnier and Turner suggested (1998, 2002), the conceptual blending presupposes at least three already established mental spaces from which a new blended mental space can arise. There must be a *generic mental space* that provides the common ground against which the integration of other mental spaces – two or more – can be meaningful. Concepts pertaining to percepts and image-schemas which stem from common sensorimotor and subjective experiences may comprise such generic mental spaces. Other conceptual representations must operate as *input spaces*, which will be blended on the ground of the generic space (Grady et al. 1999: 101). These input spaces operate similarly to source domains from which certain aspects and correspondences are projected and, after being composed, compressed or completing each other, mapped out to the target domain of the emergent blended mental space (McElhanon 2006: 48–9), which acquires its own structure (Fauconnier and Turner 1998: 144, 2002: 39–58, 113–38, 312–25).

Normally we are not aware of the process of conceptual blending. Beyond the individual mental representations that are blended during our online thoughts and behaviours, cultural models (including systems of premises, ideas, concepts and beliefs) comprise more stable blended mental spaces adopted and shared by the members of a social group through processes of cultural learning (see D'Andrade 1989; Hutchins 2005: 1557–8). Such complex blended spaces – i.e. numerical systems, systems of orientation, cosmological models, religious beliefs – which are too elaborate and thereby not easily remembered through ordinary sensorimotor and cultural experience – can be stabilized by being embedded in external structures and public representations – i.e. numerical tables, terrestrial and celestial maps, religious books, paintings and statues – that attribute representational stability to these mental spaces. Edwin Hutchins (2005) introduced the term 'material anchors' in order to describe those material structures – natural entities or material artefacts – which trigger conceptual blends.

In the aforementioned case of orientation, the metaphorical associations of the right with the east, the left with the west, the front with north and the behind with south constitute a cultural model that derives from conceptual blending. Our bodily dualisms projected and perceived on the external objects and the whole universe comprise the common ground – the generic mental space – on which blending unfolds. Our bodies and the celestial realm operate as input spaces: correspondences between our bodies and the heavens are traced, integrated and projected onto the blended mental space of our system of orientation in which we consider that the sun rises in the right, that is in the east, and sets in the left, that is in the west. However, although we have embedded such systems of orientation during cultural learning, we cannot apply and make use of this blended mental space to orient ourselves in current spatial settings without anchoring it to the phenomenally fixed movement of the sun around the earth: we have to look to the heavens to identify the points of sunrise and sunset in order to localize the universal right/east and left/west.

More elaborated material artefacts have been created in order to anchor even more complex spatial representations. Geographical maps constitute such elaborated blended spaces: they blend the input spaces of their own materials (e.g. paper, parchment, papyrus in specific dimensions), the imprinted landscapes (e.g. a drawing of the heavens, of the earth, of a continent, of a country, of a city, of a village) and the celestial cardinal points (E, W, N, S). These maps are *allocentric* since they provide representations of stable spatial relations that are independent of the current position of the reader. Simultaneously, they operate as material anchors for new *egocentric* mental spaces that blend the spatial representations on the maps with our current spatial positions and the spatial relations of the natural entities and material objects around us, enabling us to orient ourselves and plan our routes in unfamiliar landscapes (see Hutchins 2005).

Therefore, transient perceptions of space originate in our bodily presence in the world and in the immediate sensorimotor experiences of our surroundings. It is, however, the embodied human cognition that attributes shape and spatial dimensions to the perceived world, thereby generating short-term mental spaces as well as long-term image-schemas, patterns, concepts and blended mental spaces that provide the ground for more complex metaphorical spatial constructions.

From the perspective of conceptual blending theory, the ways in which initiates into the Mithraic mysteries would have perceived the actual space of the mithraeum would have been primarily grounded in their sensorimotor experiences, deriving from their physical presence in the Mithraic cult space. However, the metaphorical perception of the mithraeum as an image of the universe would have been mediated by a blending of the material construction of the cult space with the geocentric Ptolemaic cosmological model. This blending would have entailed the complex blended space of the Mithraic universal microcosm. Before we explore how the mental space of the mithraeum was layered, constructed, and experienced during the Mithraic mysteries, we need to provide some insights into the perception of time, which is intrinsically associated with the experience of space, both terrestrial and universal.

3.2 From the embodied perception of space to the metaphorical perception of time

So far we have seen how our embodied experiences mediate the formation and establishment of long-term spatial concepts pertaining to physical entities (e.g. CONTAINER), spatial relations (e.g. IN and OUT, UP and DOWN) and actions (e.g. MOVEMENT, ROTATION, INTERACTION), and we outlined how these elementary concepts are combined (projected, integrated or blended) into more complex metaphorical structures that conceptualize our multiple subjective experiences. Contrary to the perception of space which is anchored on solid material entities and observable relations that are perceived through sensory modalities, a temporal dimension is inherent in the embodied experiences without being directly traced and perceived through senses (Pöppel 1997: 56; Lakoff and M. Johnson 1999: 137-9).

The world is seemingly eternal, but its components appear to be subject to continuous change, motion and transmutation. Human existence is impermanent and the human body undergoes gradual alterations – from the time of birth, through growth, and decline to death – as well as transient changes during interaction with the surroundings. A temporal dimension is traced in the phenomenal motion and fluidity of the world and in the continual alteration of events unfolding in space (Lakoff and M. Johnson 1999: 151).

However, as Merleau-Ponty (2002: 477-8; cf. Tilley 2004: 26) pointed out, even the notion of events presupposes the presence of an observer who perceives the world from a certain point of view and distinguishes specific fragments of the spatio-temporal unity of the objective reality, which is conceptualized as distinctive units. But again, the integration of events in temporal units through the observation of motions, changes and successions presupposes complex mnemonic processes that allow the specific stages of alterations to be kept in memory, to be combined and compared in order to give a sense of gradual change – transient or enduring. As John A. Michon (1990: 38) aptly points out, 'Memory is the ensemble of the processes that temporally organize our experiences'. Indeed, our complex mnemonic systems enable us to tune ourselves to our surroundings (both natural and cultural), to trace changes both in ourselves and the external world, to store our subjective experiences as well as cultural conceptualizations of the perceived changes and to manipulate our implicit and explicit memories in order to imagine and anticipate oncoming developments, experiences and alterations (Tilley 2004: 12).

3.2.1 The rise of time in memory systems

In the interaction with the world, we continually generate mental representations of the objects and entities we interact with and keep information about these objects and entities that are temporarily accessible – often without conscious processing or decision making. In order for an object or an event to be represented in brain structures, sensory information should be transmitted to the sensory modalities and then integrated, generating, thereby, an intermodal mental representation. Although the duration of the transmission of sensory stimuli to the different sensory modalities is not the same – for example, the sensory transmission and processing of auditory stimuli lasts less than that of visual stimuli[24] – neuro-cognitive processing mechanisms overcome these temporal discrepancies quickly (in roughly *30 milliseconds*) and create seemingly real-time mental representations of objects and events as co-temporal (Pöppel 1997: 57–8). Successive events and actions that last *up to three seconds* are further integrated and experienced as happening simultaneously, comprising the subjective experience of present, or 'nowness' (pp. 58–9).

As mentioned above, from the moment that mental representations are formed and combined in perceptual units, the time that they are sustained and the amount of information that is extracted from them and retained in the mind depends on the limits and capacities of short-term memory (e.g., A. Miller 1956; Baddeley et al. 1975; Broadbent 1975; Cowan 2001). During sensorimotor experiences, short-term memory enables us to track changes and alterations in our perceived surroundings as we move in relation to others, or as others move in relation to us. These elementary 'motion situations' provide the experiential ground for the metaphorical perception of time (Lakoff and M. Johnson 1999: 151).

Previous short-term experiences, repeated transient actions, and exposure to subliminal stimuli (priming) may generate long-term storage of information in the form of implicit knowledge. Long-term implicit memories do not undergo conscious processing and cannot be verbalized (see Schacter 1987; Richardson-Klavehn and Bjork 1988) but give rise to more enduring experiences of simultaneity, of the succession of events, the successive order of actions and a sense of continuity and duration (see, e.g., Pöppel 1997, 2004) without being explicitly represented (Michon 1990: 39). The past continues to exist in the present in the form of mental representations for as long as these representations are remembered. Implicit knowledge of repeated sensorimotor experiences further enables humans to unconsciously project the immediate consequences of their actions, and thus to have an implicit, transient sense of the future in the present. Thereby, perception of 'past', 'present', and 'future' are all metaphorically instantiated in online sensorimotor experiences through the operation of implicit memory.

At this stage, primary metaphors of time that mediate the perception of temporal in reference to spatial experiences of motion are unconsciously mapped in the brain and give rise to temporal 'image-schemas' of 'past', 'present' and 'future' (Lakoff and M. Johnson 1999: 153–4). These pre-semantic image-schemas develop into long-term declarative concepts in semantic memory. Semantic memory dissociates the notions of 'past', 'present' and 'future' from the immediate embodied experiences and forms the more lasting semantic contents of these concepts that can be manipulated and combined in even more complex metaphorical schemas that structure the temporal dimensions of everyday human activities (e.g., Addis et al. 2007; Binder and Desai 2011; Gerlach et al. 2011).

3.2.2 Primary and complex metaphors of time

Time is an inextricable dimension of the world, but we cannot directly perceive and conceptualize it. The experience of temporality is extracted from spatial experiences and thereby is metaphorical per se. Spatial events and entities, which are directly and currently experienced as a perceptual unit through the sensory systems, determine the metaphorical perception of 'now' or present. In reference to immediate perceivable units, recently ended events or entities that have decayed, but which are still available in short-term memory, are perceived as having happened 'before', while oncoming predictable developments are expected to happen 'later'. At this stage, the durations of sensory experiences and the temporal segregation of embodied actions and external events are metaphorical but pre-conceptual, deriving from the time necessary for the intrinsic cognitive processes to receive, integrate and represent external stimuli and to perform related sensorimotor activities (Pöppel 1997: 59–60).

Further metaphors of time emerge and are established during our ordinary sensorimotor experiences. According to Lakoff and M. Johnson's (1999: 45, 68, 128, 143) conceptual metaphor theory, 'motion situations' – i.e. when we move in relation to others or others move in relation to us – involve inferences from the source domain of space transferred to the target domain of time and forge neural mappings between the two domains.

3.2.2.1 The MOVING OBSERVER metaphor of time

As we move in space, we perceive things that were in front of us and which we could see to flow behind us and become invisible. This very common and repeated sensorimotor experience constitutes the source domain from which mental imagery is transferred to the target domain of time and generates one of the most ordinary conceptual time-space metaphors, the so-called 'MOVING OBSERVER metaphor' (Lakoff and M. Johnson 1999: 141–8).

In this metaphorical schema, every place in the course of motion is associated with specific moments (pp. 146–7). The current position of the observer, which includes the aggregation of stimuli that are available to sensory systems and that are perceived as being co-temporal, comprises the 'present'. The places, objects, and other entities that were previously included in the observer's receptive field but are no longer perceivable, compose the 'past'. The places and objects towards which the observer moves constitute the 'future'. A major inference of this metaphorical schema is that 'past and future exist' in a certain way 'at the present', similar to how places and landscapes exist before and after the passage of the observer from each location (p. 159).

3.2.2.2 The MOVING OBSERVER metaphor in autobiographical narratives

Again invoking Fauconnier and Turner's Conceptual Blending Theory (1998, 2002), the MOVING OBSERVER metaphor can be considered to comprise a conceptual mental space that is projected into people's mental space of episodic memories to generate the blended mental space of their life-stories. Personal experiences and specific events are retained in the autobiographical memory, in which they are organized as episodic units in sequential order. The immediate human experiences in and of the world constitute the generic space from which the input space of the metaphor is extracted, abstracted and stabilized in semantic memory and then projected into the mental space of the episodic memories that it organizes and connects in autobiographical narratives.[25]

Therefore, people's lives are perceived as a continual motion from the time and place of birth to the time and place of death. The location in which people are now is perceived as the 'present'. All the episodic memories they can recall in the present simulate experiences that unfolded in times and places in which they have previously been and comprise their 'past'. Furthermore, episodic memory enables humans to imagine and 'pre-experience' places and events that may occur as they move towards the 'future' (e.g. Tulving 1983, 2002; Williams et al. 1996; Atance and O'Neill, 2001, 2005; D'Argembeau and van der Linden 2004;

Hancock 2005; Addis et al. 2007; Botzung et al. 2008). Therefore, the temporal dimension of human existence acquires the metaphorical organization of motion through spatial and temporal landscapes. This sequential movement can be structured, recalled, and narrated through the blended space of life-stories.

3.2.2.3 *The* MOVING TIME *metaphor*

A variation of the aforementioned MOVING OBSERVER metaphor is the MOVING TIME metaphor, which provides an alternative perceptual structure for embodied experiences (Lakoff and M. Johnson 1999: 141–2). This metaphorical schema arises from the short-term perception and observation of changes and alterations in the world that appear to be independent of the movements of the embodied subjects.

As people remain static and observe events unfolding in front of them, they distinguish perceptual units, which they perceive metaphorically as temporal stages of this development. From transient experiences like standing on the bank and observing the water of a river which flows from its source to its mouth, people can perceive time as flowing along with the motion of external objects or entities (cf. Merleau-Ponty 2002: 477–9). The water of the river that quickly passes in front of the observer is perceived as the flowing 'present'. The 'past' comprises all of the places that the water in the river has passed before it arrived in front of the observer, while the future consists of all the places that the water is going to pass during its travel to the mouth. Repeated embodied experiences of motion and alterations generate more enduring inferences from the space and time domains and contribute to the image-schemas of 'past', 'present' and 'future' in implicit memory.

3.2.2.4 *Metaphorical perception of the universal time*

The metaphorical perceptions of time as moving in relation to the observer that are stabilized in implicit memory can be blended with multiple motion situations that people repeatedly observe which comprises thereby their semantic knowledge of the spatio-temporal dimensions of the world. Particularly, the input mental space of the metaphor is projected to the more stable, successive and predictable iterations of physical events in space that generate the blended semantic space of the universal time. The successive phenomenal movements of the celestial elements on the heavens are perceived as defining 'same intervals of time' (Lakoff and M. Johnson 1999: 137–9). The sun's everyday movement from the point of sunrise (East) to the point of sunset (West) and its subsequent disappearance along with the appearance of the moon is integrated with the embodied experiences of the succession of light and darkness and signifies the alteration of days and nights. In addition to the sun, the moon phases as they gradually appear in the night sky also provide a material anchor for observing the passage of time.

Such primary associations of the movements of the celestial bodies on the heavens with the time passage and time intervals undergo further elaboration and sophistication in various cultures and societies. Thus, different cosmological systems have developed throughout history. These systems have been grounded on the generic space of embodied experiences in the world and have blended the primary metaphorical perception of MOVING TIME with the movements of the celestial bodies, generating complex blended mental spaces, such as models, calendars, and dating systems. Such culturally developed spaces of the universal space and time update the semantic knowledge of people who live in the relevant cultural settings and further influence the perception of their selves and the world as well their sense of history, both personal and collective.

To sum up, the perception of time is metaphorical and derives from specific features of spatial events. Inferences, interrelations and comparisons between these events presuppose the bodily presence and sensorimotor experiences of humans in space. However, the attribution of temporal dimensions to spatial events is possible only through the operation of complex mnemonic systems that enable humans to retain short-term information, to store long-term implicit and explicit knowledge about themselves and the external world, to simulate past and future experiences and events in the present and to develop more generic temporal concepts. Thereby humans can mentally move between different temporal poles (past–present–future) overcoming the temporality of their existence and the transiency of their actions and experiences (Lakoff and M. Johnson 1999: 159). Furthermore, their stored semantic knowledge and pre-established conceptual metaphors can be integrated with novel embodied experiences taking place in various cultural contexts generating new blended mental spaces of spatio-temporal integration.

Taking into account the insights provided in the previous sections into the embodied cognition and perception of space and time, in what follows we examine how the Mithraists' embodied presence and movements within the mithraeum would have affected the perception of space and time as universal categories of the Mithraic world view ascribing multiple metaphorical meanings to the cult spatial settings and mediating their perception and conception as a model of the universe.

3.3 Mithraea: from material constructions to metaphorical conception

The mithraea comprised the cult space of the Mithras cult that were situated in the terrestrial domain but were invested with certain metaphorical connotations mediating their perception as a model of the celestial realm in which initiations into the Mithraic mysteries took place. The material, rather than metaphorical, mithraea were constructed using the means and resources available. According to Porphyry (*On the Cave* 6), the prototype for the mithraeum was set by Zoroaster, who dedicated a natural cave to Mithras in Persia. Porphyry's statement here is confirmed by the archaeological evidence – in the form of epigraphy – in which Mithraists are represented as calling their cult places 'caves'. Natural caves, when they existed in the surroundings, were preferred.[26] In other places, the natural effect was achieved by cutting the tauroctony into a cliff or rock face and then building the rest of the mithraeum up against it.[27] The mithraeum was thus, as we might say today, 'grounded'. When natural caves or suitable rock faces were not available, especially in urban settings, lower levels of buildings with vaulted ceilings were selected, perhaps because they most resembled caves.[28] Selection of already built structures for the establishment of the mithraea entailed that there was no stable building orientation (Beck 1994a: 113–14, 2000: 162, 2004: 245, 2006a: 110, 2014: 249). In any event, affordability and availability would have determined the selection of places for establishing mithraea.

Well over a hundred mithraea have been discovered to date and it is estimated that hundreds or even thousands more existed throughout the Roman Empire.[29] Abundant archaeological evidence therefore enables us to outline the mithraeum's basic design. Typically, the mithraeum was a rectangular hall overarched by a vaulted ceiling giving, as we have seen, the sense of a cave. The entrance was at one of the shorter sides. The far end was dominated by the image of the bull-killing Mithras, the 'tauroctony' in modern terminology, sometimes as a fresco but usually as a sculpture often located in a central cult niche. On the longer sides, raised platforms flanked a central aisle for most of its length. These platforms ('side-benches' or *triclinia*) were functional: the initiates reclined on them during their cult meal (see preceding chapter, section 2.2.3).

The mithraeum, if Porphyry (*On the Cave* 6) is to be believed,[30] 'bore for him [i.e. Zoroaster] the image of the cosmos (*eikona kosmou*) which Mithras had created'. The perception of the cave as an 'image of the cosmos' constitutes a complex conceptual metaphor.[31] This metaphor was conventionalized in Mithraism's ritual context and would have structured the initiates' subjective experiences, actions, and movements within the mithraeum (cf. M. Johnson 1993: 165–6; Lakoff and M. Johnson 1999: 60). During the process of metaphorization, the *cave* would come to be perceived as the *universe* by focusing initiates' attention on the *correspondences* between the two. Such a metaphorical connection remains partial, not total (Lakoff and M. Johnson 1980: 12 f.): the mithraeum was not the actual universe. Nevertheless, the *connection* was especially 'real': that is what being an image or likeness of something is all about. 'To represent is to be', a matter to which we shall return below (Beck 2006a: 112 f.).

Obviously, the universe of which the mithraeum is an image is not quite the same universe we apprehend today, but rather the universe of the Graeco-Roman culture, of Mithraism's contemporaries, and of the Mithraists themselves. It is, then, a Hellenistic model of the universe, as exemplified in Cicero's 'Dream of Scipio' – described in the preceding chapter (section 2.2.2.2) and more thoroughly examined in the next section.

Again we emphasize the point we made in Chapter 2: that the universe of the Mithraists and their contemporaries was no more the 'real' universe than is our universe. It was their *cognized environment*, the universe as they apprehended it. It follows, then, that the mithraeum as universe was a *meta-model* – a model of a model – designed (consciously and otherwise) to shape the thinking of those who entered it, and who (thus) participated in the modelling.

The more immediate question that we intend to address is: *how* is the mithraeum an image of the universe, or more precisely, *how can one tell* – then and now – that the mithraeum is an image of the universe? Porphyry himself gives the answer in the continuation of the passage in which he tells us that the mithraeum is known as a 'cave' and that it functions as an image of the universe: 'and the things which the cave contained, by their proportionate arrangement, provided him [i.e. Zoroaster] with symbols of the elements and climates[32] of the cosmos (*tôn d'entos kata symmetrous apostaseis symbola pherontôn tôn kosmikôn stoicheiôn kai klimatôn*). In sum, the mithraeum would have been apprehended as an image of the universe because it contains symbols of the universe's 'elements and climates'. These cosmic symbols are 'in proportionate arrangement', by which he meant that the disposition of the symbols of the cosmic elements and climates in the mithraeum (i.e. the 'microcosm') corresponds with some precision to the disposition of the elements and climates in the universe as 'macrocosm'.

Much will be said here about the specifics of the microcosm's design and the disposition of the cosmic symbols, all of which will be addressed later – together with the seldom-asked question: what precisely are 'the elements and climates of the cosmos'? The question remains, however, of intent: *why* was the mithraeum designed as a microcosm matching the macrocosm? Once again, the Porphyry passage supplies the answer: 'the Persians perfect their initiate by inducting him into a mystery of the descent of souls and their exit back out again, calling the place a 'cave' (*houtô kai Persai tên eis katô kathodon kai palin exodon mystagôgountes telousi ton mystên, eponomasantes spêlaion ton topon*). The purpose of the Mithraic cave is clear: to enable a mystery of 'the downward descent of souls and their exit back out again'.

We shall also momentarily postpone further explication of this intent in order to first take a look into the universal model that would have comprised the Mithraists *cognized environment*.

3.4 Ptolemaic cosmology: blending terrestrial and celestial topography

As we have seen, perceptions of space and time find a stable and long-term reference frame in the observation of the heavens and the phenomenal movements of the celestial bodies in the sky. Using our egocentric embodied perspective, we are able to orient ourselves and to navigate in space in reference to the cardinal points. We are also able to organize our sensorimotor and multimodal experiences in sequential orders and time intervals in terms of the predictable successions of the sun and the moon. However, we use our egocentric spatial mappings for generating more elaborate durable allocentric maps of celestial space in order to establish stable material anchors for our spatio-temporal experiences. Cosmological systems, which are the result of more complex conceptual processing of the perceptions of the celestial objects, their positions with each other, their movements and the relationships between them, constitute such allocentric maps of the universe. Cosmological maps may develop into complex cultural models, which are based on implicit perceptions, long-term concepts and culturally available semantic knowledge, and which are blended with material anchors attributing representational stability to the world (see Hutchins 2005: 1555, 1558–62).

The cosmological system articulated by Claudius Ptolemy in the second century AD comprises percepts and image-schemas, built on earlier conceptual maps constructed by Greek, Babylonian, and Egyptian astronomers. Ptolemy used the image of the earth as a sphere (*Almagest*, 1.4) – first suggested by Pythagoras (sixth century BCE) and his student Philolaus (fifth century BCE;

Stobaeus, *Anthology* I, 22, 1d) – and borrowed the idea that the motions of the planets in the heavens defined the planetary spheres (*Almagest* 1.3; see Figure 3.1). Contrary to Pythagoras, who located the sun in the centre of the universe and to Philolaus, who had argued that all the planets together with the earth move around an invisible Central Fire, Ptolemy's model was geocentric following Plato's suggestion (fourth century BCE) that the planets follow uniform motions around the spherical earth (*Almagest* 1.3–5). Based on the image of multi-concentric planetary spheres defined by the planets as suggested by Eudoxus of Knidus (fourth century BCE; *Art of Eudoxus* or *Tehni Eudoxou*), Ptolemy argued that the rotation of the visible planets around an immobile earth defined seven successive planetary spheres. The moon is considered to be the closest planet to the earth, and determines the first planetary sphere, which separates the sublunar from the superlunar realm. The space between the 'sublunar' and the 'superlunar' realms is inhabited by 'elemental and demonic powers' who control the 'terrestrial sphere' and who are in turn controlled by the 'celestial deities' (Martin 1987: 7–8; Beck 2006a: 77–9; Panagiotidou 2008: 63–4). The other visible planets (Mercury, Venus, Sun, Mars, Jupiter, and Saturn) determine six nested spheres, with Saturn's orbit defining the outer (most distant) planetary sphere (Ptolemy, *Tetrabiblos* I.4). Beyond the planetary spheres, the stars comprise an ultimate sphere of 'fixed stars', which do not follow distinct movements around the earth as the planets do (Ptolemy, *Almagest* 1.2).

Visualizing the Ptolemaic cosmological model, we can say that the universe is perceived as a CONTAINER.[33] The sphere of the fixed stars determines the outer border of a universal CONTAINER. The wandering planets and the earth are inside the CONTAINER. People live on the earth, which remains stable in the centre of the universe, and can see the other contained celestial elements[34] but not beyond the border of the CONTAINER. Standing on the terrestrial domain and gazing at the sky they can see all the other celestial bodies rotate around them following a westward motion. The fixed stars follow this universal motion but steadily maintain their positions on the celestial border. Being in the greatest visible distance, the fixed stars comprise the most stationary benchmark of the universal motion, which marked a 'Sameness and Uniformity' for the continually changing world (Beck 2006a: 83). The planets follow the same universal motion but simultaneously rotate around the earth (within the space of the universal container, of course) usually following an easterly direction. Planetary motions affect people's lives on the earth by influencing the growth of the plants, the rise and fall of sea levels, weather alterations and so on, and thereby bring 'Difference and Multiplicity' into cosmos (Beck 2006a: 83).

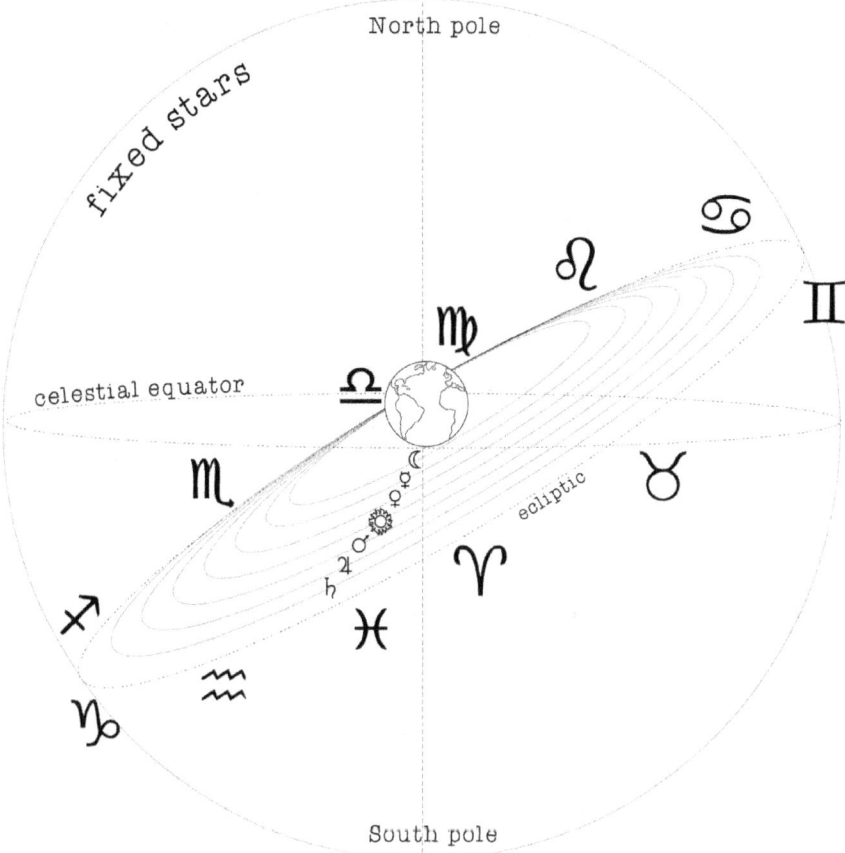

Figure 3.1 The celestial sphere

The universal spherical CONTAINER is bisected into two hemispheres by the celestial equator, which represents the circular path that all the celestial elements follow during their westward motion around the earth (Figure 3.1). The north and south celestial poles are the most remote from the earth points of the celestial hemispheres and are exactly opposite to each other. East and West respectively are not signified by specific points but are determined by the positions of the celestial bodies as they move around the earth (see Beck 2000: 162–3). The fixed stars form constellations that are visible on the northern and southern semi-spheres while they – following the celestial equator along with the planets – rotate around the diameter that connects the north and south celestial poles. The sun, the moon, and the other visible planets simultaneously follow their own routes within the universal sphere. These planetary equators are defined as the *ecliptic*, a route that is oblique to the celestial equator (Ptolemy,

Almagest 1.5, 1.8). The circle of zodiacs divides the ecliptic into twelve sequential sectors of thirty degrees each and forms the spatial background for the planetary motions (Ptolemy, *Almagest* 2.7).

The motions of the fixed stars and the planetary spheres in the celestial space provided the ground for the metaphorical perception and measurement of the MOVING TIME. The westward motion of the universal space along the celestial equator around the earth, a motion that becomes visible by the observable movement of the sun in the sky and its replacement by the appearance and movements of the moon and the stars, determines the succession of days and nights (Beck 2006a: 77–9; Panagiotidou 2008: 64). The successive positions that the sun and the moon occupy in the sky during their phenomenal motions provide the ground for the measurement of time (chronos) – its segregation to hours, moments, seconds and so on – and for the calculation that a full rotation of the universe around the earth lasts 24 hours. The eastward motions of the planets along the ecliptic within the universal CONTAINER provide a further frame of references for measuring long-term time. Taking into account the concepts of epicycles and the eccentric motions of planets introduced by Apollonius of Perga (third–second centuries BCE; Ptolemy, *Almagest* 7.1) and the Babylonian observations recorded by Hipparchus (second century BCE; Ptolemy, *Almagest* 7.2), Ptolemy modified the Platonic notion of the uniformity of planetary motions around the earth (Plato, *Timaeus* 38c3–6),[35] and elaborated a model for measuring universal time (Beck 2006a: 79; see also Beck 1994: 42).[36] Thus, he estimated that the moon needs twenty-eight days[37] to complete a full rotation around the earth, and its successive rotations defined the cycles of months. The sun, moving at the medial planetary sphere, needs one year to revolve around the earth,[38] and its rotation signifies the sequence of years. Following the ecliptic from south to north, as the sun moves westwards, it crosses the celestial equator at the spring equinox in the sign of Aries. Continuing its circular motion, the sun crosses again the celestial equator at the autumn equinox in the sign of Libra. When the sun is exactly between the two equinoxes, the summer solstice is marked at the sign of Cancer, which is the northernmost point of the ecliptic. From that point, the sun changes its course and starts moving from north to south (summer tropic). The winter solstice occurs at the sign of Capricorn, which is the southernmost point of the ecliptic, when the sun starts again to move to the north (winter tropic; see Porphyry, *On the Cave* 21–2). In this way, the orbit of the sun, passing from the spring and autumn equinoxes and the summer and winter solstices, defined the alternation of seasons (Beck 2006a: 78–9). Beyond the sun, the other planets rotate around the earth in different speeds determining different intervals of time (Ptolemy, *Almagest* 3.1; Beck 2000: 163). The period in which all the planets complete a full circuit around the earth and return simultaneously to the points of their departures constitutes the Great Year (*Megalos Eniautos*) (Beck 2006a: 114).[39]

Parallel to the celestial equator the climates determined successive bands or zones of universal latitude towards the north and south celestial poles. In particular, the signs of the zodiac that were assigned to the same celestial latitude – clima – were called 'isodynamounta' ('equally powered'), for when the sun passed from these sectors of the zodiacal circle, the day and night are of equal duration (Gordon 1976a: 131). Thus, when the sun passes from the points where the equinoxes cross the celestial equator, the length of day and night is equal (Ptolemy, *Tetrabiblos* I.11).

In short, we suggest that the Ptolemaic cosmological model can be seen as an allocentric map of the universe in the sense that it maps out the positions and movements of the celestial elements and the relations between them independently from the positions, movements and points of view of humans on the earth. However, people cannot have such a direct allocentric perception of the universal space, since they cannot stand outside of the universe and observe its overall structure. Blending this complex conceptual model with material anchors may generate more stable representations (written descriptions, visual images, diagrams etc.), which may enable mental simulations of the universe and conceptualizations of its spatio-temporal unity. As we shall see, the Mithraic mysteries involved both an egocentric and an allocentric mapping of the cosmos, anchored on the material construction of the mithraea and the scene of the tauroctony, which would have mediated the embodied spatio-temporal experience of the souls' journey to the heavens.

3.5 The Mithraic universe as a blending mental space

In the Graeco-Roman world, various architectural constructions anchored and triggered the conceptual blend between universal and terrestrial space and time as it was conceptualized in popular astrological systems that integrated the Ptolemaic cosmology.[40] Circular buildings either with a dome – like the Pantheon and the dining room in Nero's Domus Aurea in Rome – or without a vaulted ceiling – like Varro's aviary near Casinum – as well as architectural structures that indirectly referred to a circle – like the Orologium (Tower of the Winds) in Athens and the Circus Maximus in Rome[41] – were designed and operated as material anchors which instantiated popular cosmological representations and generated blended mental spaces that were metaphorically perceived as models of the universe. Mithraea constituted some of the most elaborate replicas of the cosmos, which – although constructed without great financial resources – managed to provide perhaps the most inference-rich material simulation of the universal macrocosm and to create a virtual reality of the universe that was metaphorically perceived and conceived through the bodily presence and sensorimotor experiences of the initiates within their ritual space.

Returning to Porphyry's description of the ideal mithraeum (*On the Cave* 6), we can trace the mental imagery that was projected from the cosmic space to the Mithraic cave and generated the blended mental space of the Mithraic microcosmic universe. As Porphyry wrote:

> This cave bore for him [Zoroaster] the image of the cosmos (*eikona kosmou*) which Mithras had created, and the things which the cave contained, by their proportionate arrangement, provided him with symbols of the elements and climates of the cosmos.
>
> Trans. Arethusa edition

The 'cave bore … the *image* of the cosmos'. The very term the *image* (*eikona*) indicates that people shared some major mental representations of the cosmos that they would have generated through their sensorimotor experiences and at least some internalization of the culturally developed conceptual models of universal space. Such mental representations would have comprised an integrated conceptual image of the universe. The mithraeum was not a two-dimensional depiction of this conceptual image, which could only have been perceived by an observer outside the system: it was a three-dimensional spatial model into which the initiates might enter in order to project their multi-modal representations of the universe onto the material structures of the mithraeum.

Taking into account blending metaphor theory, all the elements and components of the input mental spaces of the universe and the cave should not necessarily be projected in order to generate the blended mental space of the mithraeum as the cosmos. According to Fauconnier and Turner (1998, 2002, 2003),[42] during a process of composition counterpart elements are identified in the input mental spaces and are related to each other in order to co-exist or be fused into a new blended mental space (1998: 144, 2003: 60). The wording of Porphyry implies a primary conceptual correspondence that was implicitly perceived to exist between the Mithraic cave and the universe. The expression 'the things which the cave *contained*' (*tōn d'entos … ferontōn*) indicates without demanding further conscious processing that the cave was conceived as a CONTAINER. Actual sensorimotor experiences would have effected a conceptual fusion between the universe and the cave on the basis of the CONTAINER image-schema. Similar to the universe that people perceive as a CONTAINER only from the inside, the Mithraic cave could not be seen from the outside. Whether natural caves or artificial, windowless, vaulted halls integrated into other buildings, the mithraea had no identifiable external borders.[43] People moving around in the terrestrial domain could not distinguish a Mithraic cave within the geographical landscapes from the outside. They must go into a mithraeum in order to perceive it as a CONTAINER and such a perception largely corresponded with the ways they ordinarily perceived the universe.

Entering the Mithraic cave, initiates were cut out off from the external worlds, both terrestrial and celestial. Therefore, within the mithraeum there was no external material anchor or reference frame of orientation.[44] It was primarily the initiates' bodily presence and intrinsic body-schema along with the conceptual knowledge of the universe that would have allowed the projection and fusion of the cosmic template with that of the terrestrial cave giving rise to the blended space of the Mithraic universe as a spatial structure. During this process partial correspondences between the two input spaces would have been identified firstly through immediate egocentric spatial mappings. Recognition of correspondences is not constrained to perceived similarities. On the contrary, such cognitive processing may bypass phenomenal discrepancies in favour of metaphorical correspondences.

Building on egocentric perception, the initiates in the mithraeum looking upwards could see the ceiling of the Mithraic cave to determine its interior boundaries. These spatial boundaries, visible only from the inside, would have been perceived as counterparts of – and mentally integrated with – the internal borders of the universe; that is, the sphere of the fixed stars. The dome-shaped ceiling would have resembled the celestial concave and such perception would have extended to the rectangular hall, which would have been perceived to be metaphorically spherical.[45] However, the ceiling down to floor-level was perceived as forming only a half sphere: the initiates may have identified the floor with the plane of the celestial equator and the dome above them with the visible north hemisphere. Such perceivable correspondences between the universal sphere and the Mithraic cave would have been further completed by the initiates' conceptual knowledge of the universe. As Fauconnier and Turner (1998: 144) argue, 'A minimal composition in the blend can be extensively completed by a larger conventional pattern'. Thus, the initiates could project the cosmological model into the cave and imaginatively complete its pattern by imagining the south celestial sphere to extend below the floor.[46]

So far the physical structure of the cave provided the primary material anchors for mentally blending the mithraum with the universe. However, recall that Porphyry (*On the Cave* 6) mentioned that the 'things which the cave contained, by their proportionate arrangement, provided ... symbols of the elements and climates of the cosmos'. Among these 'things', the scene of the tauroctony, which was displayed in the great majority of the mithraea, was the most common material representation (Beck forthcoming). As we will see in the next chapter, the tauroctony was a complex symbolic structure, but for now it is enough to say that Mithras symbolized the sun and he was represented as slaying the bull, which was a symbol of the moon. Therefore, both Mithras and the moon were 'symbols of the elements'. The initiates looking at Mithras and the bull could see the sun and the moon at a specific point of the ecliptic, which could be imagined to circle the mithraeum. But at which exact point of the ecliptic did the sun appear to pass? An answer is given by Porphyry (*On the Cave* 24, 9-13):

> The equinoctial region they assigned to Mithras as an appropriate seat. And for this reason he bears the sword of Aries, the sign of Mars; he also rides on a bull, Taurus being assigned to Venus. As a creator and lord of genesis, Mithras is placed in the region of the celestial equator with the north to his right and the south to his left.[47]
>
> Trans. Arethusa edition

Porphyry's interpretation may seem to be too elaborate. However, treating the mithraeum as a simulation of the universe (cf. Fauconnier and Turner 1998: 144, 2003: 59), the initiates could correlate the available material anchors and extract further mental inferences which would have enhanced the blend. Therefore, the image of Mithras killing the bull may potentially have been perceived as representing the victory of the sun over the moon, which occurred at the spring equinox, after which the day begins to last longer than the night. At that moment the sun begins its annual rotation around the earth following the ecliptic. The long aisle that extended from the tauroctony towards the entrance of the Mithareum appeared to connect two opposite points of the ecliptic. And since the tauroctony symbolized the spring equinox, the entrance must have been the symbolic point of the autumn equinox. Therefore, the aisle corresponded to the actual cosmic diameter that connected the equinoxes at the plane of the celestial equator and further bisected the universe to the 'equinoctial colures'.[48]

Given the fluidity of 'to the left' and 'to the right' in embodied perceptions, the initiates entering the mithraeum and facing the tauroctonous Mithras have north to the left and south to the right. Transferring the egocentric reference frame of spatial orientation from the outside terrestrial domain into the Mithraic cave, if the mithraists rotated themselves by 90 degrees, so as to have north in front of them and south behind, they would identify the central cult niche bearing the tauroctony to the right hand with the east and the entrance to their left hand with the west. Just to note, the orientation within the Mithraic cave was absolutely grounded on internal frames of reference and therefore it was not necessary for any particular mithraeum to coincide with the external geographical orientations (Beck 1994a: 113–14, 2000: 162, 2004: 245, 2006a: 110, 2014: 249). The initiates could imagine the zodiacal circle to start from the cult niche and to extend westwards, circling the mithraeum and ending up again at the tauroctony. Therefore, the Mithraists who sat on the bench along the left wall that would have been identified with the northern semi-circle of the zodiac, would have perceived themselves as being more 'northerly' and thus 'higher' than the initiates who sat on the bench along the right wall that would have represented the southern semi-circle zodiac (Beck 2006a: 108–11). In addition, the various positions of the Mithraists on the benches would have corresponded to specific moments of the annual eastward (anticlockwise) movement of the sun. Thus, from an egocentric perspective, each initiate would have perceived his position as instantiating a current moment of the sun's motion, while those initiates who sat to his left would have signified past moments, while those who sat to his right would have represented the future.

Two side niches were sited exactly in the middle of the benches along the long 'north' and 'south' walls, which would have imaginatively corresponded to the points of the summer and winter solstices.[49] The imagined axis that linked the two niches was the axis of solstices, which determined the 'solstitial colure, the great circle which joins the solstices to the poles' (Beck 2006a: 111). Standing in the middle of the aisle, the axis of the solstices would have crossed the axis of the equinoxes at the heart of the universe, where the earth was sited. Above the point of intersection another axis would have been imagined to penetrate the floor in the middle of the aisle connecting the northern celestial pole on the ceiling and the southern celestial pole below the floor (pp. 103–11, 108).

In some cases the aforementioned correspondences and mental integration of the universal elements with the spatial structures of the mithraea would have been more extensively supported by additional material anchors. For instance, in the mithraeum at Vulci in Etruria (Figure 3.2),[50] twelve arches – six on each side

Figure 3.2 Mithraeum at Vulci
Source: Photo taken on 4 August 2009 by mararie (Flickr)

– support the benches along the long walls, which are intersected in the middle by two niches facing each other. Such visual representations would have provided the anchors for imagining the twelve corresponding arcs of the zodiac circling the Mithraic hall as well as the points of the ecliptic in which the summer and winter solstices occurred (see Beck 1984a: 2032–3; Gordon 1988: 53).

In the Sette Sfere Mithraeum in Ostia (Figure 3.3),[51] the zodiac circle was even more explicitly presented by mosaic representations of the zodiac signs on the benches. Starting from the tauroctony and following a westward – anticlockwise – order, the benches consecutively carried the signs of Aries, Taurus, Gemini, Cancer, Leo and Virgo towards the entrance of the mithraeum from which point they run in the opposite direction, carrying the signs of Libra, Scorpio, Sagittarius, Capricorn, Aquarius and Pisces (Figure 3.4).

Such visual signs would have enabled an allocentric mapping of the 'celestial elements' within the Mithraic universe that was irrespective of the initiates' positions and movements. The successive zodiac signs on the benches visualized the ecliptic and simultaneously delineated the annual route of the sun through the zodiac around the earth. The image of Mithras located between the signs of

Figure 3.3 Sette Sfere Mithraeum
Source: Photo taken on 9 October 2010 by Dennis Jarvis (Flickr)

Aries and Pisces was exactly at the point when the spring equinox occurred. Simultaneously, the entrance of the mithraeum was between the signs of Virgo and Libra where the autumn equinox then took place (Beck 2000: 163, 2006a: 103–11). Therefore, the image of Mithras was exactly on the axis of the equinoxes with the northern signs of the zodiac extending to his right, and the southern signs lying to his left. As we have previously seen, this was the 'proper seat' of Mithras as described by Porphyry (Beck 2006a: 185). In addition, the niche on the left appears to be between the signs of Gemini and Cancer, and would have signified the summer solstice, the most northerly point in the orbit of the sun. The niche to the right was between the signs of Sagittarius and Capricorn, and would have signified the winter solstice, the most southerly point in the orbit of the sun (Gordon 1988: 57; Beck 2006a: 111). It follows, then, that the signs of Gemini and Cancer delineated the most northern celestial clima, while the signs of Sagittarius and Capricorn determined the most southern celestial clima. Between these extreme zones of celestial latitude the zodiac signs formed 'isodynamounta' ('equally powered'), pairs which determined the intermediate northern and southern climata of the universal sphere. Simultaneously, an initiate who sat on the bench with the sign of Capricorn would have perceived an initiate who sat on the sign of Sagittarius as being at a past point of the solar

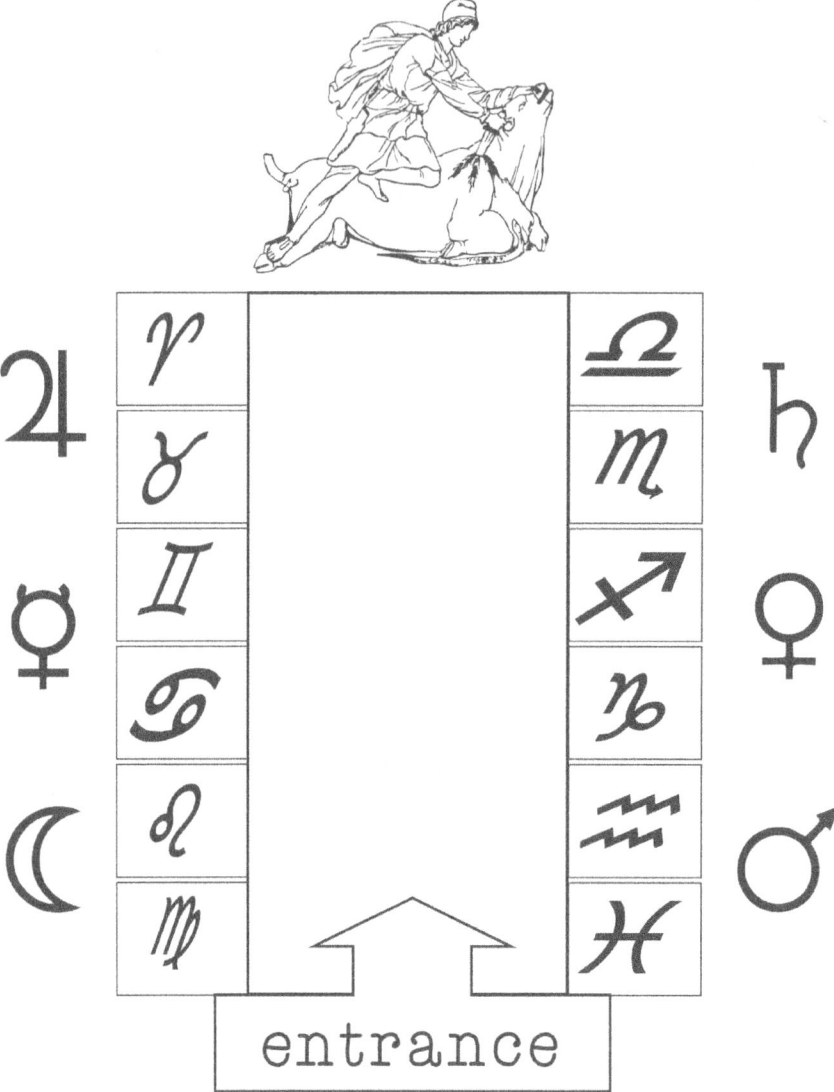

Figure 3.4 Plan of the Sette Sfere Mithraeum

rotation, and an initiate who sat on the sign of Aquarius as being at a future point of the ecliptic.

We suggest that both egocentric and allocentric mappings of the elements that compose Mithraic space would have contributed to its metaphorical perception as a model of the universe. Although we do not have evidence about the ways in which such metaphorical perception would have been instantiated in the Mithraic rituals, we can make some assumptions about the metaphorical connotations of the initiates' movements within the Mithraic cave during the ritual enactments. In particular, we can presume that the initiates departing from the cult niche and following an anticlockwise motion – a motion that followed the zodiacal signs from the sign of Aries to the sign of Pisces (as in the Sette Sphere Mithraeum) – would have perceived themselves as moving westwards along the ecliptic simulating the annual motion of the sun around the immobile earth, which simultaneously defined the succession of seasons (pp. 78–9).[52] When the initiates moved in the opposite, clockwise direction around the celestial equator, they would have delineated the daily movement of the celestial bodies along with the fixed stars around the earth, which lasted twenty-four hours and defined the alternations of days and nights (Beck 2000: 162).[53]

The assumption that ritual processions would have taken place within the mithraeum is supported by a visual representation moulded on the second side of the ritual vessel of Mainz.[54] The scene involves four figures depicted as parading leftwards, as we look at it from an outer point of view. Modern scholars have attempted to identify these figures with members of specific Mithraic grades from their visual imagery.[55] If, however, we pay more attention to the phenomenal positions and movements of the depicted figures, the scene on the Mainz vessel seems to instantiate a fragment of the ritual praxis. Although we cannot identify the ritual and its internal purpose, the leftward movement of the figures within the mithraeum seems to points out the annual eastward motion of the sun around the earth (see Beck 2000).

The metaphorical connotations and cosmological equivalences of the ritual procession depicted on the Mainz vessel are indicated by a similar representation on a vessel (Figure 3.5) found in the Köln Mithraeum in Germany. The Köln vessel seems to depict the sun between two other figures to parade on the celestial plane, on the background of which the stars are discerned. Comparing the two representations, we can assume that the Mainz vessel seemingly displays the god's cult surrogates to ritually enact on the terrestrial domain the sun's movements on the celestial firmament (see Beck 2000: 158). Therefore, the scene on the Mainz vessel might be considered as depicting the ritual enactment of the sun's motion within the Mithraic microcosm in which the movements of the initiates would have instantiated the movements of the celestial bodies on the heavens (Beck 2000: 147, 2001–2: 289).

Although we cannot be certain about how the mental integration of space and time would have worked during rituals, it seems that in some cases such integration was anchored on solid material structures within the Mithraic cave. In the mithraeum of Vulci (Moretti 1979), for instance, statues of the gods were

Figure 3.5 Köln vessel
Source: Photo taken on 9 August 2014 by Carole Raddato (Flickr)

placed in the niches that intersected the benches, and images of the planets were set between the recesses formed by the arches which supported the benches. We have no evidence about the use of these images during ritual enactment, but based on this analysis it is likely that they contributed to the perception of time in the Mithraic cult context. It seems plausible, for instance, that initiates carried the images of the planets from one zodiac sign to the other, representing time as a 'changing now' during the (real or ritual) year (Beck 2006a: 114). In this way, the niches which represented the solstices, the entrance of the mithraeum and the opposite scene of tauroctony, which determined the equinoxes, and every position on the benches would have represented specific points in the celestial space but simultaneously signified metaphorical moments in the annual and daily time as it was defined by the movements of the celestial bodies.

Thus, space and time were fused in the blended mental space of the mithraeum, where every spatial sign or movement indicated time as a moving presence in reference to past and future, which were instantiated as visually observable dimensions. Such metaphorical perceptions of time within the Mithraic cave would not have necessarily been the result of conscious processing. The image-schemas of 'past', 'present' and 'future' would have implicitly structured the short-term personal experiences of initiation and participation in the rituals. The initiation would have been stored in the initiate's long-term biographical memory as an explicit significant episode of a past that would have defined their present and determined their future. The major concepts of time would have acquired further contextual metaphorical meanings as once again the blending between the cave and the universe was run and developed its own emergent structure. Within the Mithraic microcosm, the initiates could have direct embodied experiences of a cosmos in which universal space and time were fused.

However, we cannot surmise that such fusion and conceptual blending was necessarily created in full simply by entering the mithraeum. Moreover, some of the Mithraists perhaps would *never* have reached such a coherent view of the universal space and time integrated within the Mithraic cave. A primary conceptual blend and some elementary correspondences would have more easily triggered the simpler premise that the mithraeum is the universe and Mithras is the creator and preserver of the cosmos. However, after entering the mithraeum, 'running the blend' (cf. Fauconnier and Turner 1998: 144, 2003: 59) during the mysteries and the ritual praxis, more correspondences, completions, compressions and selective projections could have gradually stimulated a mental elaboration attributing shape, structure and material ground to the blended space of the Mithraic universe. The available material anchors would have facilitated the cognitive processing, mental elaboration and imaginative fusion between the universal and terrestrial templates, but such mental processes could have gradually developed as rituals unfolded. As we see in the following section, it was via the enactment of rituals that the conceptual blending of the mithraeum and the universe, anchored on the available material representations, would have emerged as a distinct spatial structure, which would have in turn generated further conceptual inferences and elaborated metaphorical relationships between the initiates' positions and the spatial elements within the Mithraic universal space.

3.6 The mystery of the souls' journey: mental imagery and ritual enactment

The metaphorical perception of the mithraeum as an image of the universe provided the appropriate spatio-temporal background for the actualization of the mystery of the souls' journey from the earth throughout the planetary spheres towards the sphere of the fixed stars. However, there are not enough literary sources to provide exact descriptions of the rituals that would have taken place within the mithraeum. This is to a great extent reasonable if we take into account that only the initiates could participate in the rituals, keeping what happened within the cave hidden from the outsiders.

We are once again informed by Porphyry (*On the Cave* 6) that the Mithraic cave was designed as an image of the cosmos in order to provide the space where the mystery of the souls' journey would have taken place: 'the Persians [i.e. the Mithraists] perfect their initiate by inducting him into a mystery of the descent of souls and their exit back out again, calling the place a "cave". Invoking Numenius and Cronius, Porphyry (*On the Cave* 21–2) states that the gates of genesis and apogenesis were revealed within the mithraeum and from these gates the souls could travel throughout the heavens:

> Taking the cave as an image and symbol of the cosmos, Numenius and his pupil Cronius assert that there are two extremities in the heavens: the winter tropic than which nothing is more southern and the summer tropic than which nothing is more northern. The summer tropic is in Cancer, the winter tropic is in Capricorn. (21) ... Two of these [i.e. signs of the zodiac], Cancer and Capricorn, the theologians treated as gates ... Numenius and Cronius say that the gate through which souls descend is Cancer and the gate through which they ascend is Capricorn. Cancer is northerly and suited for descent, Capricorn southerly and suitable for ascent.
>
> Trans. Arethusa edition, 22

We have seen in the previous sections that the two niches at the middle of the benches along the long walls of the cave represented the two solstices, that is the gates from which the souls descend to the earth and can ascend back again to the sphere of the fixed stars. Therefore, entering the mithraeum the initiates could see the gates of genesis and apogenesis. Although we do not know if the mystery of the souls' journey was part of the initiatory rituals or how often it might have been enacted, Proclus (*In Remp.* 2.128.26–129.13 Kroll, trans. Lamberton 1986: 66 f., with minor changes and a correction [*isêmerina* = 'equinoxes', not 'solstices'] suggested and cited by Beck 2006a: 130), referring to Numenius, gives us some sense of the souls' itinerary from the earth upwards to the heavens:

> Numenius says that this place [i.e. the site of posthumous judgement] is the centre of the entire cosmos, and likewise of the earth, because it is at once in the middle of heaven and in the middle of the earth ... By 'heaven' he means the sphere of the fixed stars, and he says there are two chasms in this, Capricorn

and Cancer, the latter a path down into genesis, the former a path of ascent, and the rivers under the earth he calls the planets ... and introduces a further enormous fantasy (*teratologian*) with leapings (*pêdêseis*) of souls from the tropics to the equinoxes and returns from these back to the tropics leapings that are all his own and that he transfers to these matters, stitching the Platonic utterances together with astrological concerns and these with the mysteries (*syrraptôn ta Platônika rhêmata tois genethlialogikois kai tauta tois telestikois*). He invokes the poem of Homer [i.e. *Od.* 13.109–12] as a witness to these two chasms.

Proclus agrees with Porphyry regarding the positions of the celestial gates and further outlines the path of the souls' journey. The souls could leap from the earth to the summer tropics. From there they could move towards the equinoxes, from which they could pass to the planetary spheres. These movements would have been imaginative (*teratologian*) and as such could have been blended with material anchors within the Mithraic universe comprising, thereby, the mental blended space of the ritual enactment of the mystery of the souls' journey. Thereby, the initiates' bodily position in the middle of the cave would have mentally corresponded with their position on the earth. From there they could move bodily towards the niche to the right – as they faced the scene of tauroctony. Such movement would have mentally blended with their souls' leaping downwards, that is, southwards, towards the gate at the winter solstice at the sign of Capricorn. From there again, they could bodily move towards the entrance or the central cult niche, which was metaphorically perceived to be the equinoxes. From the equinoxes their souls could 'leap' to the planetary sphere of the moon and then successively to the spheres of the other planets in order to reach the summer solstice at the sign of Cancer and from there to get out in the sphere of the fixed stars. Such movement through the planetary spheres is described by Origen (*Contra Celsum* 6.22) as a ladder:

> These things [i.e. the celestial ascent of souls] the *logos* of the Persians and the *teletê* of Mithras intimate ... for there is therein a certain *symbolon* of the two celestial revolutions (*periodôn*), that of the fixed stars and that assigned to the planets, and of the route of the soul through and out (*diexodou*) of them. Such is the *symbolon*: a seven-gated ladder and an eighth [sc. gate] on top (*klimax heptapylos, epi de autêi ogdoê*).

Such an imaginative ladder is nicely represented in the Mithraeum of Sette Sfere, in which seven mosaic arcs are depicted as extending in sequence from the entrance, up the aisle, and have been considered to represent the seven successive planetary spheres.[56] In the same mithraeum, the mosaic depictions of the planets on the benches could have been the material anchors of the stairs of the celestial ladder from which the souls leaped from one planetary sphere to the other.[57] Therefore, starting from the winter solstice and following the ecliptic, the initiates' souls could have leapt to the sphere of the moon at the arcs of Leo and Virgo. From that point, following the moon's rotation, they could have leapt to the sphere of Mercury as they passed from the arcs of Gemini and Cancer. Rotating along to Mercury they could have leapt further to the sphere of Mars at the arcs of Libra and Scorpius and, then, to the sphere of the sun at the Spring Equinox and so on until the last planetary sphere of Saturn at the signs of Acquarius and Pisces from which, following the ecliptic, they could have jumped into the sphere of the fixed stars from the gate at the summer solstice (Figure 3.4).[58]

The metaphorical mappings between the souls' imaginative itinerary, specific material anchors and the embodied movements within the cave may sound speculative, but they indicate that similar kinds of mental blending could have mediated the actual ritual enactment of a conceptual journey towards the heavens within the Sette Sfere mithraeum. The uniqueness of these representations does not allow generalizations to all mithraea. However, even in the absence of material representations, the notion of the souls' journey could have undergone mental elaboration by the members of the local Mithraic communities generating various local metaphorical mappings, co-relations and interpretations that would have contributed to the emergent structure of the blended space of the Mithraic caves.

The primary metaphors of Time, which we examined in the previous section, would have provided the ground for such metaphorical mappings. In particular, the MOVING TIME metaphor would have been underlying the experiences of the initiates who attended the rituals, while the MOVING OBSERVER metaphor would have mediated the perception of time by those who enacted the rituals. For the observers, the movements of their co-participants within the cave would have been blended with the motions of the sun in the heavens, which instantiated the movement of time in reference to their own stationary positions, determining, thereby, the spatial background of the passage of time. Simultaneously, the ritual actors would have been identified with the sun (or other planets) and therefore their movements would have instantiated the passage of time with reference to specific points of the ecliptic at which the observers would have stood. From the actors' point of view, the present was identified with their current position, the past comprised all the signs they had passed over, and the future consisted of the signs towards which they moved. But since within the mithraeum, the whole celestial route of the sun was revealed and was directly accessible, the motion of time was not irreversible. In other words, within the Mithraic microcosm, the initiates could move forward or backward along the ecliptic, freely moving metaphorically between past, present and future.

Similarly, the metaphorical perception of TIME as LANDSCAPE could have mediated the mystery of the souls' journey. The celestial ladder which led to the heavens comprised the pathway of apogenesis. The successive planetary spheres determined the intermediate stations or stairs of this pathway. The initiates' souls would have moved in relation to the stationary spatial background of the ladder. The arrival at each sphere would have been perceived as the present, the place at which the souls were for now. The planetary spheres that were closer to the earth and through which the souls had already passed would have represented the past. The higher spheres, which were at greater distance from the earth, would have been perceived as the future, representing the successive future stations of the souls towards their final destination in the sphere of the fixed stars. Thus, the successive planetary spheres would have represented the times of the souls' journey, while the movement of the souls through the planetary spheres would have been perceived as the 'Passage of Time' (cf. Lakoff and M. Johnson, 1999: 147).

The concept of a ladder in any case compresses the notions of ascent and descent and may ground the mental imagery of the souls' journey. Therefore, what the Mithraic mysteries would have revealed to the initiates would have been the celestial gates and the ladder which their souls had once followed during genesis and which they might now follow once again towards the opposite direction upon their death. And what the mysteries would have provided to the Mithraists would have been the opportunity to carry out the journey of apogenesis while they were still alive and to travel back again to earth following the path of genesis. How often the Mithraists would have taken this journey cannot be known, but the notion of a ladder entails the possibility of infinite downward and upward movements. In any case, the general purpose of the souls' journey was not a kind of permanent salvation from the mortal life and material existence of the initiates (Beck forthcoming). Being introduced to the mysteries, the Mithraists became partners of Mithras, reached a view of universal cosmic order and participated in the preservation of this order. In order to accomplish their duties, the Mithraists should be able to move in the universe and to oversee its appropriate function. Such a view of the universe and movement within it was possible only within the Mithraic microcosm.

3.7 Cautes and Cautopates: metaphorical meaning and compression

As we have seen, from an egocentric perspective the initiates perceived themselves as being 'down' on the terrestrial domain where they spent their mortal lives. In order to release themselves from their mortality they must travel 'upwards' towards the outer level of the heavens. Thus, the image-schemas of 'up' and 'down' would have acquired specific semantic meanings and further metaphorical connotations in the ritual context of the souls' journey. And although these image-schemas were mostly instantiated as spatial dimensions and directions deriving from the initiates' embodied experiences within the mithraeum, they were materially anchored in the visual representations of the twin-figures Cautes and Cautopates, the so-called torchbearers. These figures represented secondary deities of the Mithraic cult that resembled one another in appearance and framed Mithras (the tauroctony) on each side. They were both dressed in Persian clothes and appear to hold torches,[59] which are turned in opposite directions. Cautes held the torch turned upwards, while Cautopates held the torch turned downwards. This variation, along with the locations of the torchbearers within the Mithraic caves, compressed and visually expressed multiple metaphorical meanings of 'up' and 'down'.

With reference to the direction of the torches, some primary metaphorical mappings could have been derived from the initiates' ordinary embodied perception of the daily rotation of the sun around the earth. Thereby the raised torch of Cautes could have been perceived as signifying the upward motion of the sun in the heavens, as it moves westwards from the point of sunrise in the east bringing light on the earth. Consequently, Cautes could have compressed metaphorical representations of the sun and the daylight, and also the spring and the summer when the days last longer than the nights. The lowered torch of Cautopates, on the other hand, could have signified the darkness during the night, when the sun disappears from the sky, and further the autumn and the winter when the nights and the darkness last longer than the days and the daylight (cf. Clauss 2000: 95-6).

More complex metaphorical meanings could have been ascribed to the torchbearers when they were perceived as elements of the tauroctonous scene.[60] In some cases, however, as for instance in the Sette Sfere mithraeum, Cautes and Cautopates were integrated as substantive figures in the Mithraic microcosm operating as material anchors for the metaphorical orientation and ritual actualization within the cave, and contributing to the emergent structure of the blended space (Gordon 1988: 55–6). In those mithraea, the image of Cautes was posed at the end of the south bench – towards the entrance – while the image of Cautopates was sited at the end of the north bench (Beck 2006a: 112). As we have previously seen, the south bench bore the two quadrants of the zodiac signs which corresponded to the winter and the autumn and were separated from each other by the winter solstice. On the other hand, the north bench carried the other two quadrants of the zodiacs, which determined the spring and the summer and were separated from each other by the summer solstice.

The placement of Cautes to the side of the winter solstice seems contradictory to his primary metaphorical association with the sun, the daylight, the spring and the summer. Similarly, the placement of Cautopates to the side of the summer solstice seemingly goes against his metaphorical correlation with the darkness, the night, the autumn and the winter (Gordon 1976a: 127–8, 1988: 55). Such contradiction is eliminated, however, if we integrate the torchbearers into the blended space of the mithraeum and we associate them with the unique motion of the sun around the earth as it was instantiated to run around the cave following the ecliptic. With reference to its own planetary orbit, the sun upon reaching the point of the winter solstice starts to move upwards – that is northwards – towards the summer solstice. Cautes, standing on the side of the winter solstice, would have marked the start of the upward motion of the sun, which reaches the upper point of its route at the summer solstice, from where it starts again moving downwards – that is southwards. Cautopates, standing at the point of the summer solstice signified the start of the downward motion of the sun towards the winter solstice and so on. Therefore, the torchbearers represent the upward and downward motion of the sun as it moves eastwards around the earth (see Beck 2006a: 212).

In the ritual enactment of the souls' journey the torchbearers further seem to represent the route of the souls during genesis (descent) and apogenesis (ascent). The human soul descends from the sphere of the fixed stars to the earth, where it is given birth into mortal life. The path that the soul follows begins from the gate of the summer solstice and unfolds southwards through the planetary spheres towards the gate of the winter solstice, where genesis occurs. The Mithraic mysteries provided the initiates the opportunity to ascend back again to the sphere of the fixed stars and immortality. During the mystery of apogenesis, the soul enters from the gate at the winter solstice and moves upwards to the gate of the summer solstice, from which it can exit back to the sphere of the fixed stars. Therefore, Cautopates at the north bench showed and oversaw the descending direction which the souls follow during genesis, while Cautes indicated and supervised the ascending direction which the souls could follow during apogenesis (Beck 2006a: 207, 212).

Pophyry's *On the Cave* 12–25 specifies an additional metaphorical connotation of the positions of the torchbearers within the Mithraic universe in reference to the souls' journey:

> with the north to his right and the south to his left; to the south, because of its heat, they assigned Cautes and to the north Cautopates because of the coldness of the north wind. With good reason they assigned winds to souls proceeding to genesis and departing from it because they as well drag spirit along with them, as some have supposed, and possess a like essence. But the north wind is the proper wind for souls proceeding to genesis. It is for this reason that for those about to die the breath to the north wind.
>
> Trans. Arethusa edition

Beck (1984a: 2085, 1994a: 114) has pointed out an apparent paradox in these associations suggested by Porphyry. The passage of the sun from the summer solstice, at the most northern point of the ecliptic, is accompanied by experiences of heat and light on the earth. The passage of the sun from the winter solstice, at the southern point of the ecliptic, is experienced as bringing cold and darkness to the terrestrial domain. Therefore, the raised torch of Cautes at the south bench does not seem to fit with the cold and darkness during autumn and winter. Similarly, the lowered torch of Cautopates at the north bench is incongruous with the heat and light during spring and summer. When, however, the connections are made in terms of the experiences of the winds, Cautopates at the north bench is associated with the refreshing north wind, which pushes souls downwards to genesis. Cautes is connected with the hot south wind, which may release the souls from the bodies with his melting powers enabling them to fly upwards to the heavens (Beck 2006a: 213).

As it becomes evident, the raised and lowered torches of Cautes and Cautopates within the Mithraic cave would have compressed multiple metaphorical meanings of the image-schemas of 'up' and 'down'. Some primary metaphorical mappings would have emerged from the integration of the torchbearers in the blended mental space of the mithraeum as a model of the universe. Running the blend during the rituals, the figures of the torchbearers would have acquired more complex metaphorical connotations that could have undergone further mental elaborations contributing to the conceptual structure, mental simulation, and actual realization of the mystery of the souls' journey within the Mithraic microcosm

3.8 The souls' journey in the Mithraic microcosm

Initiation into the Mithraic mysteries promised to the initiates a journey throughout the heavens that would lead them to a new view of the cosmos and apogenesis in the sphere of the fixed stars. The scanty written testimony does not provide enough evidence about how such journey would have been accomplished within the mithraea during ritual enactment. However, we suggest that the cognitive processes that underlie embodied perception and metaphorical conceptions of space and time, presented in this chapter, may allow us to make some educated guesses about how the Mithraic caves might have been perceived and conceived as the actual universe in which a journey to heavens would have been possible.

As Beck (2016) aptly puts it, 'if you want to be a cosmonaut but lack an actual space ship, build a model cosmos, not a model space ship'. In this chapter, we suggested that the basic design and furniture of the mithraea could have operated as material anchors for the conceptual blending between the caves on the terrestrial domain and the cosmological model that the caves would have represented. Metaphorical conceptions of the mithraea could have derived from the initiates' embodied presence in the caves and the blending between their immediate percepts and their conceptual knowledge of the universe acquired through cultural learning. Although the cognitive processes that underlie such blending may seem rather complex, a great part of them takes place below the threshold of consciousness, enabling the emergence of multiple metaphors and blended mental spaces.

Of course we cannot be certain about how the Mithraists would have actually perceived and metaphorically conceived the mithraeum as a universal microcosm. What we intend to underline is that the ordinary cognitive mechanisms that mediate perception of space and time and enable further metaphorical conceptions of our spatio-termporal settings could have made possible multiple metaphorical mappings and give rise to blended mental spaces that could have mediated initiates' embodied perception of the mithraeum as an image of the universe in which the journey to the heavens could have been actualized.

4

The Scene of the Tauroctony as a Symbol System

4.1 Tracing the meanings of the tauroctony

The scene of the tauroctony was the most common visual representation to be found in mithraea. Not only its presence but also its location within the Mithraic cave appears fixed, while its composition, executed either in fresco or in statuary or in relief sculpture displays an exceptional uniformity. Beginning from Porphyry's testimony (*On the Cave* 6) that 'the things which the cave contained, by their proportionate arrangement, provided ... symbols of the elements and climates of the cosmos', we have examined the role and the metaphorical meaning of the scene with reference to the mental blended space of the Mithraic microcosm. Shifting now from where the monument was sited to what the scene represented, we can trace its significance within the mysteries.

Despite its ubiquity, ancient literary sources do not preserve information about what the tauroctony meant or was thought to mean.[1] The scene itself provides the ground for many inferences and looking at its visual composition 'can allow one to conclude, predict, or project information not overtly given' (Deacon 2014: 103). We have no way of confirming most of our inferences with first- or second-hand accounts and we cannot be certain of the inferences that Mithraists would have deduced from the scene. But by exploring the processes of perception and interpretation on a cognitive level, we can derive several hypotheses as to the meaning that the scene may have carried within the cult context. To this end, in this chapter we use the theory of signs suggested by Charles Sanders Peirce as a wider framework in order to provide some insights into how Mithraists might have extracted or attributed multiple meanings to the scene of the tauroctony.

4.2 The initiate's process of interpreting the tauroctony

The tauroctony was a ubiquitous element of the material environment of the mithraeum. It was not a mere physical object but an artefact that was intentionally designed and placed within the cave. The uniformity of the scene indicates that it was not a set of signs randomly collected and represented. Rather, it was the material instantiation of the mental representations shared by people who ordered the monuments and who designed them. In Dan Sperber's terms (1996: 80–1), the tauroctony was a 'public' representation, which would have acquired meaning only through its association with the mental representations of its commissioners, designers and viewers.[2]

The representation of the tauroctony would have been, first and foremost, a means of communicating information and meanings among cult members. The extent to which the initiates would have been able to extract information and to attribute meanings to the scene would have depended on two factors: (a) on their own explicit mental representations and implicit memories established during their interaction with the world and (b) on the semantic or encyclopaedic knowledge that they would have acquired living in the Graeco-Roman world and being inducted into the Mithraic mysteries. The scene of the tauroctony would not have had inherent semantic properties immediately perceivable by its viewers. Instead, it would have comprised a complex semantic structure the perception and conception of which would have been the result of a process of interpretation.[3]

The American pragmatist Charles Sanders Peirce (1839–1914) explored the hierarchical gradation of the interpretative processes (1931–58) that mediate the attribution of conceptual meanings to mental and public representations of perceivable reality and the transmission of these meanings between people. According to his theory, every perceptible entity – including objects and artefacts, natural phenomena and cultural events, or even sensory stimuli and abstract concepts – can operate as a *sign* – a 'representamen' – of another entity if people who perceive it infer the relationship between the *sign* that *signifies* and the *object* which is *signified*.[4] This association between the *sign* and the *object* is the result of the interpretative process which takes place in people's minds and generates the meaning that connects the signifier and the signified, which is another sign, the *interpretant*.[5] The interpretant is formed on the ground of the inferred relation between the sign-signifier and the object-signified and further comprises the result of signification, which entails that a sign is interpreted as something different from itself in the human mind (*CP* 1.553; Hoopes 1991:

11–12; Sinha 1996: 485). In this view, we can say that every interpretant sign comprises a mental blended space in which certain features of the perceivable objects are merged with each other generating new conceptual entities (cf. Fauconnier and Turner 1998, 2002, 2003).

Depending on the inferential processes that mediate the blend, Peirce distinguished three modes of sign-interpretations, which are based on the different associations inferred between the signifier and the signified. The first mode[6] derives from the observable similarity between two entities that entails the interpretation of one as an *icon* of the other (CP 2.247, 2.276). The second mode recognizes the temporal and spatial contiguity or natural co-occurrence of two objects that are associated with each other. This association, established in people's minds, allows the formation of certain assumptions and predictions that interpret the presence of the signifier as an *index* of the existence of the signified (CP 2.248, 2.304). The third mode of interpretants is more complex and difficult since it is based on seemingly arbitrary correlations, which are conventionalized, learned and shared by more than one person. Such conventional associations attribute symbolic qualities to objects that are widely accepted by the members of a social group and govern a great part of their communication systems (Peirce 1868; CP 1.558, 2.293, 2.299, 2.304, 2.249; Hoopes 1991: 251–2; Deacon 1997: 70–2; Merrell 2010).

Thus, according to Peirce, interpretation is not an absolutely internal mental process independent of external reality (see, e.g., CP 5.290, 7.349). Instead, it seems to be anchored on the embodied perception of the various components of the world, which are interpreted as signs through different cognitive processes. His 'semiotic realism' goes beyond the rigid Cartesian separation between mind and body in stating that the semantic properties of perceivable reality arise and increase in complexity during human thought in the act of interpreting the world (Hoopes 1991: 8–10; see Peirce 1868). The process of interpretation moves from iconic to indexical and from indexical to a symbolic level in which the same object can be gradually interpreted as an icon, an index or a symbol of another object (Deacon 1997: 71–2).

Thus, in Peirce's view, human thought is an inherently semiotic process that involves the perception of signs, which are represented in the mind and further can be interpreted as representations of other signs.[7] His theoretical considerations seem to correspond to the insights provided by cognitive science research into the ways in which humans experience, perceive and conceive of their surroundings, form certain images and assumptions about the world, and develop complex world-view systems.

In interaction with their surroundings, people observe recurrent patterns comprising perceivable reality and develop mental representations that are perceived as icons of the various components of the world. Peirce used the term *diagrams* in order to describe these elementary icons that seem to correspond to the pre-conceptual image-schemas deriving from immediate embodied experiences. The most elementary mental diagrams develop from the inferred *iconic* similarities between perceptible spatial entities or units of bodily-sensory percepts that are mapped out in diagrammatic image-schemas (Bundgaard and Stjernfelt 2010: 64, 67, 69). Congenital perceptual mechanisms, for instance, enable humans to develop the image-schemas of textures and geometric dimensions, living organisms and material objects, faces and bodies, and to categorize perceivable natural and cultural surroundings in terms of these diagrammatic representations (p. 64).

From a cognitive perspective, once these diagrams have been fully developed and perceived as *icons*, their image-schemas make further inferences possible. Thus, people are able to mentally complete fragmentary images. They can further associate image-schemas with each other in space and time and recognize *indexical* relationships between them. Thereby, they are able to identify the image-schema of a sound with a specific sound stimulus and then to interpret that stimulus as an *index* of the nearby presence of its source. Even facial expressions, gestures, bodily movements, and sensory signals comprise image-schemas, which are connected with other mental representations like those of feelings, emotions, intentions and actions, enabling indexical associations between them. Such indexical associations comprise second-level image-schemas that are diagrammatic mappings of scripts of actions or events that enable humans to develop assumptions about the causal relations, intentions, and potential outcomes of their current actions, of others' behaviours, and of unfolding events. Thus, humans' embodied sensorimotor and perceptual experiences form the generic space in which input percepts are matched with each other on account of their observable *iconic similarities* and *indexical associations* that become projected and compressed in the blended mental spaces of the image-schemas (see Mandler 2006: 79).

The image-schemas, which comprise people's *implicit procedural knowledge*, develop into concepts during *perceptual meaning analysis* that 'analyzes perceptual displays into meanings' (Mandler 2006: 67; see also 1988, 1992). During this process, the iconic similarities and the indexical connections that structure the blended mental spaces of the image-schemas become consciously accessible, amenable to explicit thinking and verbal description, comprising people's *explicit conceptual knowledge* of the world (Mandler 2006: 64).

Conceptualization is thus an analytical semiotic process that transforms the implicit image-schemas into explicit concepts. Concepts lexically articulated in thought and communication do not necessarily resemble in appearance and do not co-exist or appear along with the entities to which they refer – that is, they do not share inherent iconic and spatio-temporal indexical connections. The associations between the linguistic signs and their referents are conventional and derive from the culturally available language developed and commonly used during social interaction. In this view words and linguistic expressions comprise symbolic representations, which attribute conceptual meanings to primitive image-schemas. Beyond language, diagrammatic mappings between seemingly irrelevant signs developing and being established through habit and habituation with certain cultural settings mediate the attribution of symbolic properties to other means of communication – like visual arts, artefacts, ritual practices – which operate as conventional vehicles of meanings widely accepted and perceivable by others (Deacon 1997: 92–3). The ability for symbolic interpretation characterizes a great part of social interaction and communication, since it enables humans to convey conceptual meanings to others either during direct verbal (i.e. spoken language) or bodily (e.g. gestures, facial expressions) communication by anchoring their own mental representations upon external material means, which operate as public representations.

Previously encoded image-schemas stored in implicit memory can be evoked and analysed into explicit concepts even when perceptible information is not displayed during *perceptual meaning analysis*. Both implicit perceptual and explicit conceptual knowledge comprise an inventory that enables humans to conceive and conceptualize their surroundings. The process of interpretation is based on the inferences extracted from the perceptible data and further on the analysis and attribution of conceptual meanings to these inferences. In addition to the role of already stored perceptual and conceptual information – which consists of dynamic and not fixed mental representations – *perceptual meaning analysis* operates online enabling humans to develop image-schemas and concepts as they perceive new – previously unknown – entities (Mandler 2006: 73, 75). And although the cognitive mechanisms that underlie the human perceptual and inferential abilities are determined and constrained by the neuro-anatomical and biological construction of the body, the range of concepts and conceptual meanings that may invest in the primitive image-schemas is largely dependent on cultural conventions and social interactions.

From this perspective, the iconography of the tauroctony constitutes a visual representation that would have been designed and constructed on the common ground of how people – not just Mithraists – experience and perceive the world. The conceptual structure of the monument and its investment with symbolic meanings would have derived from the common concepts shared by people of the Graeco-Roman world and by the purposes of cult members who intended to convey meanings to other initiates. For the perceivers, starting from the implicit recognition of the image-schemas that comprised the scene, the conceptual meanings of the representation would have emerged during a gradual interpretative process moving from identifications of iconic similarities to inferences of indexical relations and then of symbolic meanings. This process would not necessarily have reached a fully symbolic comprehension of the scene by all the members of the cult. Depending on implicit memories, explicit declarative knowledge, and the extent to which the initiates had access to astronomical knowledge and cult meanings, the process could have stopped at any of the interpretative levels: iconic, indexical or symbolic.

4.3 The iconography of the tauroctony at the first level of interpretation

Despite some minor variations, the composition, structure and articulation of the major elements comprising the tauroctony allow us to talk about *one* scene which was visually represented and was placed within all mithraea. Thus, *the scene* of the tauroctony, either depicted in two-dimensional paintings (Figure 4.1) or carved on sculptural reliefs (Figure 4.2) or on free-standing three-dimensional sculptures (Figure 4.3), was an icon in the sense that it was a visual composition drawn from real-life landscapes, objects and living organisms, which were drawn in a certain arrangement and can be perceived as representing a real-life event.

The iconic composition of the scene is easily accessible through our common perceptual abilities. Thereby, the figure–ground organization of our visual perceptual system[8] enables us to perceive the material construction of the tauroctony as an object distinguished from the spatial background of the mithraeum. We further perceive this object as a CONTAINER[9] since it has certain borders which isolate it from the surrounding space, and an internal space comprised of various visual signs. Looking at the internal space of the tauroctony, we are able to further segregate visual images that stand out from the background of the representation[10] and then to identify these images with their real-life counterparts in terms of their perceptible similarities. During this first-level inferential process, the elements that distinguish the representing signs and the

Figure 4.1 Tauroctony fresco

Source: Photo taken on 17 February 2012 by Carole Raddato (Flickr)

Figure 4.2 Tauroctony relief

Source: Photo taken on 15 August 2015 by Carole Raddato (Flickr)

Figure 4.3 Marble statue of tauroctony
Source: Photo taken on 26 October 2013 by Carole Raddato (Flickr)

referential entities – like the difference between a two-dimensional static visual representation and a three-dimensional movable living organism – are omitted. Instead, the attention focuses on the diagrammatic similarities between the signifier signs and the signified objects or the image-schemas of the latter. These similarities are projected and blended in the mental space of the interpretant, which enables the interpretation of the scene as a composition of iconic representations (Hoopes 1991: 251–5).

People of the Graeco-Roman world – like modern perceivers – could have run the same blend.[11] Those who happened to see the visual representation of the tauroctony would have been able to perceive and conceptualize the scene in terms of the elementary concepts that directly referred to primitive image-schemas, assumptions, and perceptual taxonomies of the world shared by humans and stored in long-term mnemonic systems. Running the blend, we can discern the icons of some anthropomorphic figures, of some animals (a bull, a dog, a scorpion, a snake, a raven, sometimes a lion),[12] and of some objects (a dagger, an ear – or ears – of wheat, two torches, sometimes a cup)[13] standing out from the spatial background of the scene. However, the identifications of the visual signs included in the scene with the real-life entities that they signify and the mere summarizing of these icons are not enough for perceiving the tauroctony as an iconic representation as a whole. By discerning the spatial relations between the iconic signs in terms of our elementary spatial image-schemas we can attribute to the scene its internal iconic structure as a visual representation of an event.

At the centre of the scene, we discern the icon of a clothed man whom we can take as a reference frame for the allocentric spatial mapping of the internal space of the tauroctony. The man is represented on the back of the bull. By projecting our mental body-schema on to him, we infer that he has knelt with his left leg on the back of the bull, while his right leg constrains the animal's rump. With his left hand, he has grasped the nostrils of the bull and pulls its head upwards. In his right hand, he holds the dagger, with which he stabs the bull's neck. Against all our expectations of growth in the vegetable and animal realms, the ear of wheat grows from the tail of the bull! A scorpion is presented in the act of stinging the bull's genitals. A snake and a dog are close to the neck of the animal, seeming to jump up at the wound to lick the blood, while a raven attends the scene from above, sometimes alighting on the cloak of the man who is slaughtering the bull. On the left of the scene another man is depicted holding a torch turned downwards, while on the right a third is presented holding a torch turned upwards. The positions of the torchbearers are frequently reversed (Hinnells 1976: 38–40). In the upper-left corner there is one more icon of a male, sometimes driving a four-horse chariot (quadriga), and in the upper-right corner an icon of a female figure driving a two-oxen chariot (biga).[14] More usually these figures are represented by busts only, that is facing head and shoulders.

Such a lexical description of the tauroctony with reference to the icons represented and their spatial arrangement in the scene is possible on the common ground of the conceptualization of perceptual information that people receive during the interaction with their natural and cultural surroundings and the formation of image-schemas, frames and assumptions generated during this interaction. In order, however, to dig into the deeper meanings of the iconic composition of the tauroctony, further conceptual knowledge deriving from the cultural context of the Mithras cult is demanded. Thus, someone who had previously developed the concept of the 'Persian' would have interpreted icons of Persian clothes (long trousers, a tunic with long sleeves and a Phrygian cap) worn by the man at the centre of the scene as an *index* of his relation to the Persians. Then, he would have blended the visual information received from the scene with his conceptual knowledge that Mithras was a god of 'Persian origins'. Thereby he would have inferred that the man in the scene was an *icon* of Mithras. Similarly, the twin men with the torches held in opposite ways would have been interpreted as *icons* of the torchbearers, Cautes and Cautopates. Taking into account these identifications between the represented perceptible icons and the conceptual images of Mithras and his accompaniers, the overall iconic composition of the scene would have acquired further conceptual significance. It did not represent an ordinary case of a man who kills a bull at random. It would have been conceived as a visual representation of a deed of Mithras, who slaughters the bull.[15]

Noting the ubiquity of the tauroctony and its consistent iconography, modern scholars have interpreted this deed as a mythological episode involving the deity Mithras that has not survived as a written narrative. Among these scholars, pioneer Franz Cumont (1899: 179–213) and many successive scholars (e.g. Clauss 2000: 62–101) assumed the existence of a cult myth proper, part of which might be reconstructed from the iconography, and from which a portion of the cult's doctrines and beliefs can be extracted. According to this now orthodox approach, the scene of the bull-killing Mithras, as well as a scene of the banquet of Mithras and Sun god (carried on the reverse side of the many of the same reliefs, for example V641 [Fiano Romano]), must have been significant episodes in the cult myth and would therefore have been enacted via ritual praxis. Although there came to be a consensus among scholars regarding the main outlines of the narrative that can be deduced from the monuments, the merely iconic interpretation of the tauroctony has been criticized by some who argue that the reconstruction of the myth does not exhaust the meaning and the function of the many symbols included in the scene. These symbols appear to serve little or no purpose in the construction of such a narrative (Martin 1994; Beck 2006a: 16–25).

To sum up, the process of interpreting the tauroctony begins with the initiate's inference of similarities between the signifier-signs included in the scene and the *image-schemas* of the signified entities encountered in real life. These similarities, anchored on the material construction of the representation, are blended in the mental space of the scene, which is conceived as an iconic representation of an event. The signs composing the tauroctony acquire further iconic referents in the cultural context of the mysteries, in which additional similarities between the signifiers and the *conceptual representations* of the signified entities can be inferred. During this interpretive level, the scene acquires its conceptual referent: it refers to Mithras's deed of killing the bull, and provides a visual simulation of this cult event present in all mithraea. The initiates, within the mithraeum, could perceive the public representation of the tauroctony, which would have generated a mental representation of the slaughter of the bull by Mithras. The perception and conceptualization of the scene as an iconic representation of Mithras's feat would have provided the ground for further associations and meanings. Being displayed in the microcosm of the mithraeum, the scene would have acquired referential and conceptual significance by its integration and placement within that universe.

4.4 From iconic to indexical and symbolic interpretations of the tauroctony

As argued above, iconic correlations between signifier-signs and signified-objects are grounded on the human embodied perceptual mechanisms and derive from the cognitive ability to infer similarities between percepts. New iconic associations between perceptible entities and conceptual representations can emerge and be supported and enhanced by the implicit and explicit knowledge, acquired during cultural learning and social interaction.

Scholars have interpreted the tauroctony's iconography with reference to different contexts, notably the surrounding Graeco-Roman culture and the postulated Iranian origins of the cult (Beck 2006a: 26–30). However, the abundance of what appear to be astral signs in the tauroctony triggered alternative interpretations of the scene as a symbolic representation of the heavens (30–9). Specifically, the tauroctony was approached as 'a sort of astral encoding' (Beck 2004: 235) which could be deciphered through the interpretation of the various elements in the scene with reference to the constellations that were visible in a particular tract of the heavens.[16] The tract in question comprised the constellations along the zodiac from Taurus eastward to Scorpio, together with their southern pararanatellonta (i.e. those constellations that 'rise alongside').[17]

The conceptualization of the scene in astronomical terms was to be expected, since the tauroctony was a fundamental component of the mithraeum and the mithraeum, as we know, was 'an image of the universe' 'equipped with symbols of the elements and climates of the cosmos' (Porphyry, *On the Cave* 6), and of course the primary 'elements' of the cosmos are the celestial bodies, namely stars and planets. Those of the initiates who were familiar with the astronomical imagery of their time would have been able to infer more iconic representations and further indexical associations and symbolic meanings of the signs which comprised the tauroctony.

Looking at the starry sky, the ancient astronomers – Babylonians, Mesopotamians, Egyptians, Greeks – discerned patterns of stellar formations. In order to attribute representational stability to these patterns, they projected already-established conceptual imagery of perceptible entities into the sky and used the stars as anchors in order to draw the diagrams of these images on the celestial background. These rough diagrammatic drawings deriving from the imagined similarities between the images of the perceptible entities and the discerned patterns[18] on the celestial plane comprised the mental blended spaces of the constellations.

Ptolemy, in his *Almagest* (ca. 150 CE), provides the best definitions of the Graeco-Roman constellations, which drew on Babylonian astronomy and Mesopotamian nomenclature, further elaborated by the Greek astronomers during the Hellenistic era. In almost the same period, *Catasterismi*, a work attributed to pseudo-Eratosthenes, narrated the mythical sagas which explained the projections of the visual imagery onto the constellations and the indexical and symbolic connotations of their names (see Beck 2007: 1, 7). According to this testimony, the constellation of Taurus was created by Zeus, who wished to venerate either the bull which transferred Europa from Phoenix to Crete or Io, whom he transformed into a cow to save her from Hera (Pseudo-Eratosthenes, *Catasterismi* 14). Zeus also created the constellation of Gemini in memory of the twin brothers Dioskouri, Castor and Pollux (*Catasterismi* 10). The constellation of Scorpio signified the animal which killed the Titan Orion when he tried to rape Hera (*Catasterismi* 7). Different versions of mythical origins are associated with the constellation of Virgo. According to Hesiod and Aratos, Virgo represented Dike, the goddess of justice, daughter of Zeus and Themis, who was prosecuted by humans and was transferred into the sky. Others, however, associate the constellation with Demeter or Isis or Atargatis because of the ear of wheat which she holds in her left hand (indicated by Spica, the brightest star in the constellation) (*Catasterismi* 9). Canis Major or Cyon was a stellar formation that represented the dog which protected Europa or one of the hounds that accompanied Orion (*Catasterismi* 33). The other hound of Orion was represented in the constellation of Canis Minor, or Procyon, which rose just before the Cyon (*Catasterismi* 41). The constellation of Leo was a representation of the leader of the quadrupedal animals, or more specifically of the Nemean lion, which Hercules killed as the first of his twelve labours (*Catasterismi* 12). The constellation of Aquarius was a representation of Ganimede, the cup-bearer of the Olympian gods (*Catasterismi* 126). The constellation of Corvus was close to the constellations of Crater and Hydra, and together were created by Apollo when the raven, which he had sent to bring water, came back with a water snake in the cup (*Catasterismi* 41; see Chapter 2).

In the process of interpreting those constellations that were visible on the northern celestial hemisphere, we can infer that their drawings would have been intended to represent diagrammatic similarities with the real-life referent entities and would have operated as icons of the latter. Further, they would have indicated the figures starring in the mythical stories that had been transferred on the sky. Once these iconic and indexical associations between the signifier stellar patterns and the signified entities would have been blended on the mental spaces of the constellations, the signifier icons of the real-life perceptible entities would have operated as indices of the signified constellations in specific contexts. Thus, in the context of the Mithraic cosmos, the placement and iconic composition of the tauroctony within the mithraeum, which was perceived as within the universe, would have evoked indexical associations with the celestial elements and would have provided the ground for further symbolic inferences in reference to the celestial realm.

According to Porphyry (*On the Cave* 6 [8–9]), the cave at the mouth of which Mithras is represented to slaughter the bull signified the celestial firmament. This signification is most obvious in the tauroctony depicted in fresco at the Marino mithraeum, in which the stars on the transparent wavy cloak of Mithras operate as indices of the starry sky (Beck 1994b: 269). Interpreting the tauroctony as an indexical mapping of the heavens, the image of Mithras, 'the Unconquered Sun', would have been seen as an index of the Sun on the celestial plane. The icon of the bull could have been perceived as indicating the Moon[19] on the heavens or the constellation of Taurus. Cautes and Cautopates would have indicated the twin Dioskouri and thereby the constellation of Gemini. The torchbearers defined the margins of the scene and occasionally carried or were closely represented to a bull's head[20] and to a scorpion respectively, icons which could have indicated the constellations of Taurus to the right and of Scorpio to the left (e.g. V335 and V693). The icon of the dog would have been perceived as pointing to Canis Minor or Canis Major. The icon of the snake would have indicated the constellation of Hydra. The icon of the raven would have been an index of the constellation of Corvus. When the icon of a lion was depicted, it would have indicated the constellation Leo. When the icon of a big two-handled cup was included in the scene, it would have pointed to the constellation of Crater.[21] In some mithraea – mainly in those found in the provinces of Rhine and Danube

– the icon of the lion which sinks into the crater could have indicated the vessel of Aquarius. The ear of wheat at the tip of bull's tail would have indicated Spica and would have signified the constellation of Virgo.[22]

The human-like icons at the upper corners of the scene, along with the secondary iconic representations which accompanied them, seem to indicate the anthropomorphic conceptualization of the sun and the moon in the ancient Greek world. The anthropomorphic representations of these planets did not derive from the blend of iconic similarities between these celestial elements and humans. They were more conventional symbolic representations that were established by the mythical sagas and promoted though cultural learning. In the *Hymn to Helios* (*Homeric Hymns* 31), the sun (Helios) was presented as a Titan who bore a radiant bonnet and drove the quadriga across the heavens. In the *Hymn to Selene* (*Homeric Hymns* 32), the moon (Selene) was represented as the daughter of the Titans Hyperion and Theia, and sister of the sun, which drove the biga. Therefore, the image of a man bearing the solar bonnet and driving a quadriga would have been an iconic visualization of the symbolic representation of the sun, which was conventionalized in mythology. Similarly, the image of a woman with a crescent and a biga would have been an icon of the mythological figure who, in turn, symbolized the moon.

Therefore, the scene of the tauroctony comprises signs that would have been perceived as icons of physical beings and objects being perceived and conceptualized on the terrestrial realm. Further, the same icons, when observed on the celestial plane, operated as indices of the constellations and planets. These indexical associations between the real-life entities and the celestial elements were stabilized and conventionalized in mythical sagas that entailed the conception of these icons as symbolic representations of the referred constellations and planets. At this interpretive level, the associations between signs and objects, which derive from their perceivable spatio-temporal co-occurrence in the natural world, are replaced by systematic indexical associations between them established through cultural learning.[23] Therefore, the *iconic* composition of the tauroctony within the Mithraic universe could have *indicated* that the scene represented a section of the sky on which the *symbolized* constellations were observable (cf. CP 1.559).

At the indexical level of interpretation, the presence of more than one sign indicating the same celestial entities may seem contradictory. If the tauroctony merely comprised an indexical mapping of a part of the heavens via token-by-token representations of the celestial elements on the material background of the scene, the co-existence of two signs of the sun – e.g. Mithras and the man with the quadriga – or of the moon – e.g. the bull and the female figure with the biga – would have been impossible in an ontological frame of reference. This polysemy of the signs is, however, possible at the symbolic level of interpretation in which elements projected from the input mental spaces may be compressed to the same sign or may be mapped to more than one sign in the mental blended space articulating multiple semantic meanings by being combined and correlated with each other in the emergent structure of the blended space (Deacon 1997: 100; Beck 2004: 240; cf. Fauconnier and Turner 2002: 312–25, 2004: 63–72). In symbolic representations, the signs are associated with each other, not on the ground of their perceptible co-occurrence or contiguity in the natural world but in reference to their positions and roles in the blended mental space which gives rise to token-to-token associations (Deacon 1997: 92–3). As Deacon aptly points out, 'The structure of the whole system has a definite semantic topology that determines the ways symbols modify each other's referential functions in different combinations' (p. 99). In this way, symbolic representations do not comprise unstructured collections of sign-tokens that refer to real-life entities. They constitute mental blended spaces, which develop their own internal structure governed by principles which are commonly accepted by the people who develop and use this specific symbolic system (p. 100). Thus, the symbolic associations between signs can be perceived and conceptualized within a wider pre-established symbolic system that produces and promotes conventional relationships between signs.

In the Mithraic context, the celestial firmament viewed from the Earth would have provided the generic space on which were blended the popular astronomical knowledge (based on the Ptolemaic cosmology), with monumental iconography, thereby generating the blended mental space of the tauroctony as a representation of the heavens. On this conceptual ground, modern scholars have suggested a great range of symbolic interpretations of the scene. Reinhold Merkelbach (1984: 81) correlated the tauroctony with the initiatory grades and interpreted each icon in the scene as the index of a grade, which in turn indicated its tutelary planet (see Beck 2006a: 38). Arend J. Rutgers (1970: 305–15) was the first to directly associate the tauroctonous scene with the heavens and to propose the solar identity of Mithras. In particular, Rutgers claimed that the icons of Mithras and the bull in the tauroctony were respectively the symbolic counterparts of the sun and the moon. The fight between Mithras and the bull was thus a symbolic representation of the continuous pursuit of the Moon by the Sun, which regularly ends up with the disappearance of the former from the sky every month and the victory of the latter. The appearance of a 'new moon' a few days later marks the resumption of the chase. More importantly, the tauroctony could symbolize the exceptional victory of the Sun over the Moon during the lunar eclipses, when the latter is suddenly hidden and immerses Earth into darkness (see Beck 2000: 236, 2006: 37).

The identification of Mithras with the sun was also suggested by Bruno Jacobs (1999), who interpreted the tauroctony as a symbolic representation of the spring equinox. In his interpretation, the bull at the scene symbolizes the constellation of Taurus at the moment in which it is visible for the last time on the sky just after sunset before it enters into conjunction with the sun (the heliacal setting of Taurus). Thereby the scene proclaims the end of winter and the beginning of the spring (see Beck 2000: 126, 2006a: 37). Similarly, Roger Beck (1994b: 29–50) identified Mithras with the Unconquered Sun and has interpreted the whole scene of the tauroctony as a representation of the image of the heavens at the time that the sun is in the constellation of Leo.

Not all of the interpretations suggested by modern scholars argue for the solar identity of Mithras. Alessandro Bausani (1979: 503–13), for instance, identified Mithras with the constellation of Leo and the bull with the constellation of Taurus. In his approach, he interpreted the tauroctony as a visualization of the Near Eastern image-pattern of the 'bull-killing lion' (Beck 2006a: 36), which symbolized the dominance of the constellation of Leo in summer over the constellation of Taurus who dominates in spring. Looking for the astral identity of Mithras, Michael Speidel (1980) identified him with the constellation of Orion, and Kurt-Gustav Sandelin (1988: 133–5) with the constellation of Auriga (see Beck 2000: 236, 2006a: 36–7). The most influential identification was suggested by David Ulansey (1989),[24] who interpreted the icon of Mithras in the tauroctony as an index of the constellation of Perseus, which supervised the mysterious, but fundamental cosmic phenomenon of the 'precession of the equinoxes'.[25] Avoiding any attempt to associate Mithras with a specific celestial element, Maria Weiss (1998: 1–36) interpreted this icon as an index of the whole firmament, as it is seen from the Earth during the night (Beck 2006a: 37).

Shifting the interest from searching the astral referents of the signs in the tauroctony to the implicit fusion of space and time in the scene, some scholars focused their attention on the meaning of the composition in reference to the perception of time in the cult context. Beginning from the principle that the celestial elements and their motions on the heavens provide the most solid ground for the measurement of time, Stanley Insler (1978: 519–38) interpreted the tauroctony as a calendar that represented the time at which spring is coming as signalled by the heliacal setting of the constellation of Taurus. John D. North

(1990: 115–48), on the other hand, interpreted the tauroctony as a clock that instantiated a particular hour of the day during which the indicated constellations set seriatim (see Beck 2006a: 37–8).

The plurality of interpretations suggested by modern scholars begin from the working hypothesis that the tauroctony was not an unstructured collection of icons each of which could have had certain symbolic connotations independent of the others. The signs composing the scene would have acquired symbolic meanings via association with each other in reference to the wider astrological symbolism of the cult. The semantic properties of the signs would have derived from the initiates' abilities and qualifications to receive the meanings that the tauroctony intended to communicate. The scene would have operated as an anchor for the blend between the signs that compose it and the conceptual meanings that the signs referred to giving rise to the emergent structure of the tauroctony as a symbolic representation.

4.5 'Star talk' and the tauroctony as a view to the heavens

In order for Mithraic initiates to perceive the tauroctony as a symbolic representation, they should be able to project their internal mental representations of the heavens onto the scene. The tauroctony would have provided the anchor for the projected representations, instantiating their positions and the spatial relations between them. However, this projection and subsequent interpretation of the scene would not have been grounded in the blend of similarities and natural indexical associations between the signified celestial elements and the signifier signs on the map. The referential connection between the signified and the signifiers would have emerged from the symbolic system developed in the cult context and shared by the initiates.

Beck (2006a: 7–8, 153, 194–5) has described this system as a kind of language, which he calls *star talk*, originally developed and used by astrologers and astronomers of the Graeco-Roman world. Resembling a linguistic idiom, star talk would have used signs–symbols of the celestial elements in order to articulate and communicate conceptual meanings. Interpreting the symbolic composition of the tauroctony in terms of star talk, its represented components appear to have multiple symbolic connotations and semantic properties. Beck (p. 200) has suggested a two-fold interpretation of the scene. In his view, the tauroctony could be perceived as representing a specific track of the heavens as it appeared in the sky during the daily motion of the celestial elements or as a star-chart or map that represented a particular time of the annual rotation of the planets around the Earth.

Interpreting the tauroctony as a view of the heavens, its physical borders would have signified the celestial cardinal points. Thus, the bottom of the scene would have indicated the line of the horizon which determined the visible field. The top line would have signified the highest points reached by the celestial bodies, that is, the zenith of the northern celestial hemisphere. East would be signified to the left by the symbolic icon of the sun with the quadriga and west to the right by the image of the moon with the biga. Thereby the celestial elements represented towards the left of the scene would have been perceived as being close to their rising, while the elements towards the right of the scene would have been perceived as being close to their setting (pp. 203–4). In this mapping, the icon of Mithras at the centre would have symbolized the sun when it reaches the zenith of its daily motion around the earth as part of the westward rotation of the whole universe (p. 215). The bull would have been a more polysemous sign, which would have simultaneously operated as a symbol of the moon and of the constellation of Taurus – or a symbol of the moon passing from the point of its exaltation at the constellation of Taurus (cf. Porphyry, *On the Cave* 18). Reading the star talk of the tauroctony rightwards – that is westwards – the represented signs instantiate the planetary motion around the earth, which assigns the alteration of days, months and seasons and, from this point of view, the time in the scene flows from right to left. On the left/east side of the scene, the icon of a Scorpion would have indicated the rise of the constellation that was surrounded by the zodiacal constellations of Libra, Virgo and Leo, and by their 'paranatellonta'[26] Hydra, Corvus, Crater and Canis Minor. On the right/west side of the view, the second icon of the head of a bull would have signified the setting of Taurus, which is followed by the zodiacal constellations Gemini, Leo and Virgo, and by their 'paranatellonta' Canis Major, Canis Minor, Hydra, Crater and Corvus. This specific arrangement of the celestial elements on the actual heavens took place during the passage of the sun from the constellation of Taurus in the spring to the constellation of Scorpion in the autumn. Since, however, it happened at the zenith of the sun's daily motion, the sunlight made this view of the heavens invisible. A similar view was, however, visible on the winter sky and especially at around midnight during January and February when the constellations of Cancer and Leo were at the points of their culmination (Beck 2006a: 200–1).

The interpretation of the tauroctony as a window to the heavens from which a particular section of the celestial vault was visible does not seem well-grounded on the embodied perception of the celestial vault as it is seen from the terrestrial surface. As people gaze to the sky, the visible constellations on the sky slowly alter during the 24 hours of the day and therefore the view from a window that looks at the heavens would have included different celestial bodies as the time passed. The iconic composition of the tauroctony is, however, static in comparison to the continuous alternation of the celestial view. Therefore, the tauroctony can be more easily perceived as an image of the heavens in which space and time have been frozen instead of a dynamic representation of the daily motion of the celestial bodies. Even better, the tauroctony can be interpreted as an astral map that represents the celestial bodies and the spatial relations between them, and their arrangements on the heavens. Beck's interpretation of the tauroctony as an astral map or chart seems to attribute a coherent structure to the scene and to support further inferences in the context of the Mithraic mysteries.

4.6 The tauroctony as a map or star-chart

The tauroctony designed as a star-chart would have mapped the positions of the celestial bodies, the constellations and the distances between them in ways resembling a geographical map. Contrary to terrestrial mapping, however, which represents largely static benchmarks and landscapes, the spatial arrangement of the heavens has an inherently temporal dimension, since it constantly changes as the time passes during both the daily universal rotation and the annual planetary motions. Thereby, the spatial mapping of the heavens was simultaneously a mapping of space and time. The spatial and temporal relationships were independent of the positions and the movements of the perceivers within the mithraeum, that is, within the universe. Thereby, the tauroctony would have operated as a material map that would have anchored the allocentric cognitive mapping of the sky as it would have been perceived by people at a specific moment of overall motion of the universe and of the planetary motions around the earth.

As someone looks at the scene from an external point of view – it is impossible to get into the scene – the symbol of the sun as a man with the quadriga to the left would again have indicated the east, the point at which the planets and constellations rise and become visible to the northern celestial hemisphere. Respectively, the icon of the female figure with the biga to the right would have symbolized the moon which appears when the sun has set and further would have indicated the west, the point at which the celestial bodies set and become invisible on the northern celestial vault. The bottom of the scene would have represented the celestial equinox above which the northern celestial hemisphere extends while the southern celestial hemisphere remains hidden beneath. Thereby, the lower border of the scene would have been at the south, the upper border at the north.

The icons of the torchbearers placed at the left and right edges of the scene would have communicated various semantic meanings. As twins they would have indicated the Dioskouri, and further the constellation of Gemini. The myth of Castor and Pollux claims that the twin heroes shared Pollux's immortality and spent by turns the one half of the year in heaven and the other half in the underworld. Some ancient Greek mythological traditions presented the northern hemisphere as being above the earth, while the southern hemisphere was connected with the underworld and remained invisible during the daily rotation of the celestial sphere around the earth.[27] Therefore, the celestial twins could have also symbolized the two celestial hemispheres – Cautes with the torch upwards would have symbolized the visible northern hemisphere, Cautopates with the torch downwards the invisible southern one (Ulansey 1989: 114–16; Beck 2004: 282, 2006a: 201–2).

In the mithraea from Rome and Italy, the icon of Cautes is represented to the left of the scene, that is to the east, and Cautopates to the right, that is to the west. At these positions, Cautes could have also symbolized the rise of the celestial bodies and the sun in the east during their daily westward motion around the earth. Consequently, Cautopates would have signified the setting of the sun and the other celestial bodies in the west (Beck 2004: 283, 2006a: 208). In other words, the torchbearers would have symbolized the directions of the daily journey of the sun and the planets in the heavens (Beck 2004: 283).

In the mithraea in the Rhine and Danube provinces, the torchbearers are placed in the reverse positions. Cautes is located to the right/west and Cautopates to the left/east. In these representations, the torchbearers acquire additional semantic properties by being associated with the signs of Taurus and Scorpion. In particular, Cautes to the right, close to the head of the bull, would have symbolized Taurus. The raised torch at this point would have signified the ascent of the sun through the constellation of Taurus in the spring. Respectively, Cautopates to the left, close to the scorpion, would have signified the constellation of Scorpion and his lowered torch would have indicated the descent of the sun through the constellation of Scorpion in the autumn (Beck 2006a: 208).

Reading the tauroctony leftwards – that is eastwards – the constellations of Taurus, Gemini, Leo, Virgo and Scorpio are sequentially signified as representing the successive thirty-degree sectors comprising the half zodiac. The placement of Mithras as a symbol of the sun in the centre of the scene and his association with the sign of Leo, which is the middle constellation of the represented zodiac signs, could have signified the passage of the sun from the zodiacal sector of Leo, which takes place during the last third of July and the first two-thirds of August.[28] The sixth sector of the half-zodiac, which seems to be missing from the representation, is that of Cancer. But since the bull was a sign of the Moon, which has its astral house in Cancer, then the bull could have also signified the constellation of Cancer (Beck 2004: 287–8).

The other iconic representations included in the scene would have supplemented the mapping of the northern hemisphere signifying the southern 'paranatellonta' of the represented zodiacal constellations (Beck 2006a: 196–7, 200). Therefore, the dog would have signified Canis Minor instead of Canis Major (or perhaps both), which was the paranatellon constellation of Gemini. The snake would have signified Hydra, which was the paranatellon of Leo. The raven would have signified Corvus, the paranatellon of Virgo. The cup – when present – would have been connected with the constellations of Hydra and Corvus.[29]

The design of the tauroctony as an astral map would have comprised a static spatial and temporal representation of the northern celestial hemisphere, which was placed as a material structure within the Mithraic cave. As we have seen in the previous chapter, the initiates perceived the mithraeum as the universe inevitably from an interior, egocentric angle. Within the Mithraic cosmos, the spatial and temporal dimensions would have been fluid, continually determined by the initiates' movements, positions and altering points of view. In this spatial framework, the tauroctony would have provided the steadiest representation of the universe that could have been perceived from the outside, while its spatio-temporal dimensions were firmly fixed, irrelevant to the initiates' positions and movements. Thereby, the tauroctony would have been an allocentric mapping of a specific section of the celestial firmament as it appeared at a specific moment providing a frame of reference for the ritual praxis during the mysteries.

The symbolic references to the mysteries of the souls' journey can be traced in the multivalent connotations of the icons composing the tauroctony. The bull being a symbol of the moon was considered to be the agent of genesis during which people's souls descend to Earth. The sun represented by Mithras in the context of the scene was respectively the agent of apogenesis who oversaw the ascent of the souls back to the sphere of the fixed stars.[30] The fight of Mithras with the bull at the centre of the tauroctony could have indicated those times of the year during which the sun and the moon reach the same longitude and come into conjunction, when and only when a solar eclipse can take place. Similarly, they could signify the moments at which the two planets are in opposition, occupying diametrically opposite degrees of longitude, when and only when a lunar eclipse can happen.[31] Paying more attention to the positions of Mithras and the bull in the tauroctony in relation to the other signs, the association of the symbol of the sun with its astral house in Leo and of symbol of the moon with its astral house in Cancer imply which of the possible syzygies the tauroctony could have referred to. The sun is in Leo and the moon is in Cancer just before the conjunction of the two planets, which happens at the end of July or in August. Thereby the tauroctony could have mapped the heavens at that time of the year, when the sun reaches to the closest distance to the earth and its light blurs the lunar light. During that period, a solar eclipse can happen when the moon passes between the earth and the sun, dimming the sunlight. Referring to Plutarch's description of the souls' descent and ascent through the heavens (*De genio Socratis* 591), a lunar eclipse is the best moment at which the souls can jump on the moon, beginning the journey of apogenesis. And this moment, happening in August, would have been frozen in the spatial mapping of the tauroctony, pointing the path of the souls' ascent (cf. Lactantius Placidus scholium).[32]

In this frame of reference, the positions of the torchbearers would have borne multiple semantic meanings in the scene. Similar to the symbolic references they acquired when they were placed in the mithraeum, in the tauroctony Cautopates with his lowered torch would have indicated the downward route that the souls had followed during their descent to Earth, while Cautes with his raised torch would have pointed to the upward route from which the souls could ascend back again to the sphere of fixed stars. In this pattern, north is once again associated with 'up' and south with 'down'. In the spatial symbolic mapping of the heavens, the torchbearers could have further represented the points at which the orbit of the moon crosses the ecliptic, and which are determined as the *lunar nodes*. Cautes with his raised torch would have indicated the 'ascending' node, when the moon moving upwards from south to north crosses the sun's orbit. Cautopates with his lowered torch would have been an index of the 'descending' node, when moon crosses the sun's orbit moving downwards from north to south. Referring to the ascending and descending movement of the moon, the torchbearers could have simultaneously represented the upward and downward movements of the initiates' souls during the mysteries. Therefore, the conjunction of Sun and Moon and the potential solar eclipse represented in the tauroctony would have been signified as happening between the lunar nodes, when the moon moves northwards, that is, upwards (Beck 2004: 268–74, 2006a: 206–7).

In this interpretation of the tauroctony as an astral symbolic text, the iconic composition of the scene provides the signifier-structure for anchoring an allocentric spatial mapping of the heavens. Such spatial mapping grounds the metaphorical perception of universal time and underlies the spatio-temporal organization of the scene. The spatio-temporal diagram is further blended with the script of an action providing a stable material representation of the blended mental space of the souls' journey.[33] Although we cannot infer the role of the tauroctony in the cult context with certainty and the accurate conceptual meanings that were intended to be communicated to the initiates, the scene could have operated as a material anchor and a representational guide for the actualization of the rituals.

4.7 The plausibility of meanings in the process of interpreting the tauroctony

As a system of symbols, we may attribute multiple and contrary meanings to the signs composing the tauroctonous scene by tracing multivalent associations between them. According to Peirce's theory of signs, these associations could be innumerable at the symbolic level of reference. The multitudinous symbolic inferences elicited from the signs are evident in the various interpretations of the tauroctony suggested by modern scholars in reference to the context of the Mithras cult and to Hellenistic and Roman astrology. Our intention here is not to judge the validity of these approaches. What we mostly intend is to trace the interpretive process that could have mediated the conception of the scene by the initiates.

Beginning from the perception of the tauroctony as an iconic representation, do we need to presuppose the existence of a myth or myths in order to conceive the story represented in the scene? That does not seem necessary. By asking someone to describe the visual representation of the bull-killing scene, the construction of a narrative is inevitable. The perception of implicit image-schemas grounds the conceptualization of the perceptible representation, which acquires an inherent narrative structure when it becomes an object of conceptual analysis. Conscious thinking presupposes the use of an explicit knowledge that is acquired during social interaction and cultural learning. Depending on our established concepts, the representation acquires certain semantic properties. But again, all these semantic properties are not randomly represented in our minds. Explicit thinking and conceptual interpretation as well as verbal description and communication of meanings are inherently temporal processes which attribute spatio-temporal coherence to the perceivable fragments of reality.

Therefore, as we have seen, identifying the icons in the scene, recognizing the spatial relations between them and recalling the conceptual knowledge acquired in the context of the Mithras cult are sufficient mental processes to interpret the represented scene as a significant deed of the god Mithras. Could this deed have been part of a cult myth or alternative mythical sagas developed in local Mithraic communities? Probably it could have been, but such an inference cannot be deduced, and most importantly it does not seem to contribute any further meaning to the scene. Whether there was a myth or not, the killing of the bull by Mithras can be recounted as an important deed of the god. However, focusing on the reconstruction of an overall narrative of mythical events constrains the interpretive process at the iconic level of inferences.[34]

Looking for the possible symbolic references of the scene, the next step of interpretation is to trace the indexical associations between the signs and the signified entities, which would have been established and learned by initiates in the cult context. Taking into account the grade hierarchy, the signs were interpreted as signifying the initiatory grades (cf. Merkelbach 1984). Could these indexical associations have been inferred from the scene? When the grade hierarchy was used as an organizational structure of the Mithraic communities, such associations could have been traced in the tauroctony. There is nothing that excludes the possibility for the initiates to have 'seen' signs of their grades in the scene. However, since the initiatory grades were not a ubiquitous element of the cult, we can hardly assume that the overall scene would have intentionally been designed as a symbolic representation of the grade hierarchy.

The astrological symbols included in the tauroctony comprise another class of referents for interpreting the scene. The represented signs have been associated with specific constellations, planets and sections of the heavens as they were determined by the Graeco-Roman popular cosmology and the Ptolemaic cosmological system. By mapping in the tauroctony, the celestial bodies that appear on the sky at specific moments or periods of their phenomenal universal and planetary motion around the Earth, different interpretations suggested different tracks of the heavens and similarly different moments of the day or the year that were signified in the scene. Whether interpreting the tauroctony in spatial terms (cf. Bausani 1979; Jacobs 1999; Beck 1994b) or focusing on its temporal connotations (cf. Insler 1978; North 1990), the perceptual fusion of space and time influences these interpretations and manifests how the perception of time is grounded on the metaphorical interpretation of the spatial percepts.

The interpretations that promoted sign-to-token indexical associations between the signifier-signs and the signified-celestial bodies had difficulties explaining the presence of more than one sign for the same signifier or the reverse. This problem is resolved when the multivalence of symbols is taken into account. Interpreting the tauroctony as a symbol system, its conceptual meanings become accessible and could have been communicated on the ground of a common idiom – star talk – shared and used by its perceivers.

In this view, the separation between learned and vulgar initiates pales in significance, since this distinction is based on assumptions about the extent of *a priori* astrological knowledge that people of the Graeco-Roman world would have had. Being introduced into the Mithraic mysteries, initiates would have been introduced to the wider symbolic reality of the cult. That means that communication of internal meanings would have taken place in terms of the symbolic system that would have developed within the cult context and that would have been shared and used by the cult members. If all the initiates acquired the same amount of knowledge, which is something that we cannot infer, this knowledge would have intentionally imprinted on the Mithraic monuments and would have been implicitly available for access.

Similarly, given the deficiency of the ancient records and the inherent multivalence of symbols, we cannot conclude how the Mithraists would actually have interpreted the tauroctony in the cult context. All the interpretations suggested by modern scholars would have been possible to the extent they can be inferred from the iconic composition of the scene. In parallel, we cannot exclude the possibility that there would not have been *one* interpretation of the tauroctony that would have exhausted its potential symbolic referential. The multivalent inferences reached by modern scholars could also have been extracted by the ancient initiates depending on the extent to which they would have had access to the conceptual knowledge and mental imagery of the universe articulated in the cult. Therefore, the suggested identifications between the signs in the tauroctony and the celestial elements are not mutually exclusive interpretations, but alternative approaches to the multiple levels of meaning of the scene (Beck 2004: 240).

In any case, the iconic composition of the tauroctony and its symbolic connotations would have articulated conceptual meanings conceivable by the initiates in the wider context of the cult, even if there was no coherent myth that would have narrated the story and the meanings of the scene. In the next chapter, we will see that the interpretation of the scene could have acquired personal significance for the initiates during the initiatory rituals that could have triggered high emotional arousal.

5

The Communities of Mithraists: From Personal Self to Social Identity

So far in this book the focus has been on ways in which individual participants in the Mithraic mysteries would have perceived, conceived, and conceptualized the various components of the cult reality from their own personal, embodied perspective. In particular, we have described the perceptual mechanisms and cognitive processes that would have mediated the lived experience of initiates taking part in the Mithraic rituals and how 1) general perceptions of the world, and 2) knowledge acquired during interaction with the material and conceptual surroundings of the Graeco-Roman era (updated through cultural learning) would have affected the ways in which the initiates perceived themselves as well as their fellow cult members and shared a common world view both within and outside the cult context. The focus of this last chapter shifts from the individual level of analysis to the *social* level, exploring the possible mechanisms that would have integrated the Mithraic communities.

As we argued in Chapter 2, not only initiates' self-perception, but their social identities, would have been re-defined within the cult context; the wider structure and function of the cult would have prompted group members towards pro-social behaviours in the generation of social cohesion. In this chapter we explore how participation in the Mithraic rituals would have contributed to the development of social cohesion and relationships similar to kinship that bonded the initiates with each other (sections 5.1–5.2). In particular, we briefly present the theory of modes of religiosity suggested by Whitehouse (1995, 2004) and Whitehouse and Lanman (2014), and we argue that the Mithras cult displayed the main features of religious systems of the imagistic mode (section 5.3). The imagistic quality of the Mithras cult along with the absence of concrete cult narratives would have allowed mutations and variations of its cultural representations during transmission (Sperber's epidemiology of representations; section 5.4). However, we suggest that there was a specific component of the Mithras cult that is met in most mystery cults of the Graeco-Roman era but is not included in the modes theory, which would have increased the accuracy of transmission of the scene of the tauroctony and of the design of the mithraeum, and also would have significantly contributed to social cohesion among the cult members. This component was the demand for secrecy and concealment of the ritual enactments and symbol systems, which we believe would have connected the Mithraists with each other in such exclusivistic communities (section 5.5).

5.1 Social cohesion and group characteristics

Social cohesion has attracted the interest of scholars in a wide range of disciplines (e.g. sociology, psychology, anthropology, cognitive sciences, social network analyses), who have generated numerous studies suggesting different definitions of the concept of social cohesion, exploring its various components, causes, factors and effects, and developing methods of measuring group cohesiveness.[1] Far from building a consensus, what these studies have collectively achieved is the revelation of the multifacetedness and complexity of the phenomenon and the production of multileveled approaches to its various aspects.

Although attempting to provide a single, united definition of the phenomenon is a hazardous – and perhaps ultimately impossible – task, we may at least highlight some general prerequisites for the existence of social cohesion. Social cohesion appears wherever a group or a community is formed.[2] The size of the grouping can vary significantly, but it cannot include fewer than two persons. There should be at least some distinctive, identifying characteristics, though the characteristics themselves may be arbitrary. The *minimal group paradigm* developed and employed by Henri Tajfel (1970, 1974, 1985; Turner 1978) and the *self-categorization theory* suggested by John Turner and his colleagues (1986, 1987) have shown that groups may develop on the grounds of even the most trivial characteristics. These characteristics can derive from biological impulses, shared emotions, or cognitive traits, practical goals, social and financial interests, political ideologies, religious beliefs, shared world views, or even arbitrary imposed preferences. Such 'minimal group characteristics' (Carron and Spink 1995: 86–7), even though one may know that they are artificial, nevertheless motivate individuals to associate themselves with each other and to discriminate in-group members from out-group persons or other groups, and to favour – consciously or even unconsciously – the former over the latter. According to the *social identity theory* suggested by Tajfel and Turner (1986), the perception of membership within a group generates some social self-construals, which are shared by group members and which affect their self-perception and intragroup behaviours. Whether at any given time one's identity as an individual overshadows – or is overshadowed by – one's social identity depends in part on the amount of social cohesion achieved within the group and the strength of the bonds which tie the members to each other.

In the following sections we shall examine those cult traits that would have been conducive to the development of cohesion between Mithraists. Given that any theoretical approach, empirical evidence, or experimental analysis cannot provide a complete account of social cohesion, we will attempt to trace which of the organizational principles, mechanisms, structures, emotional experiences, and cognitive processes would have forged relations between the initiates, especially during rituals, and would have contributed to their integration into the cult communities of Mithraists.

5.2 Rituals contribute to social cohesion

Many studies have highlighted collective rituals as a crucial kind of social practice that promotes cohesion and solidarity between participants and contributes to the integration of social communities (e.g. Frazer 1922; Malinowski 1944; Radcliffe-Brown 1952; Leach 1954; Douglas 1970; Sahlins 1972; Foucault 1975; Comaroff and Comaroff 1993; Durkheim 1997 [1893]; 1995 [1912]; Kertzer 1988; Bloch 2004). Different theoretical models explore multiple sociopolitical aspects as well as psychological and cognitive processes that establish and strengthen the connection between rituals and social cohesion (e.g. Robertson-Smith 1889; Fustel de Coulanges 1980; Tomasello 1999; Irons 2001; Sosis 2006; Henrich 2009; Wiltermuth and Heath 2009; Lanman 2012). Among the more recent approaches, Harvey Whitehouse and Jonathan A. Lanman (2014) have developed a dichotomous theory that identifies two kinds of social cohesion, 'fusion identity' and 'group identification', and connects these with two different modes of religiosity, 'imagistic' and 'doctrinal'. After we briefly present the modes theory, we endorse the classification of the Mithras cult as an example of the imagistic mode of religiosity and we explore the new possibilities opened up by this classification for our understanding of the Mithraic communities

5.2.1 Modes of religiosity, group identification and identity fusion

The modes theory, as first formulated by Whitehouse (1995, 2004), makes a distinction between two modes of religiosity, the so-called 'imagistic' and 'doctrinal' modes, based on common features displayed by the religious systems classified in each case.

Echoing Max Weber's (1947) insights into charismatic authority and routinization, the religious traditions classified in the doctrinal mode typically have a founder, a historical or legendary authority who was believed to have proclaimed the major creeds of the cult, determined its internal norms and established the cult community. Subsequently, other authoritative figures, as religious specialists, undertake the task of spreading the word of the founder and overseeing adherents' compliance with the sacred norms. Usually the cult creeds comprise a complex body of sacred knowledge that is often written down in sacred texts and is orally pronounced during frequent and highly routinized rituals. Participation in rituals of such frequency is accompanied by low emotional arousal and motivation and requires the storage of transmitted knowledge in semantic memory. This semantic knowledge, which can be subject to explicit reflections, is associated not with specific episodes under which it was acquired, but with its origins in the authoritative figures who determine the orthodoxy of the cult and police the believers' observance. Routinization reinforces the ability to learn complex bodies of semantic knowledge through repetition and the stabilization of this knowledge in the people's minds; routinization also limits personal speculations on the meaning of the transmitted knowledge. The material means for preserving the creeds (e.g. sacred texts) and the existence of a priesthood that performs public rehearsals and repeated causally opaque rituals leads to a fixation of the sacred knowledge and further facilitates its transmission to large-scale groups of adherents (Whitehouse 2008: 108–10; see also Whitehouse 1995, 2002, 2004).

Whitehouse and Lanman (2014: 678) recently updated the modes theory taking into account the association of each mode with certain kinds of social cohesion. In particular, they claimed that the cult communities of the doctrinal mode are characterized by anonymity, in the sense that all members do not necessarily know each other, a logical necessity in religious traditions that have expanded throughout great geographical areas and that claim large populations.[3] The authoritative figures[4] of the cult are the nodes through which members of the cult are indirectly connected with each other generating a kind of 'organic solidarity' in Durkheimian terms.[5] But what establishes and perpetuates this connection is the sharing of a stable body of cult beliefs, values and attitudes that are expressed in routinized ritual practices, secured by the religious authorities that bind the members of the community through processes of group identification – that is 'the *perception* that one belongs and is committed to a social group' (Whitehouse and Lanman 2014: 678, emphasis added, referring to the work of Tajfel and Turner 1985, and Mael and Ashforth 1992).

The shared beliefs, values and attitudes are the key factors in any group identification since they comprise the 'prototypical characteristics' for the self-classification of individuals into groups, re-determining their social self-concepts as members of these groups (Whitehouse and Lanman 2014: 678, referring to Tajfel and Turner 1979, and Turner 1985). Shared beliefs further operate as social markers allowing individuals to identify others, even *anonymous* others, as members of their group, facilitating the concomitant development of coalitional feelings[6] and bonds between who would otherwise be strangers. The psychological processes that motivate people to commit to a group of co-believers and to conform their behaviours to shared social norms is enhanced by conditions of uncertainty the threats of failure, and even death highlight the benefits, or even necessity of cooperation and coalition (Whitehouse and Lanman 2014: 678; see further Greenberg et al. 1990; Boyer 2002: 234–41; Navarrete et al. 2004; Kay et al. 2008). However, people connected with each other in terms of such group identification are less eager to sacrifice their personal well-being for the general good of the community and demonstrate low levels of pro-social and altruistic behaviours (Whitehouse and Lanman 2014: 676–8).

Pro-sociality is most evident in religious traditions classified in the imagistic mode of religiosity. Such traditions tend to develop and to be established in small-scale communities in which the members know each other and are connected by personal relationships. These relationships are forged from shared participation in causally opaque, rarely performed rituals (Whitehouse and Lanman 2014: 679).

The infrequency of ritual performances in the imagistic mode does not provide the necessary conditions for the transmission of a clearly defined body of creeds. Even if conceptual knowledge *is* transmitted in these settings, typically complex and counterintuitive information is soon forgotten because of the lack of cognitive supports, such as repetition of the ritual, 'rote' memorization of creeds, and so on. As there is no fixed body of creeds to be perpetuated, there is less need for a powerful centralized authority (e.g. priesthood) to enforce consistency: founding figures and leaders may still play an important role, but not as enforcers of orthodoxy, since there is no demand for policing members' compliance with this orthodoxy. In these contexts, any religious hierarchy has mainly symbolic significance in ritual performances without playing a crucial role in the transmission and maintenance of the cult system (Whitehouse 2008: 110–11; see also Whitehouse 1995, 2002, 2004).

In the absence of religious leaders, members of imagistic communities develop a kind of 'organic solidarity', to use Durkheim's phrase, which derives from a perception of their equivalent positions and roles within the cult context. This solidarity is locally generated. The spread of the cult is not via authoritative individuals who travel in order to convert new members – rather, a small number of members bring the community with them intact or comprise the core of new local communities established in other places. And since there is no strict orthodoxy to which all the cult members should adhere, the beliefs and ritual practices that occur in new communities may have mutated with translocation: local variations are not only possible but acceptable (Whitehouse 2008: 111).

According to Whitehouse (2008: 110–11; see also Whitehouse 1995, 2002, 2004), the flexibility and variations of the beliefs and values of such religious traditions mainly derive from the fact that individual participants have the freedom to reflect subjectively on the meaning of their experiences in the cult context. Participants in infrequently performed, causally opaque rituals that are accompanied by high emotional arousal tend to attribute great significance to their personal experiences, which they perceive as 'life-shaping episodes' (Conway 1995), and store them as 'self-defining memories' (Singer and Salovey 1993) in their autobiographical mnemonic systems (Whitehouse and Lanmnan 2014: 680). *Spontaneous exegetical reflection* on those episodic memories may develop long after the ritual performance and lead to the conception and conceptualization of the ritual experiences as results of personal communication with supernatural agents, inspiration or divine revelation. But since the meanings of the rituals that emerge from personal reflections tend to be extremely personalized and idiosyncratic, they contribute a 'multivalence and multivocality' to 'religious imagery' (Whitehouse 2008: 111). And further, since the meaning of religious imagery and the exegesis of the rituals are not predetermined by an external authority and are not the same for all participants, they do not constitute the crucial factors that connect the group members with one other.

Whitehouse and Lanman (2014: 680) suggested that it is sharing experience of emotionally arousing – and in particular of extremely dysphoric[7] – rituals that establish psychological bonds between co-participants by creating the feeling that 'only those who have experienced the same thing can possibly understand how it feels and what it means' (Whitehouse and Lanman 2014: 680). They defined this kind of social cohesion as 'identity fusion', which creates 'a durable sense of psychological kinship with other group members' (p. 681). The development of such relations is especially characteristic of small-scale societies, for participants remember the other persons who participated with them in the same ritual actions and shared similar experiences. These shared memories entail a fusion between participants' social and personal self-concepts with their social identity and play a crucial role in their self-perception (p. 677; see also Bruner 1990; Conway 1996; McAdams 2008; Boyer 2009; Damasio 2010).

The development of shared-identity relationships among the members of a social community entails perception of other members as family. Humans have evolved a kin-detection mechanism that enables them to recognize their relatives through processes of phenotypic matching of physical, facial, and histocompatible characteristics (Villenger and Waldman 2012). According to Whitehouse and Lanman (2014: 677), this kin-detection mechanism expands to trace 'cues of shared experience and personal essence'. Therefore, what connects members of a fused community with each other is the recognition during direct interaction of a shared component of self-essence. Such self-essence emerges and is defined by similar episodic memories that comprise parts of the individuals' life stories. The sharing of similar autobiographical memories instead of a set of prototypical semantic characteristics classifies even non-acquaintance individuals in the same group (p. 676; see Swann et al. 2012). The entailed psychological bonds motivate members of the group to perform behaviours similar to those that they display towards their physical relatives. Therefore, when there is a threat against the community or members of the group, the individuals may perceive this threat as being addressed against themselves or their family and are prompted to fight for the survival of the community, displaying extreme altruistic and even self-sacrificial behaviours (Whitehouse and Lanman 2014: 676; see Swann et al. 2010; Buhrmester et al. 2014).

As individual cultures continually change over time, the two modes of religiosity, Whitehouse and Lanman (2014: 681) claimed, comprise two cultural attractors towards which cultures (e.g. religious traditions) all over the world and throughout human history seem to evolve (cf. Whitehouse 2004; Whitehouse and Laidlaw 2004; Whitehouse and Martin 2004; Whitehouse and McCauley 2005; Whitehouse 2008: 112). The emergence and development of the two modes derived from environmental challenges and selective pressures under which co-operation, coalitions and forms of social organization increased the possibilities of individual survival. Rituals comprise cultural practices that developed to contribute to social cohesion. Although Whitehouse (2004) and later Whitehouse and Lanman (2014) attribute crucial significance to semantic memory in the doctrinal mode and to episodic memory in the imagistic mode in the emergence of group identification and identity fusion, the partial sociopolitical and psychological parameters that they determine for each mode provide a broader theoretical ground in order to explore the involvement of further cognitive and psychological processes in the emergence and forging of social cohesion.

5.2.2 Rituals contribute to social cohesion

As mentioned above, the modes theory suggests a distinction between the 'doctrinal' and the 'imagistic' mode of religiosity and determines a range of cognitive and psychological processes as well as sociopolitical conditions under which each mode develops in response to external challenges that contribute to different kinds of social cohesion (Whitehouse 1995, 2002, 2004, 2008; Whitehouse and Lanman 2014). The modes theory of religiosity provided the theoretical framework for the first cognitive approaches to religious movements such as the Mithras cult.

However, before the publication of Whitehouse's theory, the primacy of visual imagery in the Graeco-Roman religions and in Mithraism in particular was pointed out by scholars who focused on the imagistic quality of religious practices and the ways in which these practices would have been apprehended by their contemporaries. A primary distinction between different types of religious traditions, suggested by A. D. Nock in 1933, foreshadowed the later classification suggested by Whitehouse. Nock distinguished the 'religions of tradition', in which 'the essential element is the practice and there is no underlying idea other than the sanctity of custom hallowed by preceding generations and 'prophetic religions' in which 'reason is all-important and the practice flows from it and is in a sense secondary even if indispensable' (Nock 1933: 3). Referring to the mystery cults, Walter Burkert (1987) also underlined that:

> the magical or even religious effect is possible without antecedent conceptual clarification, even if Plato evidently prefers those priests and priestesses who are not content with manipulating things but endeavor to find a plausible explanation, an 'account' than can be communicated to others. This account, however, is not fixed by tradition, nor does it ever become dogma.
>
> Burkert 1987: 72

The imagistic quality of the Mithras cult was particularly highlighted by Beck (1984), who shifted interest from reconstructing a mythical saga to the exploration of the symbolic connotations of the Mithraic iconography.[8] Extending Burkert's suggestion, Luther Martin (1994, 2015) was the first to argue that the apprehension of Mithraic imagery might not have necessarily presupposed the existence of a myth or of a body of creeds. Manfred Clauss (2000), though without giving up the attempt to reconstruct a sacred mythical narrative, nevertheless underlined the pre-eminence of images in Mithraism as an instance of the imaginative character of the ancient Greek religious practices[9] and indicated a different way of perceiving and conceptualizing these images.[10]

The modes theory of religiosity, based on universal psychological and cognitive processes shared by humans, provided a solid theoretical framework that could ground the speculations suggested by earlier historians about the imagistic character of the Graeco-Roman cults. Martin (e.g. 2004a, 2004b, 2004c, 2006, 2015: 29–56) and Beck (2004b, 2006a: 93–4) were the first to discern the possibilities offered by this new theoretical approach for deepening a historical understanding of the Mithras cult and the ways in which initiates would have perceived the cult imagery and experienced initiation into the mysteries. They classified the Mithraic mysteries as an example of the imagistic mode of religiosity based on the criteria suggested by Whitehouse (1995, 2002, 2004). Although their insights inspired young scholars (e.g. Chalupa 2009; Panagiotidou 2009, 2010, 2012a, 2012b) to become involved in cognitive studies and to apply Whitehouse's theory – along with other cognitive theories – to the Mithras cult, their overall approach was not well received by the majority of historians. However, most of the criticism seems to have focused on the terminology used in Whitehouse's theoretical model and the association of each of his modes with certain mnemonic systems and not so much on the criteria by which any religious tradition might be classified into one of the two modes of religiosity (e.g. see Dirven 2015: 25–6). The same points have proved to be the major vulnerabilities of Whitehouse's theory from the side of cognitive scientists of religion whose critique focuses mainly on the association of the ritual practices with specific systems of memory and the implications of this connection for the transmission of the religious ideas (e.g., Schjoedt et al. 2013; Xygalatas et al. 2013).

Whitehouse and Lanman (2014) updated the theory of modes of religiosity and explored both the cognitive processes and the sociopolitical conditions in which each mode mediates the development of different kinds of social cohesion among group members. As they acknowledged (Whitehouse and Lanman 2014: 683–90), there are limitations to this modified theory: it does not cover all aspects of rituals nor the full range of cognitive and psychological mechanisms that may mediate the development of social cohesion in social communities.

However, their theoretical model does provide a conceptual framework for discerning recurrent patterns in various religious traditions, and for organizing our knowledge about specific ritual practices. Further, it allows space for further inferences about the sociopolitical and cognitive processes involved in the development of social cohesion in groups. As we shall show in following sections, the classification of the Mithras cult as an example of the imagistic mode of religiosity throws light on multiple aspects of the cult and provides the ground for further inferences about perceptions of the cult's symbolic systems and imagery, and the sharing of a common world view by the initiates.

5.3 The imagistic mode of religiosity and the Mithras cult

According to the modes theory, in religious systems that mainly involve and promote a dogmatic mode of religiosity (such as Christianity), we expect to find certain features: a centralized myth, an authoritative founder and centralized authority, consistent rituals, and frequent repetition of low-arousal rituals. In contrast, from what we can infer from the archaeological remains and the scanty written testimony, the internal organization, the ritual practices, the symbolic systems and the structures of membership of the Mithras cult seem to cluster around the attractor of the imagistic mode of religiosity. Fractionating the main components of the cult further enables us to trace the cognitive mechanisms and the psychological processes that would have mediated the establishment of the Mithraic cult system, its transmission in the Roman world, and the kind of social cohesion that would have bound the members of Mithraic communities together.

5.3.1 No myth of Mithras, fixed body of creeds or sacred texts

Although – as we have discussed in the previous chapter – modern scholars have tried very hard to extract and reconstruct the lost Mithras myth from the cult imagery, we have yet even to discover evidence that a comprehensive mythic system ever existed. There is no reference to the mythology of the god preserved in ancient sources. No sacred texts have been found that recount a myth of Mithras.

The apparent lacuna does not mean that individual Mithraists did not develop and share stories about the mythical deeds of the worshipped god. Quite similar to modern scholars, the initiates would have projected a narrative structure in the visual imagery and would have been able to deduce narrative episodes from the visual representations in the cult context. The visual representations could have themselves been the products of locally generated narratives that would have developed and been shared by the members of local or even contiguous cult communities as a result of local exegesis or communication of personal exegetical reflections. This could explain the variations of the iconographic and statuary representations that embellished the mithraea and framed the omnipresent scene of the tauroctony. Variations in local imagery might in turn have encouraged the generation of new local narratives (see Martin 2004b: 195–6).

Along with the absence of a mythology of Mithras, there is no evidence that Mithraists maintained any specific body of creeds that was established, standardized, and shared by all cult members. Once again modern scholars have attempted to deduce the beliefs and values of the cult from the visual imagery. Their attempts seem to presuppose that in the absence of sacred texts that would have clearly defined the orthodoxy of the cult, the visual imagery could have provided the ground for the deduction of major cult principles and beliefs by the initiates. This could possibly have been the case, and modern historians could be right. But the cognitive and psychological processes that mediate the deduction of precepts from visual representations are quite different from those that underlie the memorization of a fixed body of creeds, and cluster around different kinds of sociopolitical factors and organizational principles.

5.3.2 Impotent founders and absent priests in the Mithraic communities

As there is no evidence for a specific mythology or body of creeds for the Mithraic cult, there is nothing that can be attributed to an authoritative founder except the foundation of the cult itself. Porphyry's reference to Zoroaster (*On the Cave* 6 15–18) as the first who devoted a cave to Mithras indicates the Iranian origins and the putative founder of Mithraism, but there is no evidence that his figure played any role in the cult context.

According to the modes theory, the absence of any authoritative source for cult beliefs and values is regularly accompanied by the absence of a dynamic centralized leadership. In the Mithras cult, there was not a focal priesthood that held the sacred knowledge of the cult, and that had the duty to transmit this knowledge to other adherents and to oversee the latter's conformity to the cult norms. As an example of how tangential centralized authority was, recall the grade hierarchy (the intricate pattern of seven grades of initiation as described in Chapter 2) that was a Mithraic symbolic system conspicuously absent from many locales. Most likely it constituted a local variation that developed as a result of the lack of strict cult rules and sacred norms that left some space for organizational and operational flexibility.

Where it is documented, the grade hierarchy mainly pertained to the individual ascent of the initiates and their roles and positions in the ritual praxis. Although it is not known if there was an initiatory ritual to each grade, we have explored in Chapter 2 how the acquisition and holding of a particular grade would have re-determined the initiates' personal self-concepts and the perception of their relationships to their co-participants in the cult context.

5.3.3 Rituals and transmission of the Mithras cult in small groups of adherents

Since there was no official body of creeds and no centralized priesthood and authoritative figures with the mission of proclaiming these creeds in other places and to bring in new adherents, the major means of transmission of the Mithras cult would have been the ritual praxis. It was through rituals that the volunteers were initiated into the mystery of the souls' journey and comprised the cult community.

But only one initiate was not enough for the ritual performances. For the transmission and establishment of the cult in a new region, a whole group or at least a sub-group of a Mithraic community should have moved from one place to another where it would have constituted the core for the formation of a new local community. This pattern seems to fit the lifestyle of most Mithraists who either were enrolled in the armed services or were ranked in the imperial administration. Soldiers and bureaucratic officials could be transferred from one region to another throughout the Roman Empire. Being settled in a new place they would have retained their Mithraic identity and possibly they would have wanted to be integrated into an already existing Mithraic community or to establish a new one with the members of their current social networks. Simultaneously, they could have kept relations to their previous co-participants creating 'strings of contacts' between cult groups (Martin 2004b: 195–6, 2006: 140; see Whitehouse 2000: 14, 36–7). However, this mode of transmission would have been quite unwieldy, since it presupposed not the dissemination of the cult creeds but the actual movement of people and their settlement to new regions. The small scale of the Mithraic communities, as it can be inferred from the size of their meeting places,[11] seems to confirm that participation in individual Mithraic cells was not massive.

5.3.4 Infrequent rituals, emotional arousal, episodic memory, autobiographical self and social identity

Although we do not know how often the Mithraic rituals – such us the cult meal shared by the participants – were performed, we can assume that initiation into the mysteries – or into each grade – would have comprised unique events for each initiate. As we have seen in the second chapter, there is no evidence for a general script of ritual actions that was standardized and shared by all the Mithraic communities. However, the general pattern of the initiatory rituals that comprise practices of low frequency and high emotional arousal is reflected in the references to the Mithras cult in Christian sources and in the secondary visual representations displayed in some mithraea (see Chapter 2). This pattern corresponds to the wider imagistic quality of Mithraism in which the active performance of ritual actions by the participants instead of the passive perception and conception of creeds orally disseminated by the priesthood would have been the main means of integration into the Mithraic communities.

Entering the mithraeum, the new candidates – or one candidate at a time – of a local community would have participated in the initiatory practices and experienced dysphoria: unpleasant emotions (e.g. fear, humiliation, uncertainty) or even physical pain. As Whitehouse and Lanman (2014) point out, this condition of high dysphoric arousal would have resulted in initiates storing the full details of the whole initiatory episode in their autobiographical memory. Later, they would have been able to recall this memory and explicitly reflect on its meaning for their personal lives. In the absence of any official interpretation, spontaneous exegetical reflection would have attributed personal significance to the initiatory experiences, which would have further altered the initiates' self-perception (cf. Chapter 2).

Recalling the episodes of initiation, the initiates would have remembered also their co-participants who had undergone the same dysphoric rituals. According to Whitehouse and Lanman, this sharing of dysphoric experiences by initiates and of their episodic memories would have generated a fusion between the initiates' personal self-concepts, creating the sense that they shared an essential similarity with those who participated in the same group and had undergone the same ritual practices. Therefore, the Mithraists comprised close, exclusive communities that would have been connected to each other by bonds of psychological kinship. New members could enter in the community only if they were willing to participate in the common ritual practices and to undergo the same dysphoric initiation(s). These rituals forged the Mithraic identity of initiates as an essential component of both their personal and social self-concepts, which they shared with their co-participants.

Within the ritual context, the perception of the symbolic space of the mithraeum and of the scene of the tauroctony would have comprised a wider background for the initiatory experiences and would have been further subject to exegetical reflection. The participants could have reflected on the meaning of the symbolic complexes and explicitly communicated their speculations with the other members of the local communities generating, thereby, local or even regional mythical narratives and secondary visual representations.

5.4 Mutations and variations during transmission: modes theory and Sperber's epidemiology of representations

The record of narratives and conceptual reflections in written form attributes a great amount of fixity, systematicity and coherence to the transmitted stories and contemplations that cannot be achieved in occasional oral communication on account of certain constraints on human cognition. In religious traditions, the written texts comprise material anchors that attribute representational stability to the conceptual constructions and mental spaces developed and promoted by these traditions (cf. Hutchins 2005: 1555, 1558–62). Although implicit personal reflections on the religious meanings are not completely absent from dogmatic religions (see Slone 2004), the sacred texts and the routinized rehearsal of standardized precepts by the religious officials purport to obtain a religious orthodoxy by denying individual deviations and rejecting alternative explanations as heretical (Whitehouse 2005: 310; cf. Goody 1977).

In the absence of material anchors, stories that are orally transmitted tend to involve more unstable and unfixed mental spaces, amenable to gradual mutations and transformations. As we have seen in Chapter 2, the narrative organization of human thought tends to trace causal chains in the unfolding of events, to produce stories from lived experiences, and to construct autobiographical narratives. In the imagistic religions, participation in rituals of high emotional arousal are the core events around which participants develop their personal narratives of participation. Although Whitehouse (2002, 2004, 2008) and Whitehouse and Lanman (2014) argued that such events tend to be stored as *flashbulb memories* (cf. Brown and Kulik 1977) retaining all the experienced details, perceptions and sensory inputs – such as colours, odours, images, the faces of co-participants[12] –

dysphoric rituals may also suppress the memories of the experienced events. These memories can later be reconstructed and supplemented with details that are inferred and derived from logical integration of the remembered components in the cult context.[13] Similarly, people are adept at keeping in memory coherent and logically integrated stories they perceive. Although they will most likely forget the exact wording and the secondary details of the original narratives they heard, they can recall the 'gist' of these stories, completing the forgotten particulars with reasonable features or simplifying and shortening the recalled narratives over time (Whitehouse 2005: 312; see further Bartlett 1932; Sperber 1985: 86).

Dan Sperber (1985, 1996) has likened the transmission of stories, concepts and ideas to the epidemiology of viruses across populations. He defines those 'distributed, long-lasting' stories, concepts and ideas[14] as cultural representations, which are mental representations that are internalized, transmitted and shared by more or less widespread groups of people for shorter or longer time intervals.[15] Similar to our immune system, which determines the nature of the viruses that can afflict human organisms, our cognitive system predefines the principal features of cultural representations to which our mind is predisposed or susceptible to keep and recall (Sperber 1985: 74). On the one hand there are cultural representations with direct correspondences to pre-semantic image-schemas and cognitive dispositions which make these representations easily learned and transmittable, comprising the conceptual deposit developed in every cultural group. On the other hand, there are more elaborate concepts and conceptual constructions that develop in reference to complex world views and whose survival and transmission across a human population depend on their appeal to cognitive susceptibilities. In both cases, there is a difference between the epidemiology of viruses and the transmission of cultural representations. While viruses tend to be amenable to minimal transmutations during transmission, cultural representations continually undergo mutations and alterations as they are transplanted from one mind to another (p. 75). The length of time that an idea will survive and the accuracy a concept or narrative will retain during transmission depends on their appealing either to pre-semantic perceptions of the world or to specific cognitive dispositions, susceptibilities[16] and psychological processes, and the means of transmission employed in different cultural traditions.

Religious concepts, stories and ideas usually comprise elaborated cultural representations, the success of which depends on their integration and coherence with wider conceptual contexts and the techniques of transmission employed in these contexts. Combining the insights provided by Sperber's epidemiology of representations and the theory of modes of religiosity, we may argue that in the doctrinal mode concrete representations, such as sacred texts and preaching, comprise public representations that are external entities and sensory inputs that undergo perceptual and conceptual processing within the mind generating individual mental representations. Although these mental representations may not be exact replications of the perceived public representations, the material anchoring and the routinized rehearsal amplify the potentiality for internalization and transmission of acute cultural representations.

In the imagistic mode of religiosity, the absence of solid material anchors makes public representations more mutable and evocative. Infrequently experienced rituals and occasionally perceived visual imagery comprise such external public representations that generate internal mental representations and call for further conceptual processing in order to be conceived as meaningful. Although such mental representations may decline and finally be forgotten over time, when the experiences during which they were generated are perceived as salient and personally significant episodes, people tend to meta-represent the mental representations generated by the perceptible public representations and to reflect on their consistency and rationality in the relevant conceptual context. According to Sperber (1985: 85), half-understood public representations that appeal to and are consistent with the perceiver's semantic representations of the world – but do not provide the ground for definite interpretations – tend to be more evocative and susceptible to cultural transmission.[17]

As we have seen in the previous chapters, the *mithraeum* and the *scene of the tauroctony* were material representations that would have anchored complex mental spaces pertaining to the Mithraic world view. In the absence of official explanations, the conception and comprehension of the meaning of these representations would have depended on their consistency with the images and assumptions about the world promoted by the cult, as well as by the participants' exegetical reflections in terms of semantic knowledge acquired during participation in the rituals.

Being initiated into the mysteries, the initiates would have developed narratives about their personal experiences in reference to the wider cult context. Even if they would have suppressed the exact memories of dysphoric initiations immediately after their participation in them (cf. Xygalatas et al. 2013; Schjoedt et al. 2013 vs Whitehouse and Lanman 2014), they could have later reconstructed the episodes as remembered. In addition, participation in the ritual community would have provided them with the semantic framework and conceptual apparatus for reflecting on the meaning of the encoded experiences long after the experienced episodes (cf. Whitehouse 2008: 110–11).

In addition, during participation in the cult community the initiates would have articulated or heard stories about Mithras's deeds that they could later remember, forget or transform, embellishing thereby the implicit narrative of the tauroctony with secondary framing events. Thus, mythical narratives about Mithras could have developed in local Mithraic communities, which could have been materialized in the visual representations found to frame the scene of the tauroctony in some mithraea. These narratives could have been transmitted by those initiates who moved from one place to another. During transmission, the mythical stories could have undergone mutations and transformations. In some cases they could have been forgotten or ignored. Other times, they could have been adjusted to local pre-established concepts and ideas, a process that may explicate the variability of the secondary representations in the mithraea.

Autobiographical memories of ritual experiences as well as remembered narratives about Mithras would have been the primary transmissions of the cult. Along with local visual imagery, they would have contributed further to the conversion of the remembered and of the visually or orally represented episodes to the bodily actions and the re-enactment of rituals in the Mithraic communities. Variations in the personal and collective memories and in the local visual representations would have mediated variations in the ritual praxis as well as in the symbolic structures of the cult developed in local communities (e.g. the regional appearance of the grade hierarchy).

The variations observed between local communities of Mithraists and the inferred resemblances among Mithraic groups of contiguous regions find a reasonable explanation in the classification of the Mithras cult as an imagistic mode of religiosity and its transmission in terms of the epidemiology of representations suggested by Sperber. However, there are two crucial features of Mithraism that cannot be explained by the aforementioned theoretical insights. First, in the absence of any material anchors for transmission, the design of the mithraeum and foremost the scene of the tauroctony displays an exceptional uniformity and complexity and an acute replication that is difficult to explain. Taking into account Sperber's argument that (1985: 86) 'hard to remember representations are forgotten, or transformed into more easily remembered ones, before reaching a cultural level of distribution', it is astonishing how the complexity of the tauroctonous scene and the multi-layered meanings and symbolic connotations of its composition could have been orally transmitted in the Mithraic tradition.

Second, in the framework of the imagistic mode of religiosity, the sharing of initiatory experiences and the autobiographical memories of the initiates would have provided the major psychological bond that would have connected the Mithraists with each other in close, exclusive communities. However, since members of local communities would have been transferred from one place to another, it would have been difficult for them to forge bonds of psychological kinship grounded on their original initiatory experiences with the members of the new community that they would have established or the pre-existing community that they would have participated in. Therefore, in addition to emotional arousal during initiation and the sharing of similar episodic memories, there should have been something more that would explain the development of social cohesion between Mithraists and would have separated them from the others – the uninitiated outsiders.

5.5 Social cohesion, secrecy and the mysteries of Mithras

Although modern scholars from different disciplines have long studied certain aspects of ritual practices (e.g. causal opacity, emotional arousal) that are associated with and appear to contribute to social cohesion, there is a largely neglected feature of the Graeco-Roman mystery cults that seems to take advantage of a particular cognitive proclivity shared by humans that produces solidarity, and that is people's love of secrets (see Genkin 2010: ix).[18]

Sociologist Georg Simmel (1906) noticed quite early the significance of secrecy in human societies.[19] He observed that we find the sharing of secrets fascinating merely be virtue of being privileged (p. 466). People enjoy the idea that they know a secret, because this knowledge makes them feel superior to others who know that there is a secret but ignore its content, and even to those who don't know that the secret exists at all (Rigney 1979: 52). Although Simmel (1906: 471) notes that a secret shared by two persons is no longer a secret,[20] the satisfaction of having a secret nevertheless increases when someone shares it with others.[21] This sharing generates a fundamental distinction between 'us and others' and seems to generate internal cohesion among the secret-keepers (Rigney 1979: 52).

Secrecy was a major aspect of the Graeco-Roman mystery cults.[22] The secret consisted not so much in a body of ideas and precepts that were orally transmitted to the initiates who had to keep them hidden from the uninitiated. Rather, the secrecy pertained to participation in the initiatory rituals and the reservation of the details and particulars of the ritual praxis between the initiates and their concealment from the outsiders.

In the Mithras cult, the initiates participated in rituals that took place away from any public observance. The uninitiated had no access to the ritual space and were not allowed to attend the mysteries' enactment. Initiation was itself a secret script of actions that the initiates enacted in front of or along with other co-participants but they were not permitted to reveal to the outsiders. Along with the enactment of ritual practices, Mithraists gradually gained access to a secret knowledge that was not constrained to a set of ideas and beliefs but consisted in the gradual revelation of a new world view in the cult context. They reached a new view of the universe not through learning a semantic knowledge of major conceptual images and assumptions about the world, but through direct experience of the Mithraic microcosm.

In what follows we explore secrecy as one of the most fundamental features of the Mithras cult, which crucially affected its material structures and the representations shared by its initiates. We further suggest that secrecy played a crucial role in the transmission of the cult and the establishment of close, exclusive communities of high social cohesion throughout the Roman world. Thereby, we intend to point out a significant aspect of the mystery cults whose underpinnings require further investigation by the cognitive scientists and by the scholars who are interested in the association of rituals and social cohesion.

5.5.1 Secrets, social sharing and close communities: what secrets Mithraists shared

Although a secret can be constrained to one individual, its sharing between at least two persons has certain implications for intra- and extra-group social relationships (Genkin 2010: 1). As Michael Genkin (p. ix) pointed out, the notion of secrecy refers to 'a situation where 1) members of a group share information known only to them and 2) those group members are aware of this fact and 3) they deliberately conceal the information from non-group members'.

The concealed information may involve explicit beliefs and shared attitudes, performed actions and behaviours, common pursuits and plans, social identities and self-concepts or even objects and artefacts that pertain to the social domain (p. ix). That means that the act of concealment is meaningful when people who intentionally hold a secret believe that the concealed information is considered to be of high social value and can be exploited by them (Simmel 1906: 466–7). Those who hold the secret believe that they possess a knowledge that puts them in an advantageous position relevant to the ignorant. The outsiders who know the existence of the secret but ignore its content may desire its revelation.

Thereby, secrecy may provide the ground for a separation between sub-groups of insiders and outsiders within a social community (Genkin 2010: 1–2).

Simmel (1906: 468–9) suggests that in small communities whose members know each other and have close personal relationships, secrets are difficult to keep. In larger, more anonymous societies, concealment of information is easier by people who form close sub-groups of secret-keepers within the greater communities. In those cases, it seems that the secrecy that connects people with each other in small sub-groups contributes to intra-group social cohesion.

The Mithraic communities comprised such close, exclusive communities, which developed and were established across the Roman Empire. As mentioned in the previous sections, the Mithraists shared the common experience of initiation, high emotional arousal during the initiatory rituals and the episodic memories of their lived experiences. Participation in the cult would have established new roles and developed new concepts of self and social identities in the mystery context. The participants would further have gained access to a new view of the universe as it was materialized in the mithraeum and the scene of the tauroctony and was instantiated in the ritual practices. Following Whitehouse and Lanman (2014), the sharing of common experiences and memories as well as images and assumptions about the world would have connected the Mithraists with each other in relations of fictive kinship. We suggest that, simultaneously, group cohesion would have been amplified by an awareness that the whole range of experiences, perceptions, sensory inputs, and conceptual knowledge provided during initiation and participation in the Mithras cult was reserved only for the initiates and should be concealed from the uninitiated. The material structures (e.g. mithraeum, the tauroctony) and the internal organization (e.g. membership, grade hierarchy) of the cult would have promoted and enhanced the condition of secrecy. Secrecy and the demand for concealment would have certain impacts on the individual psychological reactions and the intra-group relations advocating the distinction between insiders and outsiders and amplifying social cohesion within the community.

5.5.2 Means and techniques for secrecy: grade hierarchy and the scene of the tauroctony

A secret shared by a group of people always runs the risk of being disclosed. As the size of the group expands, the nodes of the network of secrecy can increase in number and the possibilities of disclosure are amplified. The maintenance of secrecy depends largely on individual discipline and commitment to the group.

However, secret communities[23] do not exclusively rely on their members' loyalty for their survival and maintenance but develop more elaborate means for the preservation of secrecy (Rigney 1979: 52).

A common practice employed by secret communities is the selective distribution of duties, roles and information to the insiders. The development of internal hierarchical structures determines the members' access to the secret knowledge (p. 52). The grade hierarchy developed in some Mithraic communities could have operated as such a means of control of individuals' access to the new world view revealed during the mysteries. Initiatory rituals of high emotional and physical arousal would have amplified the initiates' morale and would have increased the salience of both the experienced episodes and the revealed images of the world. The gradation of initiations would have further led to the preservation of secrecy by classifying the initiates' access to the Mithraic world view and by limiting the information provided to the members of each grade that would have been necessary for the accomplishment of their cult roles and duties.

Along with the graduated membership and the classification of information, secret communities may develop artificial means for safeguarding secrecy and preventing external invasions. These means may include physical obstacles (e.g. hedges, locks, sealed gates), live guardians (e.g. door keepers, guards, watchdogs) or even complex symbolic devices and systems that block the cognitive access of intruders from the secret information and knowledge even if they manage in some way to get physical access to the communities' settlements (p. 53).

In the case of Mithraism, the establishment of the mithraea that could not be identified from outside would have contributed to the secrecy of the cult places, which remained hidden from the eyes of the curious. In addition, we have seen in Chapter 4 that the scene of the tauroctony anchored and represented multi-layered mental spaces, the perception and conception of which would have derived from a hierarchical interpretative process. Initiation into the Mithraic mysteries would have revealed those images and assumptions about the world that would have been necessary in order for the initiates to trace the multiple conceptual templates of the tauroctony. Where the grade hierarchy developed as a distinctive symbolic system, the gradation of the initiation could have entailed a gradual access to the conceptual meanings of the scene. Therefore, the scene of the tauroctony might have comprised a complex secret code, the decoding of which would have demanded physical participation in the Mithraic rituals and the gradual cognitive access to its meanings and connotations within the cult context. The uninitiated, on the one hand, who ignored the world view revealed in the Mithraic mysteries, would not have possessed the necessary conceptual means to perceive the multivalent meanings of the tauroctony and they could not have reached beyond the iconic level of interpretation. The initiates, on the other hand, would not have immediately been able to trace and perceive the multiple mental spaces represented in the scene. Participating in the mysteries, however, they would have directly lived and experienced the Mithraic cosmos and would have gradually acquired the necessary conceptual knowledge of the symbolic construction of the tauroctony.

Although it remains a mystery how the acute replication of the scene was achieved by the local Mithraic communities, the omnipresence and uniformity of the tauroctony indicates that its composition was not a matter of personal or collective reflections that would have favoured regional variations. Instead, the complex system of signs represented in the scene would have comprised a covert means for transmitting the major precepts of Mithraism, and in particular a covert, codified allocentric map for the actualization of the mysteries of the souls' journey within in the Mithraic universe.

5.5.3 Secrecy, mechanisms of social cohesion and the Mithraic rituals

The very existence of secret communities presupposes the willingness of their members to be integrated into the secret group, to collaborate with their co-participants, to abide by the norms of the group, and to make efforts to keep the intra-group secrets concealed from outsiders. Therefore, the maintenance of secrecy by groups and communities demands complex personal motivations and social mechanisms that generate cohesion and bind the members with each other with the common purpose of keeping the secret hidden.

Many causal explanations have been suggested to throw light on the underlying mechanisms that motivate people to be engaged in secret communities (see Genkin 2010: 22–30). Simmel pointed out the psychological attraction of secrecy that may increase the salience and social value of the concealed information (e.g. beliefs, practices, attitudes, plans). Even when the secrets are just fictitious or ordinary concepts, objects and conditions, their investment with an aura of mystique make them attractive and desirable targets. Access to the mystery gives people the sense that they have acquired a privileged knowledge and corresponds to their desire for exclusiveness and uniqueness, which may increase their self-esteem (Simmel 1906: 486–7; Snyder and Fromkin 1980; Genkin 2010: 22, 28).

Mystery cults promised initiates the establishment of a privileged personal relationship with the worshipped deity who puts adherents under its protection. The development of such a relationship was not available to just anyone, but presupposed the complex ritual practices that the participants voluntarily enacted in secret. Initiation into the Mithraic mysteries involved such secret rituals which integrated initiates in close communities that were under the protection of Mithras. This personal relationship with the deity, the revelation of the secret cosmic order and the assignment of duties and roles to the initiates for the preservation of this order would have given them their sense of exclusiveness and superiority over the uninitiated.[24]

The sharing of secrets among the members of a community provides at least a 'minimal group characteristic' for the self-classification of individuals into a group which influences both their self-concepts and social identity (cf. Carron and Spink 1995: 86–7; also Tajfel 1970, 1974, 1985; Turner 1978). However, this sharing of secret information, attitudes and beliefs does not comprise the only criterion of classification into a group. Along with the high emotional arousal of initiatory rituals in secret communities, the demand for secrecy and for the concealment of information about the intra-group activity may induce feelings of stress and anxiety that may urge the individuals to avoid the risks of disclosure (Simmel 1906: 480; Genkin 2010: 6–7). Such feelings of anxiety may be relieved within the group, where people can freely discuss their experiences and personal reflections. The precaution against the outsiders and the comfortability of being among co-participants may increase the identity fusion between the members of a group and contribute to the bonds of psychological kinship. Therefore, the psychological bonds between initiates into the Mithraic mysteries would have been amplified by the fact that they should conceal any information about their experiences and personal memories in the cult context from their extra-group relatives, friends, and acquaintances. They could only share their thoughts and reflections with their co-participants and other cult members (see Genkin 2010: 13).

The social cohesion that develops in secret communities further presupposes and depends on a mutual trust that their members are not going to disclose the secrets. The secret-keepers jointly enjoy the privileges entailed by the secret knowledge, and any disclosures of it will discount these privileges for the whole community. Thereby, maintenance of the positive emotions of uniqueness and exclusiveness derived from knowing a secret may be a personal motive for the reservation of the secrecy that further contributes to intra-group solidarity (Genkin 2010: 28; cf. social exchange theory; Blau 1967; Emerson 1976; Cook and Emerson 1987).

However, not only do the individuals need to keep the secret hidden, but they need to believe that their co-participants will behave in the same way in order for all of them to continue to enjoy the privilege of sharing a secret. Therefore, there may be a demand for the members of a secret community to explicitly demonstrate their trustworthiness and loyalty. Costly and dysphoric rituals have been suggested as the means of signalling the individuals' commitment to the group, which further contributes to social cohesion and intra-group solidarity (Irons 2001; Bulbulia 2004).

In the Mithras cult, the initiatory rituals would have served multivalent purposes. As mentioned above, the ritual practices would have themselves been part of the secret that the initiates should conceal from the uninitiated. The high emotional arousal during the rituals would have increased the personal significance of the lived episodes and would have mediated their storage as salient episodic memories. The sharing of the initiatory experiences and of episodic memories of the rituals, as well as the demand to keep the details of ritual practices concealed, would have altered both the personal and social self-concepts of the participants, who would have connected with each other with terms of psychological kinship. The integration of Mithraists in Mithraic communities different from those in which they were originally members would have been facilitated by the sharing of the cult secrets by all of its members. At the same time, the rituals would have operated as a costly means of signalling the initiates' commitment to the Mithraic communities. Therefore, although the Mithras cult exemplifies the criteria for its classification in the imagistic mode of religiosity, the transmission of its religious ideas, the uniformity of its major symbolic systems, the establishment of Mithraic communities throughout the Roman Empire, and the development of social cohesion among its members would have been mediated by complex cognitive and psychological processes with the notion of secrecy to have multiple impacts on both the internal organization of the cult and the personal and social identity of its members.

Conclusion

The Mithras cult provides a fertile ground in order to highlight how a *religious institution* developed and was influenced by specific *cultural contexts* to generate a coherent world view that would have been conceived, conceptualized and embedded by *individual* adherents through the operation of multiple *neuro-cognitive*, *mental*, and *psychological* processes.

As we have repeatedly noted throughout this book, the Mithras cult does not provide in abundance the typical evidence for the historical research – that is, written testimony and epigraphical material. Nevertheless, the cult has drawn the interest of historians and has been the subject of numerous and extensive historical studies. We can trace the attractiveness of the Mithras cult to modern scholars in the available evidence as well as in the apparently wide distribution of its local cells throughout the vast Roman Empire.

The historians who wish to study this Graeco-Roman cult confront a unique puzzle: we face a cult that has left abundant archaeological evidence that refuses to allow one to ignore its presence in the Graeco-Roman world. At the same time, we have no narratives at our disposal that would explicate the story of the cult – its mythical origins, its ideas and precepts, the processes of its diffusion and personal accounts of members' initiations. These features, which may seem to be shortcomings at first glance, have proven to be the major part of the allure of the cult. In the absence of written testimony, which would have provided explicit details and constrained the possibilities for historical accounts, the archaeological evidence operates as the material foundation on which historians have proposed many stories about the worshipped god Mithras, articulated different scenarios of the cult dissemination, traced various cultural influences on its main features, and suggested multiple interpretations of the symbolic connotations of its common elements.

Taking into account the apparent multivocality of the major Mithraic symbol systems – that is the mithraeum, the tauroctony, and representations of the hierarchy of seven initiatory grades – what we have attempted to do throughout this study is not to articulate a new historical account of the cult or to suggest interpretations of its structures alternative to those suggested by historians before us. In our study of the personal experiences of initiation in the Mithras cult and the appropriation of the Mithraic world view by the initiates, we found in modern neuro-cognitive research useful theoretical tools in order to approach Mithraists as embodied and embrained individuals who would have 'lived' the initiatory rituals and embedded the religious ideas, beliefs and practices promoted by the cult. By employing modern cognitive theories to interpret a past religious tradition such as the Mithras cult, we did not hope to offer definite conclusions about historical facts and ritual practices that are not known today. We mainly looked for probable ways in which the initiates could have experienced their initiations, could have made sense of the rituals and symbolic systems of the cult that could have modified their wider world view. In other words, we used cognitive theories in order to gain some insight into what would have gone on in the bodies and brains of the people who created, used and developed the Mithraic mysteries as a system of cultural practices, and in turn how these practices would have affected the initiates' minds – perceptions, conceptions, thoughts and world views.

Beginning from the theoretical premise that the Mithras cult would have provided to its members a concrete world view, in this volume we explored how the universal world-view categories, as defined by Kearney (1984), would have been instantiated in the Mithraic cult context and would have mediated the comprehension and acceptance of the Mithraic world view by the cult members. In particular, in our study we employed a variety of modern cognitive theories in order to shed some light on the cognitive underpinnings of the major world-view categories and to explore how the specific historical, social, and cultural contexts of the Graeco-Roman world would have influenced the contents and demonstrations of these categories in the Mithraic world-view system.

Particularly, we examined how the specific neuroanatomy, embodiment and situatedness of Mithraists in the Graeco-Roman world and particularly in the Mithraic cult context would have affected their *self-perception* as well as *perception of space* and *time* within the mithraeum. Taking into consideration Johnson's (1993) theoretical insights into the narrative conceptualization of the human lives, we examined how the initiatory experiences would have been integrated into the wider life-stories of Mithraists as significant turning points that would have modified their self-perception and social identities (Bruner 2003). In particular, we explored the metaphorical perception of the grade hierarchy as a gradual ascent that would have been perceived as taking place both within the mithraeum and across the heavens, and that would have been accompanied by a new view of the universe and entailed new cult identities.

Further, we explored those embodied cognitive mechanisms that mediate perception of space and time and could have enabled metaphorical conception of the mithraeum as the universe. We argued that the construction and perception of the mithraeum as an image of the cosmos would not necessarily have presupposed *a priori* knowledge of the Hellenistic cosmology but would have been grounded on the embodied presence of initiates within the Mithraic caves, participation in the mysteries, and metaphorical mappings between perceptible entities and known components of the cosmological models. We also saw that metaphorical perception would have neither presupposed complete mappings between all the elements which comprised the cosmos and the mithraeum. We rather argued that selective projections and blends mediated by the cognitive processes of composition, completion, elaboration and compression of particular elements – processes explored by Fauconnier and Turner (1998, 2002, 2003) – would have underlain the metaphorical perception of the mithraeum as the actual cosmos. In this light we argued – contrary to the suggested dichotomy between those educated Mithraists that would have possessed the necessary astrological knowledge in order to conceive the symbolic connotations of the cult and those who derived from lower classes and were considered to be more 'naive' participants – that all initiates shared the same cognitive abilities to comprehend the symbolic meanings of the lived experiences and of the perceived material structures within the cult context.

In the same vein, we suggested that comprehension of the scene of the tauroctony by the initiates could have been the result of a gradual interpretive process that presupposed participation in the mysteries, embodied perception of the cult structures, and conceptual knowledge acquired during participation. In particular, employing the semiotic theory articulated by Peirce (1931–58), we argued that the absence of any explicit background myth of the represented scene that would have further clarified its significance for the ritual enactments would have provided as remarkable a cognitive freedom to the initiates as it does to modern scholars who have traced multiple meanings and semantic connotations in the scene. The inherently temporal and narrative structure of the human thought can be traced in the historians' attempts to extract a mythical story from the visual representation. We consider that similar attempts could have been made by the initiates who, recognizing the iconic composition of the scene, could have generated stories about the god Mithras who killed the bull. Such narrative constructions, however, do not entail the existence of a common myth of Mithraism that has been lost. Simultaneously, the derivation of different stories from the tauroctony could explicate the variations of secondary visual representations that framed the main cult-scene in local sanctuaries.

We further suggested that these secondary variations in visual representations collateral to the tauroctony and also observed in the internal arrangement of the mithraea could have derived from spontaneous exegetical reflections and local exegeses that develop in religious traditions of the imagistic mode of religiosity (Whitehouse 1995, 2008). Employing modes theory (Whitehouse and Lanman 2014), we further explored how the sharing of the initiatory experiences by Mithraists would have reformed the relationships between them, making possible the formation of close Mithraic communities. In particular, we suggested that the sharing of common episodic memories of the highly arousing initiation rites would have facilitated an 'identity fusion' and the development of psychological kinship between the initiates of the exclusive local communities.

However, we argued that spontaneous exegetical reflections and local exegeses do not seem enough to fully explain the regional multivalence of Mithraic visual imagery and the transmission of the Mithraic beliefs across the Roman Empire. Simultaneously, the main design of the mithraeum and the omnipresence and uniformity of the tauroctony does not seem to fit the fluidity of the secondary representations that could have derived from mutations during transmission. In addition, we consider that the great significance that Whitehouse and Lanman (2014) attribute to episodic memory does not exhaust the cognitive mechanisms and psychological processes that would have forged bonds between the Mithraists and would have mediated the formation of close, exclusive communities.

Looking for further functions and semantic connotations of the shared initiatory experiences, which would have forged the social cohesion between the intra-group members and would have drawn the lines of separation from the extra-group people, we pointed out an aspect of the Mithraic mysteries that characterizes the majority of the mystery cults but has not received enough attention from the cognitive scientists who study the connection between rituals and social cohesion. It is the parameter of secrecy and concealment, we argued, that would have significantly contributed to the development of social cohesion and relations of fictive kinship among the members of the Mithraic communities. Recalling Simmel's early theoretical insights (1906), we suggested that along with the shared dysphoric initiatory experiences (Whitehouse and Lanman 2014), the gradual revelation of a secret world view in the mystery context and the sharing of this world view by Mithraists, who should conceal the cult knowledge and ritual details from the uninitiated, would have operated as an effective means of forging close kin relationships between them. In this framework, the hiding of the mithraea from public view, the hierarchy of initiatory grades and the multilayered semantic composition of the tauroctony would have operated as collateral means for ensuring the secrecy of the cult and for preventing the access of external intruders to the Mithraic world view.

We have shown that applying modern cognitive theories to the Mithras cult is compatible with traditional accounts; they may also offer unique insights into past agents' minds. In this light, we consider that modern research on human cognition introduces an additional level of analysis into historical studies and particularly in the study of past religious systems, bringing to the fore the *people* who created and used various cultural practices throughout history. Historians have long been interested in approaching *people* who lived in the past, focusing on the ways in which *cultural influences* and *social interactions* would have affected self-identities and world views, making commonsensical assumptions about those people's reasoning, thoughts and decisions. We believe that we can find in modern neuro-cognitive research new methodologies and theoretical insights that improve on our commonsensical assumptions about past agents' perceptions and conceptions and thus deepen our modern understanding of the past. Particularly, taking into consideration the *neuro-biological* and *cognitive mechanisms* that operated in those people's *bodies* and *brains* as well as the *psychological processes* that would have taken place in their *minds*, we can gain insight into how the *external* contextual influences would have been *internalized* by individuals, affecting their self-perceptions and their conceptions of reality. From this perspective, cognitive approaches to historical agents do not seek to undermine traditional historical approaches. Mostly they enrich historical studies by deepening our modern understanding of past agents.

In the same vein, we think that the involvement of historians in cognitive studies is equally important for the investigation and understanding of human cognition. Our cognitive capacities, as well as mental and psychological processes that mediate our perception of the world and conception of reality, are largely influenced by our current cultural and social contexts. However, these same capacities and processes developed throughout our history, influenced, affected and (re)modulated by continually altering physical, cultural and social conditions. Therefore, we cannot reach definite and generalized conclusions about 'human cognition' without taking into consideration its development throughout history. Thus, we suggest that collaboration between cognitive scientists and historians is of crucial significance if we wish to reach a diachronic understanding of human cognition.

We moderns cannot understand ourselves as embrained, embodied, and encultured agents without taking into consideration how the long history of our species led to the present. Paraphrasing a phrase of James Baldwin, 'we are trapped in history, and history is trapped in us' (*Notes of a Native Son*, 1955).

Notes

Introduction

1. Also across northern England at Hadrian's Wall.
2. On this distinction drawn in the sociology of religion see Dawson (2008).
3. In worship one tends to the gods just as in *agri-culture* one tends to the fields. The same basic 'you take care of us and we'll take care of you' contractual idea underlies both activities. Ancient religion, especially Roman religion, was nothing if not practical.
4. For overviews of public worship in the Empire see Beard et al. (1998); Rüpke (2007a, 2007b); Rives (2007).
5. The scare quotes indicate that the concept of *a* religion, let alone the concept of a *single* religion, actual or potential, is something of an anachronism. What can be safely said is that communities had their patron deities to whom special attention was paid: e.g. Athena for Athens, the Capitoline Triad (Jupiter, Juno, Minerva) for Rome; and for the Empire, an ever-growing array of deified emperors and their wives.
6. For a discussion of the term see Bremmer (2014: vi–ix).
7. As the saying goes, 'it all depends on' what one means by 'oriental'. See Bremmer (2014: xi).
8. This assumed 'Persian' identity is all the more remarkable in that Persia was the Empire's most serious foe; and yet the Mithraists were never, as far as one can tell, suspected of disloyalty.
9. Our translation is adapted from that of the Arethusa edition of the essay (Buffalo 1969), referenced as Porphyry (1969) in the References.
10. For many decades following the foundational work of Franz Cumont (1896–98), this was the major question in Mithraic scholarship. Nowadays the focus for those studying Roman Mithraism has shifted from its putative Iranian antecedents to its fashioning as a cultural enterprise in and of the Roman Empire: see esp. Alvar 2008.
11. For an account of this transmission and of the genesis of the mysteries in the West see Beck (1998).
12. Interestingly, the title of the English translation of R. Turcan's *Les cultes orientaux dans le monde Romain* (Turcan 1992) dropped the reference to the Orient, becoming simply: *The Cults of the Roman Empire* (Turcan 1996).
13. According to Paul Thagard (1996: 6), six scholars are considered the founders of cognitive sciences: George Miller (1956: 81–97), who focused on the study of

memory, John McCarthy (McCarthy and Hayes 1969), Marvin Minsky (1963), Allen Newell and Herbert Simon (Newell et al. 1958: 151–66), who dealt with artificial intelligence, and Noam Chomsky (1957) in the field of linguistics, who conceived of language in terms of cognitive grammars; see A. Geertz (2004a: 350); Xygalatas (2006: 13–14).

14 For an introduction to cognitive sciences that outlines compendiously their development and methods as well as the theories and studies of the most prominent scholars involved see A. Geertz (2004a: 347–400). See also Xygalatas (2006: 9–87).

15 It would serve no purpose for us to enter the debate on how 'scientific' in a grand sense CSR is or can ever be. Although rigorists on both sides would probably deplore it, one might even think of CSR as an umbrella term covering the cognitive *study* of religion too. This is why as authors we shall speak more inclusively of a/the cognitive *approach*.

16 Particularly, theories and methods derived from cognitive psychology, evolutionary psychology, cognitive anthropology, artificial intelligence, cognitive neuroscience, neurobiology, zoology and ethology. As examples of the employment of these methods, see Lawson and McCauley (1990); Boyer (2002); Pyysiäinen (2003); Whitehouse (2004).

17 The reviews of Beck's 2006 book, describing the mysteries of Mithras in terms of the making of representations and of the initiates' apprehension of symbol systems, were generally unfavourable. Since Beck is one of the two present authors, it would only smack of sour grapes to attempt a rebuttal here.

18 Martin's pre-eminence will be readily apparent from a look at his titles in our References. Other scholars active in the new field are Colleen Shantz and Hugo Lundhaug, who have published monographs (2009 and 2010 respectively), and the contributors to the following collections: *Past Minds: Studies in Cognitive Historiography* = Martin and Sørensen (eds) (2011); *Mind, Morality and Magic: Cognitive Science Approaches in Biblical Studies* = Czachesz and Uro (eds) (2013); finally, the first issue of the new *Journal of Cognitive Historiography* (1 (1), 2014) which is devoted to the religions of antiquity (see esp. Martin's 'Introduction to the Issue').

19 Our debt to Martin throughout this section will be readily apparent.

20 According to Margaret W. Matlin (2004: 2), 'Cognition, or mental activity, describes the acquisition, storage, transformation, and use of knowledge'.

21 Martin's account is itself a meta-narrative. Theoretically, this might pose a problem, but not, we think, in practice for our present endeavour.

22 On icons of theophany see Verity Platt's brilliant monograph (2011).

23 For our previous treatment of religions in general and Mithraism in particular as streams of representations see Beck (2006a): esp. 9, 65, 88–101); Beck (2010). In both works our debt to the anthropologist Dan Sperber's (1996) theory of cultures as 'epidemics' of representations is acknowledged. Sperber, incidentally, intends the terms 'epidemic' and 'endemic' quite literally in reference to cultural representations.

24 On human bias towards narratives see, e.g., Turner (1996); Carroll (2001); Herman (2003).
25 On the narrative mind of humans see, e.g., Fauconnier and Turner (2002); Sjöblom (2005).
26 See, however, Martin (2004a: 8), on cognition and *l'histoire des mentalités*.
27 See also Pachis and Panagiotidou (2017).
28 Gordon here anticipates the cognitive turn in the study of historical religions by several decades. Not coincidentally, he was at that time influenced by Dan Sperber's then recently published *Rethinking Symbolism* (1975). See also Gordon (1980a). On Sperber's importance to the present authors see above n. 20.
29 By 'minds' we do not mean just the thoughts, intentions, representations, etc., of persons, but rather, to use a common metaphor, the 'software' on which these applications all run. 'Mind' is not to be confused with 'what's on one's mind' or what one 'has in mind'.
30 On the function of the initiate's 'apprehension of symbols', see esp. the 'Template for a re-description of the Mithraic mysteries' in Ch. 1, sect. 3 of the earlier study (Beck 2006a: 10 f.).
31 Whether Dirven came to the Plutarch passage via Beck is not made clear. Dirven references Beck's use of the passage (2015: 27, n. 33), but she seems unaware of its centrality to Beck's entire enterprise.
32 See also p. 29: 'To judge from Plutarch's description of the mysteries of Isis, the underlying mythological narrative not only inspired the *eikones* and *mimêmata*, but was also the basis for the *hyponoiai*, or allegorical interpretation of the mysteries.' Beck's rendering of *hyponoiai* as 'underthoughts' was intentionally both etymologically literal and semantically vague. Such *hyponoiai* would include, but not be limited to, 'allegorical interpretation of myth'.
33 Collected in Martin (2015).
34 Although Dirven quotes and discusses Porphyry's statement about the mithraeum as 'cave' and 'image of the universe' (2015: 36 f., quoted in n. 74), she has nothing to say about his explication of *why* the mithraeum was so designed and furnished, i.e. to enable 'induction into a mystery of the descent of souls and their exit back out again'. This oversight is of a piece with Jan Bremmer's complete omission of the Porphyry passage from his recent book about 'Initiation into the Mysteries of the Ancient World' (Bremmer 2014: title), to which we shall return in Chapter 2.
35 'So little is known of this theology that an honest account of the complexity of the iconographic evidence easily turns into an incomprehensible list of apparently insignificant details' (Gordon 1988: 59).
36 Modern attempts to reconstruct the Mithraic doctrines reflected the transfer by earlier scholars of their own way of thinking to a past religious tradition whose ideas and precepts were less systematized and coherent, more dependent on the immediate contexts which generated them. We briefly overview these attempts in

Chapter 4. Ron Brunton, cited by Whitehouse (2005: 309), calls this tendency of past scholars the imposition of 'misconstrued order'. For a critique of the traditional ways of reconstructing Mithraic 'doctrine', see the first four chapters of Beck (2006a).

37 Nor, of course, was Gordon explicitly concerned with 'world view'.
38 Gordon here alludes to the fact that promotion through the grades places the initiate under the protection of a new planet – but in an order unique to the mysteries.
39 In his monograph on the Mithras cult, Beck made particular use of a stream of cognitive inquiry known as 'biogenetic structuralism' or 'neurotheology' (2006a: 136–48). The usefulness of this method should not be judged by its rebarbative names! Though we shall not use it to any great extent in our present study, we are certainly not repudiating it.
40 Each chapter begins with a brief description of the cognitive theoretical premises that then are applied to the Mithraic world view.

1 The World View of the Mithras Cult

1 For a preliminary application of Michael Kearney's theory to the Mithras cult see Panagiotidou (2008).
2 A description of this construct will be presented in Chapter 3.
3 Unless noted otherwise, all citations in this section are to Kearney (1984).
4 See Kearney (1984: 45), quoting U. Neisser (1976: 54): 'The schema accepts information as it becomes available at sensory surfaces and is changed by that information; it directs movements and explanatory activities that make more information available, by which it is further modified.' On the role of schemata in the organization of knowledge see also Barsalou (1992: 156–8).
5 Kearney distinguishes 'assumptions', which are 'images of reality' that exist 'in the mind of the people whose world view is being analyzed', from 'propositions', which comprise 'the model that the anthropologist constructs in order to replicate that world view' (p. 48).
6 Apprehension of space in a rather concrete way is enabled through the instantiation of mental spatial images on material artefacts such as those we call 'maps'. Maps are not a modern invention. From Roman antiquity, we might note (1) the *Forma urbis* (see *OCD s.v.*), a plan of the city of Rome, on a scale of c. 1:240, originally mounted on a temple wall in the form of stone slabs, and (2) the Peutinger Table, essentially an itinerary (Talbert 2010) showing the roads of the Empire. Such maps are instruments for the control of space, first cognitive control, then physical control: one uses the map to 'cover the ground' (essential reading, for a cognitive perspective, is Daniel Lord Smail's *Imaginary Cartographies: Possession and Identity in Late Medieval Marseille* (1999)). Maps were but one manifestation of the Roman tradition of land

surveying and the habit of 'centuriation' (see *OCD* s. 'centuriation', '*gromatici*'), of dividing land into squares and rectangles bounded by *limits*, running east–west (*decumani*) and north–south (*cardines*). Military camps and new towns were laid out on the same principle and practice.

7 Perception of space plays a crucial role in religious rituals, since it may ascribe specific symbolic meanings and values to certain places. A peculiarly Roman institution, for instance, was the augural *templum*, a sacred space defined according to certain rituals for *watching birds* (literally 'auspicy'), listening to *bird cries* (literally 'augury'), and analyzing and interpreting what is seen and heard (i.e. in what part of the defined *templum*, flying in what direction etc.). Augury and auspicy were official business: only certain magistrates of state and pro-magistrates (e.g. governors of provinces and military commanders) could 'take the auspices', and there was at Rome a high 'college' of 'augurs', which was the repository of official augural knowledge; on the augural *templum* see Beck (1977: 9–11, 1994a, 2006a: 205).

8 Historically, humans have experienced time through the succession of day and night, and the annual cycle of the seasons. Day, put crudely, is when you see things; night is when you don't – or only with difficulty. During the seasons you see vegetable matter change its appearance in the alternation of growth and decay. You also experience alternations of heat and cold; wet and dry. The passage of time is manifestly linked to the movements of the sun and the moon in the heavens. Sunrise (whether you can actually observe it or not) brings on the day, sunset the night. In summer the sun is high in the sky at midday, in winter low; in spring it climbs day after day, and in autumn it descends. Similarly, the lunar phases indicate the passage of months. We shall examine perception of time in the Mithraic world view in Chapter 3.

And so develop the first artefacts for watching and measuring time: sundials, on which the sun's shadow creeps across the dial and thus counts out the hours of day, and up and down the meridian line from its shortest length on the day of the summer solstice to its longest on the day of the winter solstice (Beck 2006a: 126–8, esp. 127: 'The sundial is a special map for the representation of the Sun's daily and annual progress ... It converts Time into Space, or rather into Change of Place.' For Mithraists, as for other denizens of the Empire, *time was visible in and on the sundial*.

9 According to Kearney (1984: 52), 'logico-structural integration ... is concerned with the ways in which the assumptions of a world-view are interrelated and with how they in turn affect cultural behavior'.

10 For a detailed analysis of the way in which the received knowledge is cognitively organized see Barsalou et al. (2005: 14–18).

11 Not for the first time, and not for the last, we quote Porphyry's *On the Cave of the Nymphs in the Odyssey* 6, as the warrant for advancing these statements:

> Similarly, the Persians perfect their initiate by inducting him into a mystery of the descent of souls and their exit back out again, calling the place a 'cave'. For

> Eubulus tells us that Zoroaster was the first to dedicate a natural cave in honour of Mithras, the creator and father of all ... This cave bore for him the image of the cosmos which Mithras had created ...

See also *On the Cave* 24, where Mithras is called 'creator and master of genesis'. We are of course well aware that we still have to establish Porphyry's credibility for these second- and third-hand statements.

12 We examine perception of self in the Mithraic cult context more thoroughly in Chapter 2.
13 Firmicus Maternus, *On the Error of Profane Religions* 5.2 (subsequently 'Firmicus *De. Err.*'). Firmicus is of course a hostile source, a Christian propagandist, turning the Mithraists' hierarchic values against them. His main point is that the sun-worshipping Mithraists absurdly 'transmit his rites in secluded caves, and so, plunged in the obscure squalor of darkness, they ever avoid the grace of splendid and serene light'. We have here an excellent and striking illustration of a clash of world views. A positive in one system becomes a negative in another. In effect, Firmicus asks of the Mithraists: how can you possibly glorify an acknowledged cattle-thief as your god and worship him as a god of light in the darkness of a 'cave'?
14 See Gordon (1980a: 41, 44 n. 44); Cumont (1975: 202 f.). The *sophists* acclaimed is called Gerontius, and one wonders if this might not be an esoteric name alluding to the wisdom and 'seniority' of the old.
15 See note 11. The structure and design of the mithraeum will be presented in detail in Chapter 3. Again, we emphasize that the cogency of Porphyry's claims remains to be established. In imputing the design and the proto-mithraeum itself to Zoroaster, Porphyry and his sources (and in all likelihood the Mithraists themselves) are merely adhering to the Greek tradition of attributing religious foundations to alien sages of long ago (see Momigliano 1975 and Bidez and Cumont 1938). By the 'Persians', Porphyry actually intends the 'Mithraists', there being no other word for the cultists of his own day.
16 Common knowledge, then as now: see Plato, *Timaeus* 38 (esp. 38c2–6 'as a result of this plan and purpose of god for the birth of time, the sun and moon and the five planets ... came into being to define and preserve the measures of time', trans. Lee); also Beck (2006a: 79).
17 However it was that, *outside* the context of the mithraeum, initiates apprehended 'space' in hierarchies from the most local up to 'the empire' and 'the *oikoumene*'.
18 For illustrations of the Felicissimus Mithraeum see www.ostia-antica.org/regio5/9/9–1.htm.
19 See http://roger-pearse.com/mithras/images/cimrm480_Mitreo_Santa_Prisca_190.jpg.
20 For planetary sequences and their significances in Mithraism, see Beck (1988).
21 On the hierarchy and classification of referential relations between signs see Hoopes (1991). In Chapter 4 we shall discuss the hierarchical processes that associated signs

to each other in Mithraism and constructed the symbolic meanings of the scene of tauroctony.
22 As Q. P. Deeley (2004: 246) put it, 'symbols are intentional, in the philosophical sense that symbols are about something, and in the psychological sense of being used for a purpose'.
23 Several theories have been advanced to explain the origins and evolution of symbolic cognition and the transition to symbolic thought that characterizes the human species. For the major theories see Donald (1991); Mithen (1996); Deacon (1997).
24 The distinction between 'models of' and 'models for' the world is of course also Clifford Geertz's (1990: 93–4).
25 In the chapters which follow, then, we must make the most of those rare examples that survive. Important general studies of ritual, for our purposes, are Bell (1992, 1997) and Rappaport (1999). A foundational study of ritual and cognition is McCauley and Lawson (2002). See also Lawson and McCauley (1990).
26 These and other representations of cult ritual we shall consider in subsequent chapters.
27 Geertz (1990: 119) wisely observes: 'The movement back and forth between the religious perspective and common-sense perspective is actually one of the more obvious empirical occurrences on the social scene.' One may safely assume that things were no different two thousand years ago.
28 The different systems of memory and the kinds of information that are stored in each of these systems will be discussed in Chapter 3.
29 The significance of the performance of religious rituals and practices in specific places in order for a relevant experience to be engraved into the participants' memory systems (Barsalou et al. 2005: 44) seems very plausible in the case of Mithraism.
30 These are often called the 'side scenes'. The classic study of their ordering and regional variations is Gordon (1980a). On the mythic episodes and their representation on the monuments in general, see Clauss (2000: 62–90, 2012: 65–88). The banquet of Mithras and Sol is a special case. As the immediate consequence of the bull-killing – the banquet is held on the hide of the slain bull – it is sometimes privileged by representation on the back of reversible taurocstony reliefs, e.g. V1896 from Konjic in Dalmatia. The birth of Mithras from a rock could also be represented by itself in sculpture, e.g. the statue from the Santo Stefano Rotondo mithraeum in Rome (Lissi-Caronna 1986: Plate XXX). (The banquet and the rock-birth, for different reasons, will be discussed more fully in the next chapter.) A final point worth noting is that several of the scenes represented on the monuments do not seem to belong to a biography of Mithras, strictly speaking.
31 The *symbolon* is a line of hexameter verse; on the educative value of such *symbola*, see Beck (2014).
32 On paganism and the 'free rider' question see Beck (2006b).

2 The Self in the Cult of Mithras

1. At the end of the preceding chapter we touched on the question of good faith, whether one joined and continued in the cult with a sense of deep conviction or opportunistically because it was a good career move or because one's friends were members (not that the motives are mutually exclusive). Here, for the sake of the argument, we assume that motives actually make little difference in the adoption of a world view. It is experience, especially experience in ritual and in group fellowship, that matters, not motive or motivation.
2. Lakoff and M. Johnson (1999: 46, 48) briefly describe the theory suggested by C. Johnson (1997).
3. Lakoff and M. Johnson (1999: 46–7, 55–8) mentions Narayanan's (1997) neurological theory of metaphor in order to clarify the neuronal structure of metaphorical thought.
4. Fauconnier and Turner's theory of conceptual blending (1998, 2002, 2003) will be more extensively used in the next chapter, where the metaphorical perception of space in the Mithras cult is examined.
5. Lakoff and M. Johnson (1999: 60) make a brief reference to Grady's theory (1997) about processes during which primary metaphors are associated with each other to produce more complex metaphors.
6. All human actions are conducted for specific purposes. Even those actions that can be viewed as functional, with particular survival and/or reproductive effects, have vital goals that ensure survival, regardless whether the agents of these actions are aware of these goals or not. As M. Johnson (1993) points out: 'Even acts of drudgery and extreme toil that are done just to survive are performed against the background ideal of a life that is worth living, or that we hope will become worthwhile if we can survive our present struggle. Every action is thus part of the living of a life that involves misfortune, luck, happiness, suffering, and fulfilment' (p. 174).
7. For a preliminary application of Mark Johnson's theory (1993) to Mithraists' identities see Panagiotidou (2010).
8. An interesting case is the Mithraic community in the Roman garrison at Dura-Europos on the Euphrates (V34–70). The language of the graffiti and dipinti is mainly Greek, with some admixture of Latin. Among the more formal dedications, as well as those in Greek, there is one in Palmyrene (V39) and one in Latin (V53). See Cumont (1975: 194–205); Francis (1975).
9. Best and most succinctly described in Clauss (2000: 33–41, 2012: 36–47). See also Clauss (1992), a catalogue of all Mithraists known at the time of publication (especially useful is the overview of membership, pp. 261–79); Gordon (1972; 1994b); Beck (1992, 1996: 177–80). Of particular importance here is the bronze *album* or membership record of a mithraeum in Virunum, published by G. Piccottini

in 1994. The album lists not only the full membership in 183 CE but also the annual intakes up to 200 CE. It also added, at a stroke, 98 'new' Mithraists to the 997 catalogued by Clauss (1992).

10 Two communities were perhaps exceptional in this respect. (1) In the most recently discovered mithraeum at Aquincum (north of Budapest), a series of dedications were made by military tribunes of *legio II Adiutrix* (Clauss 1992: 183–4). Military tribunes (*tribuni laticlavii*) were of the senatorial class. However, in our view, it is more probable that these dedications reflect a local custom of elite patronage rather than active elite participation in the mysteries in this particular Mithraic community only (Beck 2004a: 13). (2) In Rome the inscriptions from the lost mithraeum in the Piazza S. Silvestro (V400–404) attest a community led in the second half of the fourth century by members of the highest aristocracy (Clauss 1992: 296). Their positions as cult Fathers (not to mention Fathers of Fathers!) and their activities, specifically holding various grade initiations, leave no doubt that they were practising Mithraists.

11 See also Bremmer (2014: 132) ('Everything seems to indicate that, on the whole, they were neither very high nor very low on the social scale'); Gordon (1994b – a review article of Clauss 1992).

12 On 'getting it', see what we said in our Introduction (section 3 *ad. fin.*). It is worth repeating here:

> Here we need only add that the religion manifests itself particularly in *symbols and complexes of symbols* which the initiate *apprehends* in the basic sense of *grasping*, or 'getting it', as one says. 'Apprehension', too, is a key term to be carried forward from the previous study. *Katalambanein* ('to apprehend') would be the corresponding Greek verb, covering more than just mental *com*prehension in the sense of conscious (and self-conscious) understanding.

13 The distinction between 'cognized' and 'operational environment' was first suggested by the ecological anthropologist Roy Rappaport (1967) in order to describe the difference between the cultural representations of the world shared by people of a particular cultural tradition, and the actual reality and human adaptations to the external world as they are studied by anthropologists.

14 Again, we emphasize that this knowledge was not a set body of knowledge or doctrine. See Beck (2006a: 41–239).

15 Inevitably, there was leakage. For instance, the considerable amount of esoteric Mithraic knowledge embedded in Porphyry's *On the Cave* can only have reached him and his sources ultimately from inside informants.

16 In contrast to the term *true* kinship that is used to determine groups of people who connect with each other by consanguinity or relationships by marriage, the term *fictive* kinship is used to describe other kinds of social ties that develop in various cultural contexts.

17 We shall more thoroughly examine the role of secrecy for the formation of close Mithraic communities in Chapter 5.
18 Biological factors are of course crucial for the construction of self-identity and constrain someone's freedom and desire to overcome the roles that are available in each context. See M. Johnson (1993: 161–3).
19 Distinction between sexes existed in other mystery cults, but Mithraism is the only known cult which completely excluded women (Gordon 1972: 98; Bremmer 2014: 131–2).
20 You will find no women among Clauss's almost a thousand *Cultores Mithrae* (see above, n. 9). It is this absence that renders Jonathan David's attempt (2000: 121–41) to allow some role for women back in the Mithraic mysteries unpersuasive.
21 The case was brilliantly made by Richard Gordon (1980a: 42–64). 'Nymphus', he demonstrated (pp. 48–9), was a Mithraic coinage, in which a masculine ending was appended to the Greek word for 'bride', asserting thereby a blatant paradox of male autarky.
22 For the story and its representations, see Clauss (2000: 62–71, 2012: 65–72).
23 For the significance and connotations of the *hyena* in the animal lore of the Graeco-Roman world, see Gordon (1980a: 57–61). See also Bremmer (2014: 131–2, with n. 124 for further bibliographic references).
24 As the epigraphic evidence indicates, 'many Mithraists invoke the god's protection for their families and household, and there are at least 14 cases of one or more sons being associated with their father in the cult' (Gordon 1972: 98). Note also the family relationships in the Virunum *album* (above, n. 9) postulated by Piccottini (1994): two fold-out tables between pp. 28 and 29, 'Verwandtschaft' column. Brothers figure as frequently as fathers and sons.
25 On the 'deep history' of human 'dominance hierarchies' and concomitant modes of 'submission' see Smail (2008: 164–70).
26 For the analogous process of marriage see M. Johnson (1993: 176).
27 On 'turning points' see Bruner (2003: 42–50).
28 The same note contains a summary of known Mithraic rituals of initiation.
29 The possible impact of intense rituals on the Mithraists' conception of initiation will be the theme of Chapter 5.
30 Per Beskow (1979) demonstrated that branding in the Mithraic mysteries is a scholars' myth – a very hardy and persistent myth.
31 On this testimony see Beck (2014: 248–50).
32 The volume has excellent colour plates (XXI–XXIII, XXV–XXVIII). See also Clauss (2012: Plates 10–14).
33 It is pointless to speculate which of the two initiators has seniority, still less what their precise ranks in the grade hierarchy are. See, however, Gordon's perceptive observations about the pair (2009: 295–304).

34 Vermaseren (1971: Plate XXII); Clauss (2012: Plate 11).
35 As Gordon (2009: 312, n. 19) observes, a sword (the suggested alternative) makes little sense if, as here, the initiand is blindfolded!
36 For explications see Vermaseren (1971: 24–48); Merkelbach (1984: 136–7); Clauss (2000: 102–3, 2012: 99–100).
37 We have taken the term 're-representation' from Luther Martin's important study of this monument (2009).
38 Martin's note is worth quoting: 'Emphasis on the local character of Mithraic knowledge and practice did not preclude the "emergence" of certain more widely, even universally, shared Mithraic traits and practices from among the network of autonomous Mithraic cells, even in the absence of any centralized structure or organization' (2009: 288–9).
39 Illustrated in Plates XIII and XIV between pp. 174 and 175.
40 As already noted, this is a rare instance of ritual demonstrably tracking myth as encapsulated in the 'side scenes' (see Dirven 2015: 42 f.). See also Gordon (1998: 248–52).
41 The names of the seven initiatory grades were listed by Jerome in *his Letter to Laeta* CVII.
42 The reason why no English translation is offered here will be apparent when we look at the individual grades.
43 The question of whether or not the grades constituted a *priestly* hierarchy (Clauss 1990) seems to us of minor significance. Insofar as they each had special functions, which are impossible to demonstrate *systematically*, they might be seen as such. That they constituted a priestly *caste*, over against 'lay' initiates, is surely not the case. When a priest (*sacerdos*, *antistes*) is also a grade-holder, the grade is virtually always that of Father. A dedicatory inscription from Rome (V367) furnishes an exception: one of the three dedicators, Marcellinus, is an *antistes* as well as a Lion.
44 For the individuals and their names see Clauss (1992: 238–42). In the new edition of his general study of the cult, Clauss has added a section on the community at Dura as an '*Einzelbeispiel*' (2012: 42–5). On the graffiti and the community, see also Cumont (1975: 194–205); Francis (1975: 438–45). At Dura the grade terminology was slightly different from that in the West, but the system was essentially the same.
45 V59. See Cumont (1975: 203 f.); literally, *akeraios* means 'unmixed', hence metaphorically 'uncontaminated'. Grade epithets cult-wide are conveniently tabulated in Gordon (1980a: 41, with notes 44–9). They are extremely rare outside Dura.
46 For colour plates of the frescos, see *MM*: 885–910.
47 See image at http://roger-pearse.com/mithras/images/cimrm480_Mitreo_Santa_Prisca_190.jpg.
48 But see the more accurate restoration of these texts in Vermaseren and Van Essen (1965: 155–8).

49 Nama is a (genuine) Persian form of acclamation suitable in this (make-believe) Persian cult.
50 See images of V481 at http://roger-pearse.com/mithras/display.php?page=cimrm481 and of V482 at http://roger-pearse.com/mithras/display.php?page=cimrm482.
51 For the full list of names see Clauss (1992: 28–30).
52 See image at www.ostia-antica.org/regio5/9/9-1_1.jpg.
53 We are of course speaking of the 'real world' as we generally understand it, not of the 'real world' as cutting-edge physicists might construct it (if they were to offer anything as naive as a 'real world') or of some hypothetical ultimate physical reality.
54 Anthropologists confront more or less the same problems of interpretation as do historians, although anthropologists tend to be more conscious of them, and be more explicit and sophisticated in their solutions. This is why Beck (2006a: 74–81, 119–20) took as a comparator for the Mithraic cognized environment, the cognized environment of the Chamulas of the central Chiapas highlands in Mexico, as described and analysed by anthropologist Gary Gossen (1972). We invite our readers here to revisit these passages, noting in particular how 'up/high' and 'down/low' fit on grids of superiority and inferiority (Beck 2006a: 75 referring to Gossen 1972: 119).
55 We shall follow Lakoff and M. Johnson's (1980) convention of putting metaphorical expressions in small capital letters when we wish to draw attention to the metaphorical nature of the word or phrase. This will apply, in this and the subsequent section, particularly to the opposed pairs: high/low, up/down, above/below, top/bottom.
56 Lakoff and M. Johnson (1999: 53) list 'Control Is Up' in their Table (4.1) of 'Representative Primary Metaphors'.
57 Fortunately, the question of what might lie beyond need not concern us. As we shall see, the Mithraists' universe was effectively bounded, as was the universe of most of their contemporaries, including practising astronomers and astrologers.
58 The *Somnium Scipionis*, which closed Cicero's otherwise lost dialogue *De Republica*, is preserved in Macrobius's *Saturnalia*. The quotation is from *Sat.* 4.1–3 (trans. Stahl).
59 Although it is not commonplace, the ancients occasionally used the metaphor of depth (Greek *bathos*) in speaking of relative distance from earth (cf. our term 'deep space'). On this see Beck (2006a: 246–8).

Note that to talk in terms of 'inner' and 'outer', as Cicero does, is not metaphorical at all. In ancient astronomy the planets were thought, as a matter of *fact*, to be carried round on spheres, one inside another, with the stationary earth at the centre. Outside the outermost planetary sphere or spheres (that or those of Saturn) was the sphere of the fixed stars, the universal container.
60 That some stories of miraculous treatments would have violated people's common sense understanding of the world is indicated by the reactions of some supplicants reported in the inscriptions; some of them laughed, mocked others who hoped for

unbelievable treatments (e.g. *IG* IV² 1, 121, IX), or disputed Asclepius' healing powers (e.g. *IG* II² 1, 121, IV; *IG* IV² 1, 121, III).

61 See, e.g., Schacter et al. 2004; Randolph-Seng and Nielsen 2009; A. Geertz (2010); Jensen (2010); Roepstorff et al. (2010).

62 See also Gordon (2001); Beck (2006a: 72–4). For more pedestrian surveys of the individual grades see Vermaseren (1960: 115–26); Clauss (2000: 133–8, 2012: 124–31).

63 Nowadays, rather than 'in spirit', 'in ritual and cognition' would be more apposite.

64 Excellent individual illustrations of the seven panels in Laeuchli et al. (1967: 75–81, Plates 22–7).

65 Good colour illustration in Hinnells (1975, Vol. 2, Plate 29 [c]).

66 In this last scene there is also a lion-headed attendant. The paradox of the Lion as server rather than participant can be resolved if one bears in mind that the banquet represented is that of the gods themselves, not of the initiates in mimesis. On whether the initiates are actually represented wearing masks see Gordon (1980a: 69, n. 1).

67 'The raven was not just any old bird in the kept knowledge of antiquity' (Gordon 1980a: 26). Gordon explains what he intends by 'the kept knowledge of antiquity' (a body of knowledge that he also terms 'the encyclopaedia') in note 8 of the same article (p. 72). The same compliment ('not just any old bird') has been paid the raven by modern ethology. We recommend Bernd Heinrich's *Mind of the Raven* (1999). Ethology, be it noted, is the *scientific* continuation of the animal portion of the old 'encyclopedia', with some old myths dropped and some new truths added, including *cognitive* ones. The raven, we now know, is a highly intelligent bird.

68 Gordon (1980a: 26), quoting Pliny the Elder, *Natural History* 10.33. See also the charming story (Gordon 1980a: 26) about the raven who greeted the Emperor Tiberius in the Forum every day.

69 In the myth of catasterism (see Gordon 1980a: 27) the raven delays in bringing Apollo the water he requested for a sacrifice – and then lies about it. The Felicissimus cup symbol probably alludes to this story.

70 Note that 'rising' (*anatolê*) and 'setting' (*dysis*) are literal, not metaphorical, expressions when applied to the celestial bodies. Hence no 'small caps' in our text here!

71 Your best bet would be an amateur astronomer or 'star-gazer', one whose cognized environment would include the 'appearances' (to use the ancient term), i.e. the apparent sphere of the fixed stars, its daily rotation, and the seemingly erratic but nevertheless predictable revolutions of the seven 'planets' against that background. (These days that cognized environment is instantiated in an 'app': your question could be answered by anyone pointing a mobile phone so endowed at the celestial body indicated.)

72 As interpreted by Gordon (1980a: 50), following Vermaseren (1960: 118 f. (French original – Gordon cites the English translation)).

73 A Nymphus is represented in the procession of the grades in the Santa Prisca Mithraeum (V480.5). In the upper layer of the fresco his face is covered by a

flammeum, the flame-coloured bridal veil; in the lower layer he holds one in his hands (Vermaseren and Van Essen 1965: 157, 169). There may also be the representation of a Nymphus at the Pareti Dipinte ('Painted Walls') Mithraeum in Ostia: V268.5a ('standing person in short yellow tunic with red bands. In his hands he holds a red cloth (*flammeum*)'). Note also (above, section 2.2.1) Merkelbach's suggestion that the muscular 'Psyche' led by 'Cupid' in the Capua relief (V186) actually represents an initiand into the Nymphus grade.

74 On the consensus see Chalupa and Glomb (2013: 14, n. 16). Merkelbach (1984: 95, 295) proposed a Phrygian cap as part of his idiosyncratic grade identifications (see above).

75 See also the companion articles in this issue of *Religio*: Frackowiak (2013); Gordon (2013); Martin (2013); Panagiotidou (2013).

76 In *De Corona Militis* Tertullian writes in defence of a Christian soldier who, during the distribution ceremony of imperial bounty to troops, refused to wear the customary crown. Tertullian brings in the example of the soldier of Mithras who also refused to wear the crown.

77 Since 1990, new Fathers have been recovered, e.g. Atticius Tacitus and Annius Calocaerus at Virunum (Piccottini 1994), but not, to the best of our knowledge, new Lions.

78 The translation 'Leo' was perhaps unfortunate. In the original Greek, and of course without distinction between upper and lower case, becoming a 'lion' is ambiguous: one takes on the imagined nature of the creature by assuming the grade.

79 Christianity took the watery route in ritual and soteriological metaphor, reserving the fiery route for the elimination of the pollution of heretics from the body of the Church. The liquid medium of blood has also played its metaphorical part (cf. 'washed in the blood of the Lamb').

80 On honey see Gordon (1980a: 78–9, n. 37).

81 On incense and its associations with extreme heat and the sun see Gordon (1980a: 36 f). See also Detienne (1977: 5–35).

82 On these topics see Gordon (1972: 99 f.; 1980a: 36 f.); Beck (2000: 146, n. 10). A puzzling text from Dura speaks of 'fiery breath, which is for Magi too the baptism / lustration of holy (men)' (trans. Gordon). Although it references 'magi' rather than Lions, the thinking about fire and its sacred functions is close to the testimonies we have been examining. See, again, Gordon (1980a: 36).

83 Lionesses in the 'encyclopaedia' were the males' polar opposites: lustful and promiscuous, which, given the males' general distaste for sex, meant for the females' intercourse with other species of felines (Gordon 1980a: 46 f.).

84 Even today the story of Androcles and the Lion remains a favourite.

85 See, for example, the character to be expected in one born under Leo according to the astrologer Manilius (*Astronomica* 4.176–9, trans. Goold): 'Who can doubt the nature of the monstrous Lion, and the pursuits he prescribes for those born beneath

his sign? The lion ever devises fresh fights and fresh warfare on animals, and lives on spoil and pillaging of flocks.' *Not* a role model for a Mithraic Lion!
86 Contra Gordon (1972: 116, n. 42).
87 Identified as such by Richard Gordon (1980a: 87, n. 88).
88 For other views on the identities of the rod-bearers see Beck (2000:155 f). Not coincidentally, the pair evoke lictors escorting a magistrate.
89 The way in which the initiates perceived the mithraeum as 'an image of the universe' will be investigated in detail in Chapter 3.
90 An imitation of the sun's journey would be consistent with the techniques of ritual behaviour, which often use bodily movements to record rituals and retain them in the participants' memories (Barsalou et al. 2005: 44–6).
91 Gordon (1980a: 65–7), rightly in our estimation, accepts the reading of Porphyry's *On Abstinence* 4.16, which maintains that it is the Fathers who 'are addressed as eagles and hawks'. Eagles in the 'encyclopaedia', Gordon shows, had the ability to stare at the sun unblinkingly, and it was by this token that they recognized their true-born chicks. The eagle's gaze is a wonderful metaphor for the *insight* of the legitimate leaders of a solar cult.
92 The fundamental study of the gods' banquet/cult meal was made, long ago now, by J. P. Kane (1975). Kane's study is comparative in that it covers cult meals in other associations in the classical world. See also Clauss (2000: 108–13, 2012: 104–9) (good illustrations in both editions).
93 See the image at www.tertullian.org/rpearse/mithras/images/cimrm1896b.jpg
94 Turcan (1999: 256) is surely right in recognizing only these two as grade-holders.
95 See images at http://roger-pearse.com/mithras/display.php?page=cimrm483.
96 Most notably those at Tienen in Belgium, on which see Martens (2004: 43–5). See also Olive (2004); De Grossi Mazzorin (2004).
97 In Gordon's translation from Clauss's first edition (2000: 113): 'The god himself is the host.'
98 In V1137 the feast is held on the dead but unbutchered bull itself.
99 In the next chapter, where we examine the Mithraic construction of space and time, we shall see how passage to and fro through celestial space was both envisioned and imparted to the initiates in a 'mystery'.

3 Space and Time in the Mithras Cult

1 Following Lakoff and M. Johnson's theory of metaphors (1980: 117–18), we use the term 'natural' instead of 'literal' since a great part of human natural experiences – including bodily and mental states, social interactions and interactions with physical surroundings – is metaphorically conceptualized. Later in this chapter, we will show

how perception of time is inherently metaphorical because of the mind's inability to process cognitively the literal concept of time.

2 For a preliminary examination of the perception of space and time in the Mithraic mysteries, see Panagiotidou (2012a). See also above, Chapter 1, section 1.2 on the Mithraists' world view.

3 It is a recent misunderstanding that Merleau-Ponty gave a prevalent position to the human body over mind (see Raja and Rüpke 2015: 14). His materialistic approach mainly challenged previous idealistic and intellectualistic explanations of the world which were based on the Cartesian ontological dualism between body and mind (see Tilley 2004: 2; Noland 2009: 55). Merleau-Ponty disputed this dichotomy and highlighted the mediation of the body and bodily gestures in the perception of the external world, the navigation in natural and cultural surroundings, and the creation and acquisition of cultural meanings (see Noland 2009: 55–6, 86).

4 The term 'limbic system' is conventionally used, since a precise and concrete unit in the brain which mediates emotions has not been determined. Some researchers alternatively use the term the 'emotional brain', while Brodal (2010: 417) selects the term 'limbic structures'. On the criticism of the term see, e.g., Nieuwenhuys et al. (2008: 941); Brodal (2010: 417). On the neuroanatomy of the so-called limbic system see, e.g., Augustine (2008: 313–26).

5 Extensive research is being conducted on the brain structures, producing a large amount of bibliographical references. For that reason only a very limited number of references are given here. On the prefrontal cortex see E. Miller (1999); E. Miller and Cohen (2001); E. Miller et al. (2002); Alvarez and Emory (2006); Badre et al. (2010). On the role of the anterior cingulate cortex in the online emotional and cognitive processing and integration of the external stimuli see Bush et al. (2000); Allman et al. (2001); Bush et al. (2002); Luu and Pederson (2004).

6 Some researchers have disputed the term 'autonomic' since there is no clear distinction between autonomic and somatic parts of the human nervous system. However, Brodal (2010: 369) suggests the conventional use of the term 'autonomic nervous system', which he defines as '*the neuronal groups and fiber connections that control the activity of visceral organs, vessels and glands* (also the vessels and glands that are not parts of visceral organs)' (emphasis in the original).

7 *The New Shorter Oxford English Dictionary* defines homeostasis as 'maintenance of a dynamically stable state within a system by means of internal regulatory processes that counteract external disturbances of the equilibrium' (cited by Brodal 2010: 370). In addition to the operation of the autonomic nervous system, homeostasis is achieved through the regulation of the visceral, endocrine and somato-motor functions coordinated by hypothalamus (see, e.g., Nieuwenhuys et al. 2008: 293–8; Brodal 2010: 369–70; cf. Swanson and Mogenson 1981). For more details on the autonomic nervous systems see, e.g., Appenzeller and Oribe 1997 [1970]; Jänig 2006.

8 The distinction between 'interoception' and 'exteroception' was first suggested by the Nobel laureate neurophysiologist Charles Scott Sherrington in 1906.
9 Sherrington also introduced the term 'proprioception' in order to determine the human awareness of their bodies and their positions and movements in space. Although he made a clear distinction between interoceptors, exteroceptors and proprioceptors, which enable humans to perceive their internal bodily milieu, the external stimuli and their own bodies respectively, today proprioception is considered to be part of our exteroceptive system (see Evans 2010: 28–9; Henshaw 2012: 179–83; Dolins and Mitchell 2014: 23–4)
10 For example, Pöppel (1997: 59) estimates that information in short-term memory is retained for three seconds, while more recently Revlin (2012) suggests that short-term memory keeps information for eighteen seconds. However, the decay of information in short-term memory may be mediated by time while other parameters (e.g. rehearsal, chunking, focus of attention) may be involved (e.g. Broadbent 1958; Cowan 2001, 2008). Some researchers dispute the very impact of time on the information retainment in the short-term memory (see, e.g., Nairne 2002; Lewandowsky et al. 2004; Jonides et al. 2008).
11 On techniques of rehearsal that expand the time limits of short-term memory see, e.g., Baddeley et al. (1975); Guttentag (1984).
12 On how chunking may expand the content constraints in short-term memory see, e.g., A. Miller (1956); Tulving and Patkau (1962); Cowan et al. (2004); Chen and Cowan (2005).
13 That is not to say that the spatial cognitive mappings are purely subjective representations of the world. Although spatial perception does not seem to correspond to an objective Euclidian space, perceptual systems developed during the evolution of the human species in order to provide more or less accurate representations of the material reality (Dolins and Mitchell 2014: 4). In this view, it is the human perceptual abilities that mostly represent space and the external world in a three-dimensional Euclidian manner (see, e.g., O'Keefe and Nadel 1978: 11; Evans 2010: 40; cf. Fernandez and Farell 2009).
14 For more on the binocular and stereoscopic vision see, e.g., Howard and Rogers (1995); Anderson (2003); Menz and Freeman (2003); Alais and Blake (2005); Hayhoe et al. (2009); Blake and Wilson (2011).
15 We have briefly referred to the processes of perception and primary organization of the perceptual information in schemas and frames in Chapter 1.
16 We have also briefly used some elementary spatial schemas – like the universal container – and concepts – like DOWN/UP, HIGHER/LOWER, ABOVE/BELOW – in Chapter 2, when we examined the metaphorical perception of grade hierarchy as an ascent in space. Here we provide insights into those perceptual and cognitive processes that give rise to and gradually form spatial percepts, image-schemas,

concepts, primary metaphors and complex metaphorical mappings that structure and organize human perception of space. As in the previous chapter, we put metaphorical expressions in small capital letters in order to underline the metaphorical meaning of the word or phrase.

17 In the previous chapter, we have seen how the SOURCE–PATH–GOAL schema provides the ground for complex metaphorical mappings that could have structured the initiates' lived experience and conceptualization of the initiation in the Mithraic mysteries.

18 Although other sensory modalities, including proprioception (see, e.g., Yamamoto and Shelton 2005) and audition (see, e.g., Loomis et al. 2002), participate in the perception of space, vision appears to play a prevalent role in spatial perception, orientation and navigation (Mou et al. 2004: 35; see also Hrotic 2009: 120–4).

19 According to Hermer and Spelke (1994) and Wang and Spelke (2000), the locations and spatial relations between objects are not included in the allocentric cognitive maps, which mainly represent more general geometric scenes and geographical landscapes, which are available offline for orientation and navigation (geocentric representations). These findings have been questioned by Mou et al. (2004), who argue that 'an allocentric system must contain enduring representations of spatial relations among objects' (p. 38). For the research on the updating process of the allocentric spatial maps see, e.g., Mou et al. (2004); Holmes and Sholl (2005); Burgess (2006); Waller and Hodgson (2006); Xiao et al. (2009).

20 Mou et al. (2004) suggested that the egocentric system allows humans 'to avoid obstacles, walk through doorways, stay on the sidewalk, and so on, but it does not prevent the observer from getting lost' (154). However, Waller and Hodgson's (2006) experiments showed that the same system helps people to keep themselves 'oriented to specific objects in their immediate environment (i.e. not lost)' (880).

21 The distinction between the front and behind parts of three-dimensional objects presupposes that there are observable differences between their sides that correspond to the image-schemas of the 'front' and 'behind'. Thus, for example, the front side of a building is conventionally considered to be the side where its entrance is located and so on.

22 Such complex metaphorical mappings, which seem to apply in the case of Mithraists, may vary in different religious systems of beliefs and cosmologies entailing multiple cultural and ethical values in different contexts (Lakoff and M. Johnson 1980: 14–19; Tilley 2004: 6).

23 In the Mithraic mysteries, the fight between Mithras signifying the sun, and Taurus, pointing to the moon, metaphorically indicates the battle between light and darkness.

24 The duration of the transmission of sensory information is further dependent on the distance between the perceiver and the unfolding event, since visual stimuli travel faster in space than sound (see Pöppel 1997: 57).

25 On the long debate regarding the experiential relationship and neuro-biological connection between semantic and episodic memory see Yee et al. (2013: 353) citing Tulving (1972: 389) and Squire and Zola (1998).
26 Mithraea built wholly or partly in natural caves are: the Duino Mithraeum (NE Italy, Gordon 1976b, photograph VSuppl), V653 (Sutri Mithraeum, close to Rome), V2256 (Kreta in Moesia Inferior), V2303 (Tigusor, also in Moesia Inf.); the recently discovered mithraeum in Hawarti in Syria (Gawlikowski 1999, VSuppl); the remarkable twin mithraea in Doliche, Commagene (Schütte-Maischatz and Winter 2000, VSuppl), also a recent discovery.
27 Examples of this type of mithraeum are V1851 and 1852 (Arupium, Dalmatia) on which see Beck 1984b, and V895/6 (the Bourg St. Andéol Mithraeum in the Rhône Valley; see Walters 1974: 70–3).
28 The mithraeum found in a vaulted cellar in Caesarea Maritima in modern Israel was originally used for grain storage (Bull 1978: 75; photograph VSuppl). Constructed in rooms of this sort and thus potentially evoking 'caves' are the mithraeum in Santa Maria Capua Vetere (V180, Vermaseren 1971) and the Marino mithraeum (Vermaseren 1982), the San Clemente (V338), Barberini (V389), Thermae Antoninianae (V457), and Santa Prisca (V476) mithraea in Rome, and the mithraeum of the Baths of Mithras (Mitreo delle Terme del Mitra) (V229) and Mitreo di Fructosus (V226) in Ostia. On mithraea of this type see Beck (2006a: 105).
29 Based on topographical evidence, Coarelli (1979: 77) estimates that there were 680–90 mithraea just within the Aurelian walls of Rome. On further estimations of the number of mithraea as well as of the number of Mithraists see Martin (2015: 10–1; cf. Bjørnebye 2015).
30 Of course, Porphyry is not to be believed concerning Zoroaster's institution of the archetypal mithraeum in a cave 'in the mountains near Persia'. In our view, however, he is certainly to be believed concerning the design of actual mithraea, since what he says is confirmed by the archaeological evidence.
31 We introduced 'conceptual metaphors' in the preceding chapter (section 2.3.2 ff.). The essential modern works are Lakoff and M. Johnson (1980), M. Johnson (1993), and Lakoff and M. Johnson (1999).
32 The celestial climates were projections to the universal sphere of the terrestrial zones of latitude; see Beck (2016, forthcoming).
33 We have already referred to the perception of the universe as a container as it is described by Cicero in the 'Dream of Scipio'; see section 2.3.2.
34 The term 'celestial elements' was meant to signify both the fixed stars and the wandering planets, in other words all the celestial bodies which extended above the earth inside the universal CONTAINER.
35 'Wherefore, as a consequence of this reasoning and design on the part of God, with a view to the generation of Time, the sun and moon and five other stars, which bear

the appellation of "planets", came into existence for the determining and preserving of the numbers of Time' (trans. Lamb).

36 The Ptolemaic system echoes the cosmology of Plato (*Timaeus* 38c3–6) according to which the celestial bodies instantiate 'time in the cosmos', blending time and space on the heavens.

37 The 'sidereal month' defined by the orbit of the moon is 27.32 days. The 'synodic month' determined by a 'new moon' to the next 'new moon' lasts 29.53 days (Beck 2006a: 77).

38 A full rotation of the sun around the earth, starting from the spring equinox, determines the so-called solar or tropical year which, according to Hipparchus, cited by Ptolemy (*Almagest* 3.1), lasts 365 and ¼ days.

39 Plato, *Timaeus* 39d2 (trans. Lamb): 'Nevertheless, it is still quite possible to perceive that the complete number of Time fulfils the Complete Year when all the eight circuits, with their relative speeds, finish together and come to a head, when measured by the revolution of the Same and Similarly-moving.'

40 According to Franz Cumont (1960 [1912]: 32, 51–2), the Ptolemaic cosmology influenced and re-modulated the popular astrological systems, which in turn updated most of the religious cosmological models and notions from the beginning of the Roman Imperial era onwards (see Barton 1994; Beck 2007; Martin 2015a: 82).

41 For more on the architectural constructions of the Graeco-Roman world which replicated the image of the universe see Beck (2006a: 120–3).

42 Fauconnier and Turner (1998, 2002, 2003) suggest that four major cognitive processes, those of composition, completion, elaboration and compression, mediate the construction and perception of blended mental spaces.

43 Even in the exceptional cases in which mithraea were established in free-standing structures, no attention was paid to their external surfaces; Beck (2016, forthcoming).

44 Within the Mithraic cave, along with the loss of any external frame of spatial orientation, initiates would have lost any sense of time, since the motion of the sun was not observable and daylight could not reach inside.

45 For an answer to the question why the Mithraists chose to establish their cult places in vaulted rectangular halls instead of domed rooms see Beck (2016).

46 Porphyry, *De Antro Nympharum* 22, 7–9: 'since the southern pole is as yet invisible to us, Capricorn has been assigned to Saturn, the most remote and highest of the planets.'

47 According to Porphyry's testimony, the dagger held by Mithras is the zodiac sign of Aries, which, according to the basic principles of astrology, is the house of Ares and the point of the spring equinox. On the other hand, Taurus is the astrological house of Venus, which is the second house of Libra, where the winter equinox occurs. Thus, Mithras bears the symbols of the equatorial zone, and is placed exactly on the axis of

the equinoxes (Beck 1976a: 95–8, 1994a: 106, 1994b: 39–41, 2000: 160, 2006a: 103–15).

48 The 'equinoctial colure' is defined as 'the great circle of the celestial sphere which passes through both poles and both equinoxes', and 'bisects the universe' as the plane of any great circle (Beck 2006a: 108, 111).

49 Two niches facing each other in the middle of the benches along the long walls have been found in most of the excavated mithraea (Gordon 1988: 57). In some cases, there were further material objects or representations that were displayed in connection with the niches. For example, in the Sette Porte mithraeum in Ostia the niches bore two small altars with no inscriptions. In the right niche of the mithraeum of the Palazzo dell'Arte in Rome, fragments of a vessel entwined by a snake were found by the archaeologists, while the image of a crater was depicted in the space between the niches, a representation similar to that found in the mithraeum in Dura-Europos (Gordon 1976a: 132–3).

50 For more images see www.tertullian.org/rpearse/mithras/display.php?page=supp_Italy_Vulci_Mithraeum.

51 Cumont (1896: 243–5) and Becatti (1954: 47–51) have provided thorough descriptions of the mithraeum of Sette Sfere. However, according to Gordon (1976a: 146–7), these descriptions include some false interpretations of the symbols represented in the sanctuary. For more images see www.ostia-antica.org/regio2/8/8-6.htm.

52 The signs of zodiac carried on the benches were divided into four quadrants, each of which determined a season: Aries, Taurus and Gemini determined the spring, Cancer, Leo and Virgo indicated the summer, Libra, Scorpio and Sagittarius determined the autumn, and Capricorn, Aquarius and Pisces defined the winter (Gordon 1976a: 126; Beck 2006a: 209).

53 On the representations in the scene of the tauroctony of the different motions that the sun and the moon seemingly followed defining different intervals of time see Beck (1994b: 42).

54 In Chapter 2 we discussed the representation of a Mithraic initiation on one side of the Mainz vessel.

55 The first figure, which is depicted as clad in a breastplate, has been identified with a Soldier. Horn (1994: 28–30) and Merkelbach (1995: 1–6) have matched the second figure, which is represented as wearing a Phrygian cap and holding a rod turned downwards with a member of the grade of Perses. The third figure is depicted as shaking a whip which, as mentioned before, is also represented on the mosaic floor of the Felicissimus mithraeum and is considered to be a symbol of the grade of Heliodromus. Apart of the whip, both Horn and Merkelbach have interpreted a spike protruding from the figure's head as a rayed solar bonnet, which would also be consonant with the grade of a Sun-Runner (Beck 2000: 154–5). Where the two

scholars disagree is their interpretation of the fourth figure, which resembles in appearance the second one but is depicted bareheaded holding a rod turned upwards. Horn (1994: 24, 29) has matched this figure with a member of the grade of Nymphus, while Merkelbach (1995: 6) has identified it with that of Raven.

56 In the Sette Porte mithraeum, there is a representation of seven gates along the short wall between the benches in front of the entrance, which has been interpreted as representing the gates to seven planetary spheres from which the initiates' souls pass during their celestial journey (for images see www.ostia-antica.org/regio4/5/5-13.htm).

57 Similar mosaic depictions of the planets have been found in the Sette Porte mithraeum, although the order of the representations is not identical with that in the Sette Sfere mithraeum. Here, the images of Mars and Luna are depicted on the vertical side of the right bench, while the images of Venus and Mercury are represented on the left bench. The remaining images of Jupiter and Saturn are depicted on the floor towards the scene of the tauroctony.

Sun
(= Mithras in the Tauroctony)
Saturn
Jupiter

Mercury	Moon
Venus	Mars

58 Such interpretation of the order of the images of the planets on the benches in the Sette Sfere mithraeum does not exclude alternative interpretations suggested by scholars in the past. Gordon (1976a), for instance, has associated the order of the planets in the Sette Sfere mithraeum with that found in the Sette Porte mithraeum and has argued that such configuration represents the actual positions of the planets in heaven the night of the creation. Beck (1979, 1988: 13–14) questioned the astrological value of Gordon's interpretation. He also associated the representations of the planets in the aforementioned mithraea, but suggested that the planetary orders in both cases instantiate an actual celestial event, the positions of the planets on the celestial firmament during the spring equinox of 172 and 173 CE.

59 In some mithraea Cautes and Cautopates are displayed to hold rods instead of torches. On a monument found in the lower Danube, images of birds have replaced the torches. In all cases, however, these images are used to convey the same metaphorical meanings (Beck 2000: 157); on Cautes and Cautopates see Hinnells (1976); Beck (1977, 2006a, 209–12, forthcoming).

60 The symbolic meanings of the torchbearers within the scene of the tauroctony are examined in the next chapter. Here we mainly refer to the symbolization of the two figures as elements of the symbolic structure of the mithraeum.

4 The Scene of the Tauroctony as a Symbol System

1. Compare Dio Chrysostom's explication, in *Oration* 12, of the meanings conveyed by Phidias's statue of Olympian Zeus (Beck 2010).
2. On representations, private and public, see above, Introduction, sections 2 and 4; also Beck (2006a: 9–10). 'Public' representations are perceptible objects out there in the world and thus accessible to more than a single person. The term does not mean 'open to the public' in the normal modern sense. In that sense, of course, the tauroctony was not 'public'.
3. For a preliminary examination of the hierarchical interpretation of the tauroctony as a system of signs see Panagiotidou (2012b).
4. Cf. Sperber's definition (1996: 61): 'A representation involves a relationship between three terms: an object is a representation of something, for some information-processing device.'
5. Peirce repeatedly attempted to define the *sign* and the *interpretant* throughout his work (see, e.g., '76 Definitions of the sign by C. S. Peirce' collected and analysed by Robert Marty with an Appendix of twelve further definitions or equivalents proposed by Alfred Lang, published online at http://web.archive.org/web/20010127005900/http://www.univ-perp.fr/see/rch/lts/marty/access.htm). Among his many attempts, the following definition emphasizes the communicative role of the sign:

    > By a sign I mean anything whatever, real or fictive, which is capable of a sensible form, is applicable to something other than itself, that is already known, and that is capable of being so interpreted in another sign which I call its interpretant as to communicate something that may not have been previously known about its Object. There is thus a triadic relation between any Sign, an Object, and an Interpretant.
    >
    > MS 654, 7

6. Peirce used the abstract terms 'Firstness', 'Secondness' and 'Thirdness' in order to categorize the signs in terms of the process of interpretation (*CP* 1.369–72, 376–8, 532, 2.84–9, 3.422, 5.469, 8.328, 8.330).
7. Although Peirce mainly used instances of linguistic signs in order to exemplify his theoretical considerations, he believed that thought is the archetypical semiotic process, which is not necessarily linguistic but cannot unfold without signs (see, e.g., Hoopes 1991: 252; Deacon 2014: 97).
8. We have briefly referred to the figure–ground organization of the visual perceptual system, which enables humans to discern objects from the background, in Chapter 3; see, e.g., Rubin 1915, 1958; Grossberg 1994; Pind 2012; Wagemans et al. 2012.

9 As in previous chapters, small capital letters are used in order to emphasize the metaphorical nature of a word that conceptualizes pre-conceptual image-schemas, or metaphorical phrases.
10 Similarly to three-dimensional representations, the two-dimensional paintings of the tauroctony would have given rise to three-dimensional percepts extracted from perceiving and mentally representing the scene (see Evans 2010: 32).
11 Although the ancient non-initiates, unlike modern tourists and museum-goers, never did get to see a tauroctony, we can assume that they shared the same perceptual abilities and conceptual resources with the initiates that would enable them to perceive the scene of the tauroctony as a composition of icons, if they would have the opportunity to encounter the scene.
12 The icons of a lion as well as of a cup are represented in numerous tauroctonies from the Rhine and Danube provinces. In this context the lion and cup icons appear to constitute a triad with the snake icon.
13 These object icons, it is important to note, are not free-floating in the composition. In this respect they differ from the object icons on contemporary magical gems and seals. In the tauroctony a torch icon, for example, is almost always shown attached naturalistically to the hand of a person icon, whereas on magical gems, free-floating torch icons are commonplace.
14 See, e.g., V1292 (Osterburken) and V810 (London).
15 There has been a debate among scholars about whether Mithras killed the bull after hunting or as part of a ritual sacrifice. Here we follow Cumont (1899, 185–186), who referred to the scene using the more neutral term 'killing the bull' without further implying whether Mithras hunted or sacrificed the animal. On the interpretation of the tauroctony as a sacrificial scene that violated the typical pattern and traditional rules of the sacrificial practices employed during the Graeco-Roman period see Turcan (1981: 341–73); Gordon (1988: 66–9); and Martin (2004b: 196–7).
16 The astral symbolism of the tauroctony was first noted by K. B. Stark (1869). Cumont (1899: 202) disputed the interpretation of the Mithraic mysteries in astrological and astronomical terms, arguing that whatever was the astronomical symbolism embedded in the cult was a later and superficial addition, which occurred during the integration of the Iranian cult into the Roman world.
17 Described in detail in Beck (1994b: 31f., with Figs 1–3). See also Beck (2006a: 194–7, with Figs 5–7).
18 On the perceptual visual mechanisms that enable humans to group signs discerned in the visual field into coherent figures see the Gestalt Grouping Principles in Evans (2010: 33–6).
19 Referring to Porphyry, *On the Cave* 18, the moon was also known as a bull and Taurus was the constellation of the moon's 'exaltation'. Each planet has a sign of the

zodiac at which it is more powerful, that is the point of its 'exaltation', and respectively as a sign of the zodiac at which it is weaker, that is the sign of its 'humiliation'; see further Beck (1994b: 175, 2006a: 198).

20 For instance, in the tauroctony found at a mithraeum in Bologna (V694), the head of a bull is represented close to Cautes's leg, while some plants grow to his left side (Gordon 1976a: 123).

21 In some mithraea, the icon of a crater was represented in other places independent of the tauroctony. For instance, in the mithraeum S. Stephano Rotondo/Castra Peregrinorum in Rome (VSuppl.), the image of a white crater was painted to the east of the entrance. In the Felicissimus mithraeum, a crater was represented in mosaic in the middle of the space between the entrance and the cult niche, while in the Sette Porte mithrauem, a mosaic representation of a crater is located in front of the cult niche (see Gordon 1976a: 120–3, 1988: 58).

22 For a brief presentation of these associations see Beck (1994b: 269).

23 As Deacon (1997: 93) remarks, 'the process of discovering the new symbolic association is a reconstructing event, in which the previous learned associations are suddenly seen in a new light and must be reorganized with respect to one another'.

24 For a criticism to the approach of Ulansey see Beck (1994b: 36–40, 2004: 237–8).

25 The 'precession of the equinoxes' was observed and determined by the astronomer Hipparchus in the second century BCE. Today it is known that the precession is due to an unstable motion of the rotational axis of the Earth as it is manifested by an apparently very slow (one degree every 70 years) change of the position of the celestial poles and equinoxes (Beck 2004: 237–8).

26 The constellations that rise and set along with the zodiacal constellations and are placed to the north and to the south of the ecliptic were determined as 'paranatellonta'. The observation of the 'paranatellonta' contributed to the measurement and calculation of the time of the rising and setting of the zodiac constellations when the latter were not visible in the sky (see Beck 2004: 270, 2006a: 263; and also Gordon 1988: 59).

27 Ulansey (1989: 114) refers to the testimony of Philo of Alexandria (c. 30 BCE–45 CE) who attributed the mythological association of the Dioskouri with the celestial hemispheres to the mythmakers of past times. For more on the association between Dioskouri and the torchbearers see Ulansey (1989: 112–16).

28 The constellation of Leo was the astral house of the sun from which the latter passed during the warmest period of the year. Aelian Claudius, *De Natura Animalium* 12. 7. 21–3: 'and because of its excessively fiery nature, they say that it is the "domicile" of the sun; and when the sun is at its hottest in the height of summer, they say it is approaching the Lion' (trans. Gordon 1980a: 34). For more on the association of Mithras with the Sun in Leo see Beck (2004: 274–91, 2006a: 215).

29 This spatial relation between the Crater, the Hydra, and the Corvus is symbolized on the mosaic representation of a crater with a raven and a snake at its sides on the floor of the Sette Sfere mithraeum (Gordon 1988: 59).
30 These symbolic connotations comprise conceptual patterns common to the Graeco-Roman culture; see Porphyry, *On the Cave* 18 24; Julian, *Orationes* 5.172; Plutarch, *De facie*; *De genio Socratis* 943 ff.; see Beck (2004: 289).
31 The points of conjunctions or oppositions between the sun and the moon are determined as their syzygies, each of which happens once each month (Beck 2004: 290).
32 The exquisite stucco ceiling at the Ponza mithraeum seems to confirm such mapping by commemorating a real solar eclipse which took place on 14 August in 212 CE (Beck 2004: 290; see further Beck 1976b).
33 Beck (2004: 290-1) has suggested that the conception of the tauroctony as a representation of an *action* – the souls' journey of genesis and apogenesis – that takes place in *space* and *time* reveals its *relevance* to the Mithras cult and its internal *purpose*.
34 This is the main shortcoming of the recent approach suggested by Lucinda Dirven (2015) according to which, although we cannot assume the existence of a uniform myth of Mithras known to all the Mithraic communities, the iconographic and monumental evidence would have visualized mythological narratives that would have been re-enacted during the rituals. In order to describe a visual representation or an action we develop narratives that are governed by an inherent temporal structure (our first thought or oral expression leads to the next one, which in turn prepares the next one and so one, developing and unfolding our conscious thinking or verbal communication; cf. CP 5.284; Ponzio 2014: 446). Consequently, arguing that the Mithraists developed different versions of mythical sagas, which they represented on material artefacts, and that these stories would have been conceived and re-enacted by the initiates as visualization of mythical events limits the interpretation on the recognition of iconic similarities between the represented signs and the signified events. Such iconic interpretations would have probably taken place in the mithraea and would have provided the ground for further indexical associations and symbolic meanings invested on the monumental and visual imagery of the cult.

5 The Communities of Mithraists

1 For a brief review of the major conceptions, theories and approaches to social cohesion see Bruhn (2009: 31–48).
2 See Bruhn (2009: 47), citing Carron and Spink (1995: 86–7): 'It could be argued that the terms cohesion and group are tautological; if a group exists, it must be cohesive

to some degree. Thus it is probably no surprise that even in collectives where minimal group characteristics are present, manifestations of cohesion are evident.'
3 The modern world religions display the features of the doctrinal mode of religiosity to a great degree. However, many traditional societies have developed and perform routinized rituals of low arousal (see, e.g., Atkinson and Whitehouse 2011).
4 Beliefs and attitudes adopted and displayed by authoritative and prestigious individuals tend to attract people's attention and to enhance their willingness to commit to the same social norms; see, e.g., Henrich and Gil-White (2001).
5 Durkheim (1997 [1893]; 1995 [1912]) determined 'organic solidarity' as this kind of cohesion, which develops among members of mostly large societies in which division of labour entails that each participant is not perceived as equivalent with the others but possesses a specialized position and role in the group (1997: 68–87). He contrasted 'organic' with 'mechanical solidarity' (pp. 31–67), which mainly emerges in small-scale communities comprising members of equivalent status and operation. Whitehouse and Lanman (2014) explore the underlying psychological processes that mediate the Durkheimian modes of solidarity and, as they argue, are better expressed by the terms 'group identification' and 'identity fusion'.
6 On the coalitional psychology that promotes compliance with social norms of large, anonymous communities see Henrich and Henrich (2007); Kurzban and Neuberg (2005).
7 As Whitehouse and Lanman (2014: 691) admit, they refer to the dysphoric rituals because they have more evidence on those, but they do not exclude that euphoric rituals can have similar effects (cf. Atkinson and Whitehouse 2011).
8 As we have seen in the previous chapter, many scholars focused on the visual imagery of the Mithras cult and especially on the scene of the tauroctony, and suggested different interpretations of its symbolic meanings.
9 Clauss (2000: 17): 'The [Mithras] cult is an example of the primacy of images in the ancient world, in ancient thought, and of the power of the symbolic, of life lived beneath the suzerainty of symbols.'
10 Clauss (2000: 12): 'But in ancient religion images, or rather the ways in which people perceived images, were based upon a quite different psychology. They were apprehended directly, rather as a dream operates with images. In all likelihood, such images did not need to be explained conceptually ...'
11 The majority of mithraea could not accommodate more than twenty to twenty-five persons.
12 As Whitehouse (2008: 110) aptly pointed out, 'It is almost as if a camera has gone off in one's head, illuminating the scene, and preserving it forever in memory.'
13 See the research of Xygalatas et al. (2013) and Schjoedt et al. (2013).
14 According to Sperber (1985: 76), beyond stories, concepts and ideas, cultural representations may consist of perceptions, actions and meta-representations.

15 Sperber (1985: 74) pointed out: 'There exists, however, no threshold, no boundary with cultural representations on one side, and individual ones on the other. Representations are more or less widely and lastingly distributed, and hence more or less cultural.'
16 Sperber (1985: 80) made a distinction between dispositions, which are the products of selection during evolution, and susceptibilities, which are by-products of dispositions.
17 According to Sperber (1985: 85), this is the case of 'conceptual mysteries', which 'they achieve relevance because of their paradoxical character, i.e. because of the rich background of everyday empirical knowledge from which they systematically depart. By achieving relevance they occupy people's attention and become better distributed than representations which are mysterious merely by being obscure.'
18 People like to gain access to secret information, but dislike any secrecy when it excludes them from knowing the secret (Genkin 2010: 6).
19 Concealment of objects and information is not a unique feature of the human species. Primates, as well as other species, are used to hiding food from other animals (see, e.g., further Vander Wall 1990). What seems to be unique to humans is the concealment and social sharing of secrets for 'non-instrumental goals' (Genkin 2010: 2).
20 Cf. Benjamin Franklin's observation that 'three can keep a secret, if the two of them are dead'.
21 The research of Kelly and McKillop (1996) also showed that sharing harmful personal secrets tends to relieve individual stress and anxiety.
22 For a preliminary investigation of the connection between secrecy and social cohesion in the Mithras cult see Panagiotidou forthcoming.
23 As Genkin (2010: 1) pointed out, the existence of a secret community can be unknown, or its existence can be known while its members' identities remain hidden, or even its existence and the identities of its members can be known and only its practices are concealed.
24 Simmel called this desire for exclusiveness and superiority 'aristocracy-building motive' (1906: 486).

References

Abbreviations:

CP = Peirce 1931–58
EM: *Études mithriaques* = Duchesne-Guillemin (ed.) 1978
EPRO: *Études préliminaires aux religions orientales dans l'Empire romain*
IG: *Inscriptiones Graecae* (Berlin: De Gruyter, 1873–1932)
IR: *Integral Review: A Transdisciplinary and Transcultural Journal for New Thought, Research and Praxis*
JMS: *Journal of Mithraic Studies*
JRS: *Journal of Roman Studies*
MM: *Mysteria Mithrae* = Bianchi (ed.) 1979
MS: *Mithraic Studies* = Hinnells (ed.) 1975
MS 654, 7 = C. S. Peirce, Essays 1st Pref., 1910 August, page 7
OCD: *Oxford Classical Dictionary* (4th edition, 2012)
RMESF = Martens and De Boe (eds) 2004
RRE: *Religion in the Roman Empire*
SM: *Studies in Mithraism* = Hinnells (ed.) 1994
TMMM = Cumont 1896–99
V = Vermaseren 1956–60
VSuppl. = 'Supplementary items' added to Roger Pearse's website (see Pearse, R., below). These are mostly monuments discovered since the publication of Vermaseren 1956–60

Addis, D. R., A. T. Wong and D. L. Schacter (2007), 'Remembering the past and imagining the future: common and distinct neural substrates during event construction and elaboration'. *Neuropsychologia* 45 (7), 1363–77.
Alais, D. and R. Blake (2005), *Binocular Rivalry and Perceptual Ambiguity*. Boston: MIT Press.
Allman, J. M., A. Hakeem, J. M. Erwin, E. Nimchinsky and P. Hof (2001), 'The anterior cingulate cortex: the evolution of an interface between emotion and cognition'. *Annals of the New York Academy of the Sciences* 935 (1), 107–17.
Alvar, J. (2008), *Romanising Oriental Gods: Myth, Salvation and Ethics in the Cults of Cybele, Isis and Mithras*. Trans. R. L. Gordon. Leiden: Brill.
Alvarez, J. A. and E. Emory (2006), 'Executive function and the frontal lobes: a meta-analytic review'. *Neuropsychology Review* 16 (1), 17–42.

Anderson, B. L. (2003), 'The role of occlusion in the perception of depth, lightness, and opacity'. *Psychological Review* 110, 785–801.

Appenzeller, O. and E. Oribe (1997 [1970]). *The Autonomic Nervous System: An Introduction to Basic and Clinical Concepts*. Amsterdam: Elsevier.

Ashwell, K. W. S. and P. M. E. Waite (2004), 'Development of the peripheral nervous system'. In G. Paxinos and J. K. Mai (eds), *The Human Nervous System*. San Diego, CA: Elsevier, pp. 14–30.

Atance, C. M. and D. K. O'Neill (2001), 'Episodic future thinking'. *Trends in Cognitive Science* 5 (12), 533–9.

Atance, C. M. and D. K. O'Neill (2005), 'The emergence of episodic future thinking in humans'. *Learning and Motivation* 36, 126–44.

Atkinson, Q. D. and H. Whitehouse (2011), 'The cultural morphospace of ritual form: examining modes of religiosity cross-culturally'. *Evolution and Human Behavior* 32 (1), 50–62.

Atkinson, R. C. and R. M. Shiffrin (1968), 'Human memory: a proposed system and its control processes'. In K. W. Spence and J. T. Spence (eds), *The Psychology of Learning and Motivation*. Vol. 2. New York: Academic Press, pp. 89–195.

Augustine, J. R. (2008), *Human Neuroanatomy*. London: Academic Press.

Baddeley, A. D. and G. Hitch (1974). 'Working memory'. *Psychology of Learning and Motivation* 8, 47–89.

Baddeley, A. D., N. Thomson and M. Buchanan (1975). 'Word length and the structure of short term memory'. *Journal of Verbal Learning and Verbal Behavior* 14 (6), 575–89.

Badre, D., A. S. Kayser and M. D'Esposito (2010), 'Frontal cortex and the discovery of abstract action rules'. *Neuron* 66 (2), 315–26.

Barsalou, L. W. (1992), *Cognitive Psychology: An Overview for Cognitive Scientists*. Hillsdale, NJ: Lawrence Erlbaum Associates.

Barsalou, L. W., A. K. Barbey, K. W. Simmons and A. Santos (2005), 'Embodiment in religious knowledge'. *Journal of Cognition and Culture* 5 (1/2), 14–57.

Bartlett, F. (1932), *Remembering: A Study in Experimental and Social Psychology*. Cambridge: Cambridge University Press.

Barton, T. (1994), *Ancient Astrology*. London: Routledge.

Bausani, A. (1979), 'Notte sulla preistoria astronomica del mito di Mithra'. In *MM*, pp. 503–13.

Beard, M., J. North and S. Price (1998), *Religions of Rome*. 2 vols. Cambridge: Cambridge University Press.

Becatti, G. (1954), *Scavi di Ostia, II: I Mitrei*. Roma: Libreria dello Stato.

Beck, R. (1976a), 'The seat of Mithras at the equinoxes: Porphyry, *De antro nympharum* 24'. *JMS* 1, 95–8. Reprinted in Beck 2004, pp. 129–32.

Beck, R. (1976b), 'Interpreting the Ponza Zodiac'. *JMS* 1, 1–19. Reprinted in Beck 2004, pp. 151–69.

Beck, R. (1977), 'Cautes and Cautopates: some astronomical considerations', *JMS* 2, 1–17. Reprinted in Beck 2004, pp. 133–49

Beck, R. (1978), 'Interpreting the Ponza Zodiac, II'. *JMS* 2, 87–147. Reprinted in Beck 2004, pp. 171–231.

Beck, R. (1979), 'Sette Sfere, Sette Porte, and the Spring Equinoxes of A.D. 172 and 173'. MM, pp. 515–30.

Beck, R. (1984a), 'Mithraism since Franz Cumont'. In H. Temporini and W. Haase (eds), *Aufsteig und Niedergang der römischen Welt* II 17 (4). Berlin: Walter de Gruyter, pp. 2002–115.

Beck, R. (1984b), 'The rock-cut mithraea of Arupium (Dalmatia)'. *Phoenix* 38, 356–71.

Beck, R. (1988), *Planetary Gods and Planetary Orders in the Mysteries of Mithras*. EPRO 109. Leiden: Brill.

Beck, R. (1991), 'Thus spake not Zarathustra: Zoroastrian pseudepigrapha of the Graeco-Roman world'. Excursus in M. Boyce and F. Grenet, *A History of Zoroastrianism*, Vol. 3. Leiden: Brill, pp. 491–565.

Beck, R. (1992), 'The Mithras cult as association'. *Studies in Religion* 21, 3–13.

Beck, R. (1994a), 'Cosmic models: some uses of Hellenistic science in Roman religion'. In T. D. Barnes (ed.), *The Sciences in Greco-Roman Society. APEIRON* 27 (4). Edmonton, AL: Academic Printing and Publishing, pp. 99–117. Reprinted in Beck 2004, pp. 335–53.

Beck, R. (1994b), 'In the place of the lion: Mithras in the tauroctony'. *SM*, pp. 29–50. Reprinted in Beck 2004, pp. 267–91.

Beck, R. (1996), 'The mysteries of Mithras'. In J. S. Kloppenborg and S. G. Wilson (eds), *Voluntary Associations in the Ancient World*. London: Routledge, pp. 176–85.

Beck, R. (1998), 'The mysteries of Mithras: a new account of their genesis'. *JRS* 88, 115–28. Reprinted in Beck 2004, pp. 31–44.

Beck, R. (2000), 'Ritual, myth, doctrine, and initiation in the mysteries of Mithras: new evidence from a cult vessel'. *JRS* 90, 145–80. Reprinted in Beck 2004, pp. 55–92.

Beck, R. (2001–2), 'History into fiction: the metamorphoses of the Mithras myths'. *Ancient Narrative* 1, 283–300.

Beck, R. (2004), *Beck on Mithraism: Collected Works with New Essays*. Aldershot: Ashgate.

Beck, R. (2004a), 'Mithraism after "Mithraism since Franz Cumont," 1984'. In Beck 2004, pp. 3–29.

Beck, R. (2004b), 'Four men, two sticks, and a whip: image and doctrine in a Mithraic ritual'. In H. Whitehouse and L. Martin (eds), *Theorizing Religions Past: Archaeology, History, and Cognition*. Walnut Creek, CA: AltaMira, pp. 87–103.

Beck, R. (2006a), *The Religion of the Mithras Cult in the Roman Empire: Mysteries of the Unconquered Sun*. Oxford: Oxford University Press.

Beck, R. (2006b), 'The religious market of the Roman empire: Rodney Stark and Christianity's pagan competition'. In L. Vaage (ed.), *Religious Rivalries in the Early Roman Empire and the Rise of Christianity*. Waterloo, ON: Wilfrid Laurier University Press, pp. 233–52.

Beck, R. (2007), *A Brief History of Ancient Astrology*. Oxford: Blackwell.

Beck, R. (2010), 'Ancient and modern approaches to the representation of supernatural beings: Dio Chrysostom (*Oration* 12) and Dan Sperber (*Explaining Culture*) compared'. In P. Pachis and D. Wiebe (eds), *Chasing Down Religion: In the Sights of History and the Cognitive Sciences. Essays in Honor of Luther H. Martin*. Thessaloniki: Barbounakis Publications, pp. 1–9.

Beck, R. (2014), 'Educating a Mithraist'. In B. S. Bøgh (ed.), *Conversion and Initiation in Antiquity: Shifting Identities – Creating Change*. Early Christianity in the Context of Antiquity 16. Frankfurt am Main: Peter Lang, pp. 247–55.

Beck, R. (2016), 'The ancient mithraeum as model universe, part 1'. In N. Campion (ed.), *Heavenly Discourses*, Proceedings of the Heavenly Discourses Conference, Bristol, UK, 14–16 October 2011. Ceredigion, Wales: Sophia Centre Press, pp. 21–31.

Beck, R. (forthcoming), 'If so, how? Representing "Coming back to life" in the mysteries of Mithras'. In F. S. Tappenden, and C. Daniel-Hughes (eds), *Coming Back to Life: The Permeability of Past and Present, Mortality and Immortality, Death and Life in the Ancient Mediterranean* (e-book). Montreal: McGill University Library and Archives, pp. 161–89.

Bell, C. (1992), *Ritual Theory, Ritual Practice*. Oxford: Oxford University Press.

Bell, C. (1997), *Ritual: Perspectives and Dimensions*. New York: Oxford University Press.

Beskow, P. (1979), 'Branding in the mysteries of Mithras?' In *MM*, pp. 487–501.

Bianchi, U. (ed.) (1979), *Mysteria Mithrae*. Atti del Seminario Internazionale su 'La specificità storico-religiosa dei Misteri di Mithra, con particolare riferimento alle fonti documentarie di Roma e Ostia', Roma e Ostia, 28–31 Marzo. EPRO 80. Leiden.

Bidez, J. and F. Cumont (1938), *Les Mages hellénisés: Zoroastre, Ostanès et Hystaspe, d'après la tradition gecque*. T. I. Introduction; t. II. Les textes. Paris: Les Belles Lettres.

Binder, J. R. and R. H. Desai (2011), 'The neurobiology of semantic memory'. *Trends in Cognitive Science* 15 (11), 527–36.

Bjørnebye, J. (2015), 'Mithraic movement: negotiating topography and space in late antique Rome'. In I. Östenberg, S. Malmberg, and J. Bjørnebye (eds), *The Moving City: Processions, Passages and Promenades in Ancient Rome*. London: Bloomsbury, pp. 225–36.

Blake, R. and H. Wilson (2011), 'Binocular vision'. *Vision Research* 51 (7), 754–70.

Blau, P. M. (1967), *Exchange and Power in Social Life*. New York: J. Wiley.

Bloch, M. (2004), *Marxism and Anthropology: The History of a Relationship*. London: Routledge.

Botzung, A., E. Denkova and L. Manning (2008), 'Experiencing past and future personal events: functional neuroimaging evidence on the neural bases of mental time travel'. *Brain and Cognition* 66, 202–12.

Boyer, P. (2002), *Religion Explained: The Evolutionary Origins of Religious Thought*. New York: Basic Books.

Boyer, P. (2009), 'What are memories for?' In P. Boyer and J. Wertsch (eds), *Functions of Recall in Cognition and Culture: Memory in Mind and Culture*. Cambridge: Cambridge University Press, pp. 3–28.

Brashear, W. M. (1992), *A Mithraic Catechism from Egypt* (P. Berol. 21196). Vienna: Verlag Adolf Holzhausens Nfg.

Bremmer, J. N. (2014), *Initiation into the Mysteries of the Ancient World*. Münchener Vorlesungen zu Antiken Welten 1. Berlin: de Gruyter.

Broadbent, D. E. (1958), *Perception and Communication*. New York: Pergamon Press.

Broadbent, D. E. (1975), 'The magic number seven after fifteen years'. In A. Kennedy and A. Wilkes (eds), *Studies in Long-Term Memory*. London: Wiley, pp. 3–18.

Brodal, P. (2010), *The Central Nervous System: Structure and Function*. Oxford: Oxford University Press.

Brown, R. and J. Kulik (1977), 'Flashbulb memories'. *Cognition* 5 (1), 73–99.

Bruhn, J. (2009), *The Group Effect: Social Cohesion and Health Outcomes*. Dordrecht: Springer.

Bruner, J. (1990), *Acts of Meaning*. Cambridge, MA: Harvard University Press.

Bruner, J. (2003), 'The "remembered" self'. In U. Neisser and R. Fivush (eds), *The Remembering Self: Construction and Accuracy in the Self-Narrative*. Cambridge: Cambridge University Press, pp. 41–54.

Bryant, D. J. and B. Tversky (1999), 'Mental representations of perspective and spatial relations from diagrams and models'. *Journal of Experimental Psychology: Learning, Memory, and Cognition* 25, 137–56.

Buhrmester, M. D., Fraser, W. T., Lanman, J., Whitehouse, H. and W. B. Swann (2014), 'When terror hits home: identity fused Americans who saw Boston bombing victims as "family" provided aid'. *Self and Identity*. DOI:10.1080/15298868.2014.992465.

Bulbulia, J. (2004), 'The cognitive and evolutionary psychology of religion'. *Biology and Philosophy* 19, 655–86.

Bull, R. J. (1978), 'The mithraeum at Caesarea Maritima'. *EM*, pp. 75–89.

Bundgaard, P. and F. Stjernfelt (2010), 'Logic and cognition'. In P. Cobley (ed.), *The Routledge Companion to Semiotics*. London: Routledge, pp. 57–73.

Burgess, N. (2006), 'Spatial memory: how egocentric and allocentric combine'. *Trends in Cognitive Science* 10 (12), 551–7.

Burgess, N., S. Becker, J. A. King and J. O'Keefe (2001), 'Memory for events and their spatial context: models and experiments'. *Philosophical Transactions of the Royal Society B: Biological Sciences* 356, 1493–1503.

Burkert, W. (1987), *Ancient Mystery Cults*. Cambridge, MA: Harvard University Press.

Bush, G., P. Luu and M. I. Posner (2000), 'Cognitive and emotional influences in anterior cingulate cortex'. *Trends in Cognitive Science* 4 (6), 215–22.

Bush, G., B. A. Vogt, J. Holmes, A. M. Dale, D. Greve, M. A. Jenike and B. R. Rosen (2002), 'Dorsal anterior cingulate cortex: a role in reward-based decision making'. *Proceedings of the National Academy of Sciences of the USA* 99 (1), 523–8.

Byrne, P., S. Becker and N. Burgess (2007), 'Remembering the past and imagining the future: a neural model of spatial memory and imagery'. *Psychological Review* 114 (2), 340–75.

Carroll, N. (2001), 'On the narrative connection'. In W. Van Peer and S. Chatman, *New Perspectives on Narrating Perspective*. Albany: SUNY Press, pp. 21–41.

Carron, A. V. and K. S. Spink (1995), 'The group size–cohesion relationship in minimal groups'. *Small Group Research* 26 (1), 86–105.

Casadio, G. and P. A. Johnston (eds) (2009), *Mystic Cults in Magna Graecia*. Austin: University of Texas Press.

Cervel, M. S. P. (2003), *Topology and Cognition: What Image-Schemas Reveal about the Metaphorical Language of Emotions*. Munich: Lincom Europa.

Chalupa, A. (2009), 'Religious change in Roman religion from the perspective of Whitehouse's theory of the two modes of religiosity'. In L. H. Martin and P. Pachis (eds), *Imagistic Traditions in the Graeco-Roman World*. Thessaloniki: Vanias, pp. 113–35.

Chalupa, A. and T. Glomb (2013), 'The third symbol of the *Miles* grade on the floor mosaic of the Felicissimus Mithraeum in Ostia: a new interpretation'. *Religio* 31, 9–32.

Chen Z. and N. Cowan (2005), 'Chunk limits and length limits in immediate recall: a reconciliation'. *Journal of Experimental Psychology: Learning, Memory, and Cognition* 31 (6), 1235–49.

Chomsky, N. (1957), *Syntactic Structures*. The Hague: Mouton.

Clark, A. (1997), *Being There: Putting Brain, Body, and World Together Again*. Cambridge, MA: MIT Press.

Clark, A. (2008), *Supersizing the Mind: Embodiment, Action, and Cognitive Extension*. Oxford: Oxford University Press.

Clauss, M. (1990), 'Die Sieben Grade des Mithras-Kultes'. *Zeitschrift für Papyrologie und Epigraphik* 82, 183–94.

Clauss, M. (1992), *Cultores Mithrae: Die Anhängerschaft des Mithras-Kultes*. Heidelberger Althistorische Beiträge und Epigraphische Studien 10. Stuttgart: Steiner.

Clauss, M. (2000), *The Roman Cult of Mithras: The God and his Mysteries*. Trans. R. L. Gordon. New York: Routledge.

Clauss, M. (2012), *Mithras: Kult und Mysterium*. Darmstadt: von Zabern. (Essentially a revised and updated edition of the German original of which Clauss 2000 is the English translation.)

Coarelli, F. (1979), 'Topographia mithriaca di Roma'. In *MM*, pp. 69–79.

Comaroff, J. and J. L. Comaroff (1993), *Modernity and its Malcontents: Ritual and Power in Postcolonial Africa*. Chicago: Chicago University Press.

Conway, M. A. (1995), *Flashbulb Memories. Essays in Cognitive Psychology*. Hillsdale, NJ: Erlbaum.

Conway, M. A. (1996), 'Autobiographical knowledge and autobiographical memories'. In D. Rubin (ed.), *Remembering Our Past: Studies in Autobiographical Memory*. Cambridge: Cambridge University Press, pp. 67–93.

Cook, K. S. and R. M. Emerson (1987), *Social Exchange Theory*. Newbury Park CA: SAGE Publications.

Cowan, N. (2001), 'The magical number 4 in short-term memory: a reconsideration of mental storage capacity'. *Behavioral and Brain Sciences* 24, 1–185.

Cowan, N. (2008), 'What are the differences between long-term, short-term, and working memory?' *Progress in Brain Research* 169, 323–38.

Cowan, N., Z. Chen and J. N. Rouder (2004), 'Constant capacity in an immediate serial-recall task: a logical sequel to Miller (1956)'. *Psychological Science* 15 (9), 634–40.

Craig, A. D. (2003), 'Interoception: the sense of the physiological condition of the body'. *Current Opinion in Neurobiology* 13, 500–5.

Cumont, F. (1896–99), *Textes et monuments figurés relatifs aux mystères de Mithra*. 2 vols. Brussels: Lamertin.

Cumont, F. (1960 [1912]), *Astrology and Religion among the Greeks and Romans*. Trans. J. B. Baker. New York: Dover.

Cumont, F. (1975), 'The Dura Mithraeum'. Ed. and trans. E. D. Francis. In *MS*, pp. 151–214.

Czachesz, I. and R. Uro (eds) (2013), *Mind, Morality and Magic in the Biblical World: Cognitive Science Approaches in Biblical Studies*. Durham: Acumen Publishing.

Damasio, A. (1994), *Descartes' Error: Emotion, Reason, and the Human Brain*. New York: Avon Books.

Damasio, A. (2000), *The Feeling of What Happens: Body, Emotion and the Making of Consciousness*. San Diego, CA: Harvest.

Damasio, A. (2010), *Self Comes to Mind: Constructing the Conscious Brain*. New York: Random House.

D'Andrade, R. (1989), 'Culturally based reasoning'. In A. Gellatly, D. Rogers, and J. Sloboda (eds), *Cognition and Social Worlds*. Oxford: Oxford University Press, pp. 132–43.

D'Argembeau, A. and M. Van der Linden (2004), 'Phenomenal characteristics associated with projecting oneself back into the past and forward into the future: influence of valence and temporal distance'. *Consciousness and Cognition* 13 (4), 844–58.

Dawson, L. L. (2008), 'Church-sect-cult: constructing typologies of religious groups'. In P. B. Clarke (ed.), *The Oxford Handbook of the Sociology of Religion*. Oxford: Oxford University Press, pp. 525–44.

Deacon, T. (1997), *The Symbolic Species: The Co-evolution of Language and the Brain*. London: W.W. Norton and Company.

Deacon, T. (2014), 'Semiosis: from taxonomy to process'. In T. Thellefsen and B. Sorensen (eds), *Charles Sanders Peirce in His Own Words (Semiotics, Communication and Cognition)*. Berlin: De Gruyter, pp. 95–104.

Deeley, Q. P. (2004), 'The religious brain: turning ideas into convictions'. *Anthropology and Medicine* 11 (3), 245–67.

De Grossi Mazzorin, J. (2004), 'I resti animali del mitreo della Crypta Balbi a Roma (note preliminari)'. In *RMEFS*, pp. 179–83.

Detienne, M. (1972), *Les jardins d'Adonis: la mythologie des aromates en Grèce*. Paris: Gallimard.

Detienne, M. (1977), *The Gardens of Adonis: Spices in Greek Mythology*. Trans. J. Lloyd. Atlantic Highlands, NJ: Humanities Press.

Diamond, A. (2013), 'Executive functions'. *Annual Review of Psychology* 64, 135–68.

Dirven, L. (2015), 'The mithraeum as *tableau vivant*: a preliminary study of ritual performance and emotional involvement in ancient mystery cults'. *RRE* 1.1, 20–50.

Dolins, L. and R. W. Mitchell (2014), 'Linking spatial cognition and spatial perception'. In L. Dolins and R. W. Mitchell (eds), *Spatial Cognition, Spatial Perception: Mapping the Self and Space*. Cambridge: Cambridge University Press, pp. 1–32.

Donald, M. (1991), *Origins of Modern Mind: Three Stages in the Evolution of Culture and Cognition*. Cambridge, MA: Harvard University Press.

Douglas, M. (1970), *Natural Symbols: Explorations in Cosmology*. New York: Pantheon.

Durkheim, E. (1995 [1912]), *The Elementary Forms of Religious Life*. Trans. K. Fields. New York: Free Press.

Durkheim, E. (1997 [1893]). *The Division of Labor in Society*. Trans. W. D. Halls, intro. L. A. Coser. New York: Free Press.

Easton, R. D. and M. J. Sholl (1995), 'Object-array structure, frames of reference, and retrieval of spatial knowledge'. *Journal of Experimental Psychology: Learning, Memory, and Cognition* 21, 483–500.

Emerson, R. M. (1976), 'Social exchange theory'. *Annual Review of Sociology* 2, 335–62.

Evans, V. (2010), 'The perceptual basis of spatial representation'. In V. Evans and P. Chilton, *Language, Cognition and Space: The State of the Art and New Directions*. London: Equinox, pp. 21–48.

Fauconnier, G. and M. Turner (1998), 'Conceptual integration networks'. *Cognitive Science* 22(2), 133–87.

Fauconnier, G. and M. Turner (2002), *The Way We Think: Conceptual Blending and the Mind's Hidden Complexities*. New York: Basic Books.

Fauconnier, G. and M. Turner (2003), 'Conceptual blending, form, and meaning'. *Recherches en Communication: Sémiotique cognitive* 19, 57–86.

Fernandez, J. M. and B. Farell (2009), 'Is perceptual space inherently non-Euclidean?' *Journal of Mathematical Psychology* 53 (2), 86–91.

Foley, H. and M. Matlin (2015 [1991]), *Sensation and Perception*. Hove: Psychology Press.

Foucault, M. (1975), *Discipline and Punish: The Birth of the Prison*. Trans. A. Sheridan New York: Random House.

Frackowiak, D. (2013), 'The bull's limb theory reloaded'. *Religio* 21, 39–42.

Francis, E. D. (1975), 'Mithraic graffiti from Dura-Europos'. MS, pp. 424–45.

Frank, L. M., E. N. Brown and M. Wilson (2000), 'Trajectory encoding in the hippocampus and entorhinal cortex'. *Neuron* 27, 169–78.

Franklin, N. and B. Tversky (1990), 'Searching imagined environments'. *Journal of Experimental Psychology: General* 119, 63–76.

Frazer, J. (1922), *The Golden Bough: A Study in Magic and Religion*. London: Macmillan.

Fustel de Coulanges, N. D. (1874 [1980]), *The Ancient City: A Study on the Religion, Laws, and Institutions of Greece and Rome*. Trans. W. Small. Boston: Lee and Shepherd [repr. Baltimore, MD: Johns Hopkins University Press].
Gaddis, J. L. (2002), *The Landscape of History: How Historians Map the Past*. Oxford: Oxford University Press.
Gawlikowski, M. (1999), 'Hawarti: preliminary report'. *Polish Archaeology in the Mediterranean* 10 (Reports 1998), 197-204.
Geertz, A. (2004a), 'Cognitive approaches to the study of religion', in A. Geertz, R. R. Warne and P. Antes (eds), *New Approaches to the Study of Religion: Textual, Comparative, Sociological, and Cognitive Approaches*. Berlin: Walter de Gruyter, pp. 347-400.
Geertz, A. (2004b), *Introduction to Cognitive Approaches to the Study of Religion*. Aarhus: Laboratory of Religion, Department of the Study of Religion, Faculty of Theology, Aarhus University.
Geertz, A. (2010), 'Brain, body and culture: a biocultural theory of religion'. *Method and Theory in the Study of Religion*, 22 (4), 304-21.
Geertz, C. (1990), *The Interpretation of Cultures: Selected Essays*. New York: Basic Books.
Genkin, M. (2010), 'Simmel in the Laboratory: An Experimental Investigation into the Relationship between Secrecy and Cohesion'. Unpublished MA thesis, Cornell University.
Gerlach, K. D, R. N. Spreng, A. W. Gilmore and D. L. Schacter (2011). 'Solving future problems: default network and executive activity associated with goal-directed mental simulations'. *Neuroimage* 55, 1816-24.
Gibson, J. J. (1950), *The Perception of the Visual World*. Boston: Houghton Mifflin.
Goodman, N. (1978), *Ways of Worldmaking*. Brighton: The Harvester Press.
Goody, J. (1977), *The Domestication of the Savage Mind*. Cambridge: Cambridge University Press.
Gordon, R. L. (1972), 'Mithraism and Roman society'. *Religion* 2 (2), 92-121. Reprinted in Gordon (1996) as Chapter III.
Gordon, R. L. (1976a), 'The sacred geography of a Mithraeum: the example of Sette Sfere'. *JMS* 1 (2), 119-65. Reprinted in Gordon (1996) as Chapter VI.
Gordon, R. L. (1976b), 'Archaeological reports: Italy'. *JMS* 1 (2), 197-9.
Gordon, R. L. (1980a), 'Reality evocation, and boundary in the Mysteries of Mithras'. *JMS* 3, 19-99. Reprinted in Gordon (1996) as Chapter V.
Gordon, R. L. (1980b), 'Panelled complications'. *JMS* 3, 200-27. Reprinted in Gordon (1996) as Chapter IX.
Gordon, R. L. (1988), 'Authority, salvation and mystery in the Mysteries of Mithras'. In J. Huskinson, M. Beard and J. Reynolds (eds), *Image and Mystery in the Roman World: Three Papers Given in Memory of Jocelyn Toynbee*. Gloucester: A. Sutton, pp. 45-80. Reprinted in Gordon (1996) as Chapter IV.
Gordon, R. L. (1994a), 'Mystery, metaphor and doctrine in the mysteries of Mithras'. *SM*, pp. 103-24.

Gordon, R. L. (1994b), 'Who worshipped Mithras?' *Journal of Roman Archaeology* 7, 459–74. (Review article of Clauss 1992.)

Gordon, R. L. (1996), *Image and Value in the Graeco-Roman World: Studies in Mithraism and Religious Art*. Aldershot: Ashgate (Variorum).

Gordon, R. L. (1998), 'Viewing Mithraic art: the altar from Burginatium (Kalkar, Germania Inferior)'. *Antigüedad: Religiones y Sociedades (ARYS)* 1, 227–58.

Gordon, R. L. (2001), 'Ritual and hierarchy in the Mysteries of Mithras'. *Antigüedad: Religiones y Sociedades (ARYS)* 4, 245–74.

Gordon, R. L. (2009), 'The Mithraic body: the example of the Capua mithraeum'. In Casadio and Johnston 2009, pp. 290–313.

Gordon, R. L. (2012), 'Mithras (Mithraskult)'. In *Reallexicon für Antike und Christentum*, Band XXIV, cols 964–1009.

Gordon, R. L. (2013), 'The Miles-frame in the Mitreo di Felicissimo and the practicalities of sacrifice'. *Religio* 31, 33–8.

Gossen, G. H. (1972), 'Temporal and spatial equivalents in Chamula ritual symbolism'. In W. A. Lessa and E. Z. Vogt (eds), *Reader in Comparative Religion: An Anthropological Approach*. New York: Harper & Row, pp. 116–29.

Grady, J. E. (1997), *Foundation of Meaning: Primary Metaphors and Primary Scenes*. PhD dissertation, University of California, Berkeley.

Grady, J. E, T. Oakley and S. Coulson (1999), 'Blending and Metaphor'. In G. Steen and R. Gibbs (eds), *Metaphor in Cognitive Linguistics*. Philadelphia: John Benjamins, pp. 101–24.

Greenberg, J., T. Pyszczynski, S. Solomon, A. Rosenblatt, M. Veeder, S. Kirkland and D. Lyon (1990), 'Evidence for terror management theory II: the effects of mortality salience on reactions to those who threaten or bolster the cultural worldview'. *Journal of Personality and Social Psychology* 58 (2), 308–318.

Griffith, A. B. (2006), 'Completing the picture: women and the female principle in the Mithraic cult'. *Numen* 53 (1), 48–77.

Grossberg, S. (1994), '3-D vision and figure-ground separation by visual cortex'. *Perception and Psychophysics* 55 (1), 48–120

Guthrie, S. E. (2002), 'Animal animism: evolutionary roots of religious cognition'. In I. Pyysiainen and V. Anttonen (eds), *Current Approaches in the Cognitive Science of Religion*. London: Continuum, pp. 38–67.

Guttentag, R. E. (1984), 'The mental effort requirement of cumulative rehearsal: a developmental study'. *Journal of Experimental Child Psychology* 37, 92–106.

Haidt, J. (2012), *The Righteous Mind: Why Good People Are Divided by Politics and Religion*. New York: Vintage Books.

Hancock, P. A. (2005), 'Time and the privileged observer'. *Kronoscope* 5, 176–91.

Harland, P. A. (2003), *Associations, Synagogues, and Congregations: Claiming a Place in Ancient Mediterranean Society*. Minneapolis, MN: Fortress Press.

Harris, J. (2014), *Sensation and Perception*. London: SAGE Publications.

Harrison, J. E. (1909), 'The influence of Darwinism on the study of religions'. In

A. C. Seward (ed.), *Darwin and Modern Science: Essays in Commemoration of the Centenary of the Birth of Charles Darwin and of the Fiftieth Anniversary of the Publication of the Origin of the Species*. Cambridge: Cambridge University Press.

Hayhoe, M, B. Gillam, K. Chajka and E. Vecellio (2009), 'The role of binocular vision in walking'. *Visual Neuroscience* 26 (1), 73–80.

Heinrich, B. (1999), *The Mind of the Raven: Investigations and Adventures with Wolf-Birds*. New York: Cliff Street Books.

Henrich, J. (2009), 'The evolution of costly displays, cooperation and religion: credibility enhancing displays and their implications for cultural evolution'. *Evolution and Human Behavior* 30 (4), 244–60.

Henrich, J. and F. J. Gil-White (2001), 'The evolution of prestige: freely conferred deference as a mechanism for enhancing the benefits of cultural transmission'. *Evolution and Human Behavior* 22 (3), 165–96.

Henrich, J. and N. Henrich (2007), *Why Humans Cooperate: A Cultural and Evolutionary Explanation*. Oxford: Oxford University Press.

Henshaw, J. M. (2012), *A Tour of the Senses: How Your Brain Interprets the World*. Baltimore, MD: Johns Hopkins University Press.

Herman, D. (2003), 'How stories make us smarter: narrative theory and cognitive semiotics'. *Recherches en communication* 19 (19), 133–54.

Hermer, L. and E. S. Spelke (1994), 'A geometric process for spatial reorientation in young children'. *Nature* 370, 57–9.

Hinnells, J. H. (ed.) (1975), *Mithraic Studies: Proceedings of the First International Congress of Mithraic Studies*, 2 vols (with consecutive pagination). Manchester: Manchester University Press.

Hinnells, J. H. (1976) 'The iconography of Cautes and Cautopates, 1: the data', *JMS* 1, 36–67.

Hinnells, J. H. (ed.) (1994), *Studies in Mithraism* (papers from the Mithraic Panel, XVIth Congress of the International Association for the History of Religions, Rome, 1990). Rome: Bretchneider.

Holmes, M. C. and M. J. Sholl (2005), 'Allocentric coding of object-to-object relations in overlearned and novel environments'. *Journal of Experimental Psychology: Learning, Memory and Cognition* 31 (5), 1069–87.

Hoopes, J. (ed.) (1991), *Peirce on Signs: Writings on Semiotic by Charles Sanders Peirce*. Chapel Hill, NC: University of North Carolina Press.

Hopkins, K. (2000), *A World Full of Gods: Pagans, Jews and Christians in the Roman Empire*. London: Phoenix.

Horn, H. G. (1994), 'Das Mainzer Mithrasgefäß'. *Mainzer Archäologische Zeitschrift* 1, 21–66.

Howard, I. P. and B. J. Rogers (1995), *Binocular Vision and Stereopsis*. Oxford: Oxford University Press.

Hrotic, S. M. (2009). 'Academic Peer-Evaluation Tactics: An Evolutionary Approach'. Unpublished doctoral dissertation. Belfast: Queen's University.

Hutchins, E. (2005), 'Material anchors for conceptual blends'. *Journal of Pragmatics* 37, 1555–77.
Insler, S. (1978), 'A new interpretation of the bull-slaying motif'. In M. B. de Boer and T. A. Edridge (eds), *Hommages à Maarten J. Vermaseren*. EPRO 68. Leiden: Brill, pp. 519–38.
Iriki, A. (2014), 'Understanding of external space generated by bodily re-mapping: an insight from the neurophysiology of tool-using monkeys'. In L. Dolins and R. W. Mitchell (eds), *Spatial Cognition, Spatial Perception: Mapping the Self and Space*. Cambridge: Cambridge University Press, pp. 439–55.
Irons, W. (2001), 'Religion as a hard-to-fake sign of commitment'. In R. Nesse (ed.), *The Evolution of Commitment*. New York: Russell Sage Foundation, pp. 292–309.
Jacobs, B. (1999), *Der Herkunft und Entstehung der römischen Mithrasmysterien: Überlegungen zur Rolle des Stifters und zu den astronomischen Hintergründen der Kultlegende*. Konstanz: Universitätsverlag Konstanz.
Jänig, W. (2006), *Integrative Action of the Autonomic Nervous System: Neurobiology of Homeostasis*. Cambridge: Cambridge University Press.
Jeannerod, M. (2006), *Motor Cognition: What Actions Tell the Self*. Oxford: Oxford University Press.
Jensen, J. S. (2010), 'Doing it the other way round: religion as a basic case of "normative cognition"'. *Method and Theory in the Study of Religion* 22 (4), 322–9.
Johnson, C. (1999), 'Metaphor vs. conflation in the acquisition of polysemy: the case of *see*'. In M. K. Hiraga, C. Sinha, and S. Wilcox (eds), *Cultural, Psychological, and Typological Issues in Cognitive Linguistics*. Amsterdam: John Benjamins, pp. 155–69.
Johnson, M. (1987), *The Body in the Mind: The Bodily Basis of Meaning, Imagination, and Reason*. Chicago: University of Chicago Press.
Johnson, M. (1993), *Moral Imagination: Implications of Cognitive Science for Ethics*. Chicago: University of Chicago Press.
Johnson, M. (2007), *The Meaning of the Body*. Chicago: University of Chicago Press.
Jonathan, D. (2000), 'The exclusion of women in the mithraic mysteries: ancient or modern?', *Numen* 47 (2), 121–41.
Jonides, J., R. L. Lewis, D. E. Nee, C. A. Lustig, M. G. Berman and K. S. Moore, (2008), 'The mind and brain of short-term memory'. *Annual Review of Psychology* 59, 193–224.
Kane, J. P. (1975), 'The Mithraic cult meal in its Greek and Roman environment'. In *MS*, pp. 313–51.
Kay, A., D. Gaucher, J. Napier, M. Callan and K. Laurin (2008), 'God and the government: testing a compensatory control system for the support of external systems'. *Journal of Personality and Social Psychology* 95, 18–35.
Kearney, M. (1984), *World View*. Novato, CA: Chandler & Sharp.
Kelly, A. E. and K. J. McKillop (1996), 'Consequences of revealing personal secrets'. *Psychological Bulletin* 120, 450–65.
Kertzer, D. (1988), *Ritual, Politics, and Power*. New Haven, CT: Yale University Press.

Kimmel, M. (2013), 'The arc from the body to culture: how affect, proprioception, kinesthesia, and perceptual imagery shape cultural knowledge (and vice versa)'. *IR* 9 (2), 300–48.
Klatzky, R. L. (1998), 'Allocentric and egocentric spatial representations: definitions, distinctions, and interconnections'. *Spatial Cognition* 1404, 1–17.
Kumaran, D. and E. A. Maguire (2005), 'The human hippocampus: cognitive maps or relational memory?' *Journal of Neuroscience* 25, 7254–9.
Kurzban, R. and S. Neuberg (2005), 'Managing ingroup and outgroup relationships'. In D. Buss (ed.), *The Handbook of Evolutionary Psychology*. Hoboken, NJ: Wiley, pp. 653–75.
Laeuchli, S. (ed.) (1967), *Mithraism in Ostia: Mystery Religion and Christianity in the Ancient Port of Rome*. Chicago: Northwestern University Press.
Lakoff, G. (1990), *Women, Fire, and Dangerous Things: What Categories Reveal about the Mind*. Chicago: University of Chicago Press.
Lakoff, G. and M. Johnson (1980, with an 'Afterword' 2003), *Metaphors We Live By*. Chicago: University of Chicago Press.
Lakoff, G. and M. Johnson (1999), *Philosophy in the Flesh: The Embodied Mind and its Challenge to Western Thought*. New York: Basic Books.
Lanman, J. A. (2012), 'The importance of religious displays for belief acquisition and secularization'. *Journal of Contemporary Religion* 27 (1), 49–65.
Lawson, T. E. and R. N. McCauley (1990), *Rethinking Religion: Connecting Cognition and Culture*. Cambridge: Cambridge University Press.
Leach, E. R. (1954), *Political Systems of Highland Burma*. London: LSE.
Leach, E. R. (1966 [1961]), *Rethinking Anthropology*. London: Athlone Press.
Lewandowsky, S., M. Duncan and G. D. A. Brown (2004), 'Time does not cause forgetting in short-term serial recall'. *Psychonomic Bulletin and Review* 11 (5), 771–90.
Lisdorf, A. (2010), 'Towards a cognitive historiography: frequently posed objections'. In P. Pachis and D. Wiebe (eds), *Chasing Down Religion: In the Sights of History and the Cognitive Sciences*. Essays in Honor of Luther H. Martin. Thessaloniki: Barbounakis, pp. 233–42.
Lissi Caronna, E. (1986), *Il mitreo dei Castra Peregrinorum (S. Stefano Rotondo)*. EPRO 104. Leiden: Brill.
Loomis, J. M., Lippa, Y., Klatzky, R. L. and R. G. Golledge (2002), 'Spatial updating of locations specified by 3-D sound and spatial language'. *Journal of Experimental Psychology: Learning, Memory, and Cognition* 28: 335–45.
Lunais, S. (1979), *Recherches Sur La Lune, I: Les Auteurs Latins*. Leiden: Brill.
Lundhaug, H. (2010), *Images of Rebirth: Cognitive Poetics and Transformational Soteriology in the Gospel of Philip and the Exegesis on the Soul*. Leiden: Brill.
Luu, P. and S. M. Pederson (2004). 'The anterior cingulate cortex: regulating actions in context'. In M. I. Posner (ed.), *Cognitive Neuroscience of Attention*. New York: Guilford Press, pp. 232–42.

Mael, F. and B. Ashforth (1992), 'Alumni and their alma maters: a partial test of the reformulated model of organizational identification'. *Journal of Organizational Behavior* 13, 103–23.

Malinowski, B. (1944), *A Scientific Theory of Culture and Other Essays*. Chapel Hill, NC: University of North Carolina Press.

Mancia, M. (2006), 'Implicit memory and early unrepressed unconscious: their role in the therapeutic process (How the neurosciences can contribute to psychoanalysis)'. *International Journal of Psychoanalysis* 87 (1), 83–103.

Mandler, J. M. (1988), 'How to build a baby: on the development of an accessible representational system'. *Cognitive Development* 3, 113–36.

Mandler, J. M. (1992), 'How to build a baby: II. Conceptual primitives'. *Psychological Review* 99 (4), 587–604.

Mandler, J. M. (2006), *The Foundations of Mind: Origins of Conceptual Thought*. Oxford: Oxford University Press.

Martens, M. (2004), 'The *Mithraeum* in Tienen: small finds and what they can tell us'. In *RMESF*, pp. 25–56.

Martens, M. and G. De Boe (eds) (2004), *Roman Mithraism: The Evidence of the Small Finds*. Brussels: Institute for the Archaelogical Heritage.

Martin, L. H. (1987), *Hellenistic Religions: An Introduction*. Oxford: Oxford University Press.

Martin, L. H. (1994), 'Reflections on the Mithraic tauroctony as cult scene'. *SM* 217–24. Reprinted in Martin 2015, pp. 21–8.

Martin, L. H. (1997), 'Akin to the gods or simply one to another? Comparison with respect to religions in antiquity'. In H. J. Klimkeit (ed.), *Vergleichen und Verstehen in der Religionswissenschaft*. Wiesbaden: Harrassowitz, pp. 147–59.

Martin, L. H. (2004a), 'Towards a scientific history of religions'. In H. Whitehouse and H. L. Martin (eds), *Theorizing Religions Past: Archaeology, History, and Cognition*. Walnut Creek. CA: AltaMira, pp. 7–16.

Martin, L. H. (2004b), 'Performativity, narrativity and cognition: demythologizing the Roman cult of Mithras'. In W. Braun (ed.), *Rhetoric and Reality in Early Christianity*. Waterloo, ON: Wilfrid Laurier University Press, pp. 187–217.

Martin, L. H. (2004c), 'Ritual competence and Mithraic ritual'. In T. Light and B. Wilson (eds), *Religion as a Human Capacity*: A Festschrift in Honor of E. Thomas Lawson. Leiden: Brill, pp. 245–64.

Martin, L. H. (2005), 'Towards a cognitive history of religions'. *Revista de Estudos da Religião* 4, 7–18.

Martin, L. H. (2006), 'The Roman cult of Mithras: a cognitive perspective'. *Religio* 14 (2), 131–46. In Martin 2015 (as Chapter 3), pp. 29–40.

Martin, L. H. (2009), 'The Amor and Psyche relief in the mithraeum of Capua Vetere: an exceptional case of Graeco-Roman syncretism or an ordinary instance of human cognition?' In Casadio and Johnston 2009, pp. 277–89 (Chapter 16). Reprinted in Martin 2015, pp. 107–18 (Chapter 8).

Martin, L. H. (2012a), 'Cognition and religion'. *Culture and Research* 1, 25–42.
Martin, L. H. (2012b), 'The future of the past: the history of religions and cognitive historiography'. *Religio* 20 (2), 155–71.
Martin, L. H. (2013), 'Mithras, Milites, and bovine legs'. *Religio* 21, 49–55.
Martin, L. H. (2014a), *Deep History, Secular Theory. Historical and Scientific Studies of Religion*. Boston: De Gruyter.
Martin, L. H. (2014b), 'Introduction to the Issue'. *Journal of Cognitive Historiography* 1 (1), 10–13.
Martin, L. H. (2015), *The Minds of Mithraists: Historical and Cognitive Studies in the Roman Cult of Mithras*. London: Bloomsbury Academic.
Martin, L. H. (2015a), 'The landscapes and mindscape of the Roman cult of Mithras'. In Martin 2015 (as Chapter 6), pp. 75–88.
Martin, L. H. and J. Sørensen (eds) (2011), *Past Minds: Studies in Cognitive Historiography*. London: Equinox.
Matlin, M. W. (2004), *Cognition*. New York: Wiley.
May, M. (2007), *Sensation and Perception*. New York: Chelsea House Publications.
McAdams, D. P. (2008), 'Personal narratives and the life story'. In O. John, R. Robins, and L. A. Pervin (eds), *Handbook of Personality: Theory and Research*. New York: Guilford, pp. 241–261.
McCarthy, J. and J. P. Hayes (1969), 'Some philosophical problems from the standpoint of artificial intelligence'. *Machine Intelligence* 4, 463–502.
McCauley, R. N. and E. T. Lawson (2002), *Bringing Ritual to Mind: Psychological Foundations of Cultural Forms*. Cambridge: Cambridge University Press.
McElhanon, K. A. (2006), 'From simple metaphors to conceptual blending: the mapping of analogical concepts and the praxis of translation'. *Journal of Translation* 2 (1), 31–81.
Menz, M. D. and R. D. Freeman (2003), 'Stereoscopic depth processing in the visual cortex: a coarse to fine mechanism'. *Nature Neuroscience* 6, 59–65.
Merkelbach, R. (1984), *Mithras*. Königstein: Hain.
Merkelbach, R. (1995), *Isis Regina-Zeus Sarapis: Die griechischägyptische Religion nach den Quellen dargestellt*. Stuttgart: Teubner.
Merleau-Ponty, M. (2002 [1945]), *Phenomenology of Perception*. Trans. C. Smith. London: Routledge.
Merrell, F. (2010), 'Charles Sanders Peirce's concept of the sign'. In P. Cobley (ed.), *The Routledge Companion to Semiotics*. London: Routledge, pp. 28–39.
Michon, J. A. (1990), 'Implicit and explicit representations of time'. In R. A. Block (ed.), *Cognitive Models of Psychological Time*. Hillsdale, NJ: Erlbaum, pp. 37–58.
Mierzwińska-Hajnos, A. (2009), 'Conceptual blending vs. conceptual metaphor theory: a note on the semantics of plant names in English and Polish'. Paper presented at Poznań Linguistic Meeting, 2–5 September 2009. http://wa.amu.edu.pl/pl.m_old/2009/sites/default/files/Abstracts/PLM2009_Abstract_Mierzwinska-Hajnos.pdf

Miller, A. G. (1956), 'The magical number seven, plus or minus two: some limits on our capacity for processing information'. *Psychological Review* 63(2), 81–97.

Miller, E. K. (1999), 'The prefrontal cortex: complex neural properties for complex behavior'. *Neuron*, 22(1), 15–7.

Miller E. K. and J. D. Cohen (2001), 'An integrative theory of prefrontal cortex function'. *Annual Review of Neuroscience* 24, 167–202.

Miller, E. K., D. J. Freedman and J. D. Wallis (2002), 'The prefrontal cortex: categories, concepts and cognition'. *Philosophical Transactions of the Royal Society B: Biological Sciences* 357 (1424), 1123–36.

Minsky, L. M. (1963), 'Steps toward artificial intelligence'. In E. A. Feigenbaum and J. Feldman (eds), *Computers and Thought*. New York: McGraw-Hill, pp. 406–50.

Mithen, S. (1996), *The Prehistory of The Mind: The Cognitive Origins of Art, Religion and Science*. London: Thames & Hudson.

Momigliano, A. (1975), *Alien Wisdom: The Limits of Hellenization*. Cambridge: Cambridge University Press.

Mou, W., T. P. McNamara, C. M. Valiquette and B. J. Rump (2004), 'Allocentric and egocentric updating of spatial memories'. *Journal of Experimental Psychology: Learning, Memory, and Cognition* 30 (1), 142–57.

Nadel, L. and L. MacDonald (1980), 'Hippocampus: cognitive map or working memory?' *Behavioral and Neural Biology* 29, 405–409.

Nairne, J. S. (2002). 'Remembering over the short-term: the case against the standard model'. *Annual Review of Psychology* 53, 53–81.

Narayanan, S. (1997), *Embodiment in Language Understanding: Sensory-Motor Representations for Metaphoric Reasoning about Event Descriptions*. PhD dissertation, University of California, Berkeley.

Navarrete, C. D., R. Kurzban, D. M. Fessler and L. A. Kirkpatrick (2004), 'Anxiety and intergroup bias: terror management or coalitional psychology?' *Group Processes and Intergroup Relations* 7(4), 370–97.

Neisser, U. (1976), *Cognition and Reality: Principles and Implications of Cognitive Psychology*. San Francisco: Freeman.

Neisser, U. (2003), 'Self-narratives: true and false'. In U. Neisser and R. Fivush (eds), *The Remembering Self: Construction and Accuracy in the Self-Narrative*. Cambridge, New York: Cambridge University Press, pp. 1–18.

Newell, A., J. C. Shaw and H. A. Simon (1958), 'Elements of a theory of human problem solving'. *Psychological Review* 65, 151–66.

Nieuwenhuys, R., J. Voogd and C. van Huijzen (2008 [1976]), *The Human Central Nervous System: A Synopsis and Atlas*. Berlin: Springer-Verlag.

Nock, A. D. (1933), *Conversion: The Old and the New in Religion from Alexander the Great to Augustine of Hippo*. Oxford: Oxford University Press.

Nock, A. D. (1937), 'The genius of Mithraism'. *JRS* 27, 108–14.

Noland, C. (2009), *Agency and Embodiment: Performing Gesture/Producing Culture*. Cambridge, MA: Harvard University Press.

North, J. D. (1990), 'Astronomical symbolism in the Mithraic religion'. *Centaurus* 33, 115–48.
O'Keefe, J. (1991), 'An allocentric spatial model for the hippocampal cognitive map'. *Hippocampus* 1, 230–5.
O'Keefe, J. and L. Nadel (1978), *The Hippocampus as a Cognitive Map*. Oxford: Oxford University Press. [Available online at www.cognitivemap.net/]
Olive, C. (2004), 'La faune exhumée des *mithraea* de Martigny (Valais) et d'Orbe-Boscéaz (Vaud) en Suisse'. In RMESF, pp. 147–56.
Pachis, P. and O. Panagiotidou (2017), 'The long way from cognitive science to history: to shorten the distance and fill in the blanks'. In L. H. Martin and D. Wiebe (eds), *Religion Explained? The Cognitive Science of Religion After Twenty-Five Years*. London: Bloomsbury.
Panagiotidou, O. (2008), 'World view of the Mithras cult'. *TOTEM Tidsskrift ved Afdeling for Religionsvidenskab Aarhus University* 20, 59–70.
Panagiotidou, O. (2009), *The World View of the Mithras Cult: A Cognitive Approach*. Unpublished MA thesis. Aristotle University of Thessaloniki.
Panagiotidou, O. (2010), 'Transformation of the initiates' identities after their initiation into the mysteries of Mithras'. *Bulletin for the Study of Religion* 40, 52–61.
Panagiotidou, O. (2012a), 'From body to space and time: perceiving space and time in the Mithras cult'. *Sacra* 1, 33–47.
Panagiotidou, O. (2012b), 'The cognitive route of "star talk": the scene of tauroctony as a system of signs'. *Pantheon* 7 (1), 70–8.
Panagiotidou, O. (2013), 'Mithras and Charles S. Peirce: history needs theory'. *Religio* 21, 43–7.
Panagiotidou, O. (2014), 'Disease and Healing in the Asclepius Cult: A Cognitive Approach'. Unpublished PhD dissertation. Thessaloniki: Aristotle University of Thessaloniki.
Panagiotidou, O. (2016a), 'Religious healing and the Asclepius cult: a case of placebo effects'. *Open Theology* 2 (1), 79–91.
Panagiotidou, O. (2016b), 'Asclepius' myths and healing narratives: counter-intuitive concepts and cultural expectations'. *Open Library of Humanities* 2 (1), p.e6.
Panagiotidou, O. (forthcoming), 'Secrecy in the Mithras cult: concealment, cognition and social cohesion'. *The Mysteries of Mithras and other Mystic Cults in the Roman World*. Symposium Peregrinum 2016. Tarquinia, Vulci, Marino - Soprintendenza Archeologia del Lazio e dell'Etruria Meridionale, 16–19 June 2016.
Parslow, D. M., B. Brooks, S. Fleminger, D. Rose, J. A. Gray, V. Giampietro, M. J. Brammer, S. Williams, D. Gasston, C. Andrew, G. N. Vythelingum, G. Ioannou, A. Simmons and R. G. Morris (2004), 'Allocentric spatial memory activation of the hippocampal formation measured with fMRI'. *Neuropsychology* 18 (3), 450–61.
Pearse, R., *Catalogue of Monuments and Images of Mithras*: http://roger-pearse.com/mithras/display.php?page=selected_monuments (see Preface).
Peirce, C. S. (1868), 'On a new list of categories'. *Proceedings of the American Academy of Arts and Sciences* 7, 287–98.

Peirce, C. S. (1931-58), *The Collected Papers of C. S. Peirce*. Vols 1-6, ed. C. Hartshorne and P. Weiss; vols 7-8, ed. A. W. Burks. Cambridge, MA: Harvard University Press.

Piccottini, G. (1994), *Mithrastempel in Virunum*. Klagenfurt: Verlag des Geschichtsvereines für Kärnten.

Pind, J. (2012), 'Figure and ground at 100'. *The Psychologist* 25 (1), 90-1.

Platt, V. (2011), *Facing the Gods: Epiphany and Representation in Graeco-Roman Art, Literature and Religion*. Cambridge: Cambridge University Press.

Ponzio, A. (2014), 'Not an individual, but a dual self (at least)'. In T. Thellefsen and B. Sorensen (eds), *Charles Sanders Peirce in His Own Words (Semiotics, Communication and Cognition)*. Berlin: De Gruyter, pp. 443-50.

Pöppel, E. (1997), 'A hierarchical model of temporal perception'. *Trends in Cognitive Sciences* 1 (2), 56-61.

Pöppel, E. (2004), 'Lost in time: a historical frame, elementary processing units and the 3-second window'. *Acta Neurobiologiae Experimentalis* 64, 295-301.

Porphyry (1969), *The Cave of the Nymphs in the Odyssey*. Ed. and trans. Seminar Classics 609, State University of New York at Buffalo. Buffalo: Arethusa.

Pyysiäinen, I. (2003), *How Religion Works: Towards a New Cognitive Science of Religion*. Leiden: Brill.

Radcliffe-Brown, A. R. (1952), *Structure and Function in Primitive Society*. Glencoe, IL: Free Press.

Raja, R. and J. Rüpke (2015), 'Appropriating religion: methodological issues in testing the "lived ancient religion" approach'. *RRE* 1 (1), 11-19.

Randolph-Seng, B. and M. E. Nielsen (2009), 'Opening the doors of perception: priming altered states of consciousness outside of conscious awareness'. *Archive for the Psychology of Religion* 31, 237-60.

Rappaport, R. A. (1967), 'Ritual regulation of environmental relations among a New Guinea people'. *Ethnology* 6 (1), 17-30.

Rappaport, R. A. (1999), *Ritual and Religion in the Making of Humanity*. Cambridge: Cambridge University Press.

Revlin, R. (2012). *Cognition: Theory and Practice*. New York: Worth Publishers.

Richardson-Klavehn, A. and R. A. Bjork (1988), 'Measures of memory'. *Annual Review of Psychology* 39, 475-543.

Rigney, D. (1979), 'Secrecy and social cohesion'. *Society* 16 (4), 52-5.

Rives, J. B. (2007), *Religion in the Roman Empire*. Malden, MA: Blackwell Publishing.

Robertson-Smith, W. (1889), *Religion of the Semites*. London: Adam & Charles Black.

Roepstorff, A., Niewöhner, J. and S. Beck (2010), 'Enculturing brains through patterned practices'. *Neural Networks* 23, 1051-9.

Royden, C. S. and K. D. Moore (2012), 'Use of speed cues in the detection of moving objects by moving observers'. *Vision Research* 59, 17-24.

Rubin, E. (1915), *Synsoplevede Figurer: Studier i psykologisk Analyse. Første Del* [*Visually experienced figures: Studies in psychological analysis. Part one*]. Copenhagen and Christiania: Gyldendalske Boghandel, Nordisk Forlag.

Rubin, E. (1958), 'Figure and ground'. In D. C. Beardslee and M. Wertheimer (eds), *Readings in Perception*. Princeton, NJ: D. Van Nostrand, pp. 194–203.
Rüpke, J. (2007a), *Religion of the Romans*. Cambridge: Polity Press.
Rüpke, J. (ed.) (2007b), *A Companion to Roman Religion*. Malden: Blackwell Publishing.
Rüpke, J., R. Feldmeier, K. L. King, R. Raja, A. Y. Reed, C. Riedweg, S. Schwartz, C. Smith and M. Vinzent (2015), 'Editorial'. *RRE* 1 (1), 1–7.
Rutgers, A. J. (1970), 'Rational interpretation of the ritual of Mithras, and of various other cults'. In E. A. Leemans (ed.), *Anamnesis: Gedenkboek prof. dr. E.A. Leemans*. Brugge: De Tempel, pp. 303–15.
Sahlins, M. (1972), *Stone Age Economics*. Chicago: Aldine-Atherton.
Sandelin, K. G. (1988), 'Mithras-Auriga?' *Arctos: Acta Philologica Fennica* 22, 133–5.
Schacter, D. L. (1987), 'Implicit memory: history and current status'. *Journal of Experimental Learning, Memory, and Cognition* 13, 501–18.
Schacter, D. L., Dobbins, G. I. and M. D. Schnyer (2004), 'Specificity of priming: a cognitive neuroscience perspective'. *Nature Reviews, Neuroscience* 5, 853–62.
Schjoedt, U., J. Sørensen, K. L. Nielbo, D. Xygalatas, P. Mitkidis and J. Bulbulia (2013), 'Cognitive resource depletion in religious interactions'. *Religion, Brain and Behavior* 3 (1), 39–86.
Schütte-Maischatz, A. and E. Winter (2000), 'Kultstätten der Mithrasmysterien in Doliche'. In J. Wagner (ed.), *Gottkönige am Euphrat: Neue Ausgrabungen und Forschungen in Kommagene*. Mainz: Verlag Philipp von Zabern, pp. 93–9.
Sfameni Gasparro, G. (1985), *Soteriology and Mystic Aspects in the Cult of Cybele and Attis*. EPRO 103. Leiden: Brill.
Sgubini Moretti, A. M. (1979), 'Nota preliminare su un mitreo scoperto a Vulci'. In *MM*, pp. 259–76.
Shantz, C. (2009), *Paul in Ecstasy: The Neurobiology of the Apostle's Life and Thought*. Cambridge: Cambridge University Press.
Shapiro, L. (2011), *Embodied Cognition*. London: Routledge.
Sherrington, C. S. (1906), *The Integrative Action of the Nervous System*. New Haven, CT: Yale University Press; London: H. Milford, Oxford University Press.
Sholl, M. J. (2001), 'The role of a self-reference system in spatial navigation'. In D. Montello (ed.), *Spatial Information Theory: Foundations of Geographical Information Science*. Berlin: Springer-Verlag, pp. 217–32.
Sholl, M. J. and G. P. Bartels (2002), 'The role of self-to-object updating in orientation-free performance on spatial memory tasks'. *Journal of Experimental Psychology: Learning, Memory, and Cognition* 28, 422–36.
Sholl, M. J. and T. Nolin (1997), 'Orientation specificity in representations of place'. *Journal of Experimental Psychology: Learning, Memory, and Cognition* 23, 1494–1507.
Simmel, G. (1906), 'The sociology of secrecy and of secret societies'. *American Journal of Sociology* 11, 441–98.
Simos, P. (2002), *Vision in the Brain: Organization and Plasticity in the Visual System*. Lisse: Swets & Zeitlinger.

Singer, J. A. and P. Salovey (1993), *The Remembered Self: Emotion and Memory in Personality*. New York: Free Press.

Sinha, C. (1996), 'Theories of symbolization and development'. In A. Lock and R. C. Peters (eds), *Handbook of Human Symbolic Evolution*. Oxford: Clarendon Press, pp. 483–500.

Sjöblom, T. (2005), 'Storytelling: narratives of the mind and modes of religiosity'. *Historical Reflections* 31(2), 235–54.

Slingerland, E. (2014), 'Toward a second wave of consilience in the cognitive scientific study of religion'. *Journal of Cognitive Historiography* 1 (1), 121–30.

Slone, J. (2004), *Theological Incorrectness: Why Religious People Believe What They Shouldn't*. Oxford: Oxford University Press.

Smail, D. L. (1999), *Imaginary Cartographies: Possession and Identity in Late Medieval Marseille*. Ithaca, NY: Cornell University Press.

Smail, D. L. (2008), *On Deep History and the Brain*. Berkeley, CA: University of California Press.

Smith, R. S. and S. M. Trzaskoma (trans) (2007), *Apollodorus' Library and Hyginus' Fabulae: Two Handbooks of Greek Mythology*. Indianapolis, IN: Hackett.

Snyder, C. R. and H. L. Fromkin (1980), *Uniqueness: the Human Pursuit of Difference*. New York: Plenum Press.

Sosis, R. (2006), 'Religious behaviors, badges and bans: signaling theory and the evolution of religion'. In P. McNamara (ed.), *Where God and Science Meet: How Brain and Evolutionary Studies Alter our Understanding of Religion*. Westport, CT: Praeger, pp. 61–86.

Speidel, M. (1980), *Mithras-Orion: Greek Hero and Roman Army God*. EPRO 81. Leiden: Brill.

Sperber, D. (1975), *Rethinking Symbolism*. Cambridge: Cambridge University Press.

Sperber, D. (1985), 'Anthropology and psychology: towards an epidemiology of representations'. *Man* N.S. 20 (1), 73–89.

Sperber, D. (1996), *Explaining Culture: A Naturalistic Approach*. Oxford: Blackwell.

Squire L. R. and S. M. Zola (1998), 'Episodic memory, semantic memory, and amnesia'. *Hippocampus* 8, 205–11.

Stark, K. B. (1869), 'Die Mithrasstein von Dormagen'. *Jahrbücher des Vereins von Altertumsfreunden im Rheinlande* 46, 1–25.

Suthana, N. A., A. D. Ekstrom, S. Moshirvaziri, B. Knowltonand and S. Y. Bookheimer (2009), 'Human hippocampal CA1 involvement during allocentric encoding of spatial information'. *The Journal of Neuroscience* 29 (34), 10512–19.

Swann, W. B., J. A. Gómez, J. Dovidio, S. Hart and J. Jetten (2010). 'Dying and killing for one's group: identity fusion moderates responses to intergroup versions of the trolley problem'. *Psychological Science* 21 (8), 1176–83.

Swann, W. B., J. Jensen, J. A. Gómez, H. Whitehouse and B. Bastian (2012), 'When group membership gets personal: a theory of identity fusion'. *Psychological Review* 119 (3), 441–56.

Swanson, L. W. and G. J. Mogenson (1981), 'Neural mechanisms for the functional coupling of autonomic, endocrine and somatomotor responses in adaptive behavior'. *Brain Research Reviews* 3 (1), 1–34.

Swerdlow, N. M. (1991), 'On the cosmical mysteries of Mithras' (review article of Ulansey 1989). *Classical Philology* 86, 48–63.

Tajfel, H. (1970), 'Experiments in intergroup discrimination'. *Scientific American* 223, 96–102

Tajfel, H. (1974), 'Social identity and intergroup behaviour'. *Social Science Information* 13, 65–93.

Tajfel, H. (1985), 'The social identity theory of intergroup behavior'. In S. Worchel and W. G. Austin (eds), *Psychology of Intergroup Relations*. Chicago: Nelson-Hall, pp. 33–48.

Tajfel, H. and J. C. Turner (1979), 'An integrative theory of intergroup conflict'. In W. G. Austin and S. Worchel (eds), *The Social Psychology of Intergroup Relations*. Monterey, CA: Brooks-Cole, pp. 33–47.

Tajfel, H. and J. C. Turner (1986), 'The social identity theory of intergroup behaviour'. In S. Worchel and W. G. Austin (eds), *Psychology of Intergroup Relations*. Chicago: Nelson-Hall, pp. 7–24.

Talbert, R. J. A. (2010), *Rome's World: The Peutinger Map Reconsidered*. Cambridge: Cambridge University Press. Available online at www.cambridge.org/us/talbert/index.html.

Taylor, E., *Ostia: Mithraea*. Available online at www.ostia-antica.org/dict/topics/mithraea/mithraea.htm.

Tertullian (1966), *De Corona Militis*. Ed. J. Fontaine. Paris: Presses Universitaires de France.

Thagard, P. (1996), *Mind: Introduction to Cognitive Science*. Cambridge MA: MIT Press.

Tilley, C. (2004), 'From body to place to landscape: a phenomenological perspective'. In C. Tilley and W. Bennett (eds), *Materiality of Stone: Explorations in Landscape Phenomenology*. Oxford: Berg, pp. 1–31.

Tomasello, M. (1999), *The Cultural Origins of Human Cognition*. Cambridge, MA: Harvard University Press.

Tulving, E. (1972), 'Episodic and semantic memory'. In E. Tulving and W. Donaldson (eds), *Organization of Memory*. New York: Academic Press, pp. 381–403.

Tulving E. (1983), *Elements of Episodic Memory*. Vol. 2. New York: Oxford University Press.

Tulving, E. (2002), 'Episodic memory: from mind to brain'. *Annual Review of Psychology* 53, 1–25.

Tulving, E. and J. E. Patkau (1962), 'Concurrent effects of contextual constraint and word frequency on immediate recall and learning of verbal material'. *Canadian Journal of Psychology* 16, 83–95.

Turcan, R. (1996), *The Cults of the Roman Empire*. Trans. A. Nevill. Malden, MA: Blackwell.

Turcan, R. (1999), 'Hiérarchie sacerdotale et astrologie dans les mystères de Mithra'. *La Science des cieux: Sages, mages, astrologues. Res Orientales* 12, 249–61.

Turcan, R. (2000), *Mithra et le mithriacisme*. Paris: Les Belles Lettres.

Turner, J. C. (1978), 'Social categorization and social discrimination in the minimal group paradigm'. In H. Tajfel (ed.), *Differentiation Between Social Groups: Studies in the Social Psychology of Intergroup Relations*. London: Academic Press, pp. 235–50.

Turner, J. C. (1985), 'Social categorization and the self-concept: a social cognitive theory of group behavior'. *Advances in Group Processes: Theory and Research* 2, 77–122.

Turner, J. and O. Penny (1986), 'The significance of the social identity concept for social psychology with reference to individualism, interactionism and social influence'. *British Journal of Social Psychology* 25 (3), 237–252.

Turner, J. C., M. A. Hogg, P. J. Oakes, S. D. Reicher and M. S. Wetherell (1987), *Rediscovering the Social Group: A Self-Categorization Theory*. Oxford: Blackwell.

Turner, M. (1987), *The Body in the Mind: The Bodily Basis of Meaning, Imagination, and Reason*. Chicago: University of Chicago Press.

Turner, M. (1996), *The Literary Mind: The Origins of Thought and Language*. New York: Oxford University Press.

Ulansey, D. (1989), *The Origins of the Mithraic Mysteries: Cosmology and Salvation in the Ancient World*. New York: Oxford University Press.

Vander Wall, S. B. (1990). *Food Hoarding in Animals*. Chicago: University of Chicago Press.

Varela, F., E. Thompson and E. Rosch (1991), *The Embodied Mind: Cognitive Science and Human Experience*. Cambridge, MA: MIT Press.

Vermaseren, M. J. (1956–60), *Corpus Inscriptionum et Monumentorum Religionis Mithriacae*. 2 vols. The Hague: Martinus Nijhoff. (V + number = the number in this catalogue. Numeration is consecutive between volumes. Vol. 1 contains nos 1–1002, Vol. 2 nos 1003–2377; Vol. 2 starts [pp. 11–44] with a Supplement to Vol. 1.)

Vermaseren, M. J. (1960), *Mithra, ce dieu mystérieux*. Paris: Éditions Sequoia.

Vermaseren, M. J. (1963), *Mithras. The Secret God*. Trans. T. and V. Magaw. London: Chatto. (Translation of Vermaseren 1960, above.)

Vermaseren, M. J. (1971), *Mithraica 1: The Mithraeum at Santa Maria Capua Vetere*. EPRO 16. Leiden: Brill.

Vermaseren, M. J. (1982), *Mithriaca 3: The Mithraeum at Marino*. EPRO 16. Leiden: Brill.

Vermaseren, M. J. and E. E. Van Essen (1965), *The Excavations in the Mithraeum of the Church of Santa Prisca in Rome*. Leiden: Brill.

Villenger, J. and B. Waldman (2012), 'Social discrimination by quantitative assessment of immunogenetic similarity'. *Proceedings of the Royal Society B: Biological Sciences* 279 (1746), 4368–74.

Wagemans, J., J. H. Elder, M. Kubovy, S. E. Palmer, M. A. Peterson, M. Singh and R. von der Heydt (2012), 'A century of Gestalt psychology in visual perception:

I. Perceptual grouping and figure–ground organization'. *Psychological Bulletin* 138 (6), 1172–1217.

Waller, D. and E. Hodgson E. (2006), 'Transient and enduring spatial representations under disorientation and self-rotation'. *Journal of Experimental Psychology: Learning, Memory, and Cognition* 32 (4), 867–82.

Walters, V. J. (1974), *The Cult of Mithras in the Roman Province of Gaul*. EPRO 41. Leiden: Brill.

Wang, R. F. and E. S. Spelke (2000), 'Updating egocentric representations in human navigation'. *Cognition* 77, 215–50.

Weber, M. (1947), *The Theory of Social and Economic Organization*. Oxford: Oxford University Press.

Weiss, M. (1998), 'Mithras, der Nachthimmel: eine dekodierung der römischen Mithraskultbilder mit Hilfe des Avesta'. *Traditio* 53, 1–36.

Whitehouse, H. (1995), *Inside the Cult: Religious Innovation and Transmission in Papua New Guinea*. Oxford: Oxford University Press.

Whitehouse, H. (2000), *Arguments and Icons: Divergent Modes of Religiosity*. Oxford: Oxford University Press.

Whitehouse, H. (2002), 'Modes of religiosity: towards a cognitive explanation of the sociopolitical dynamics of religion'. *Method and Theory in the Study of Religion* 14, 293–315.

Whitehouse, H. (2004), *Modes of Religiosity: A Cognitive Theory of Religious Transmission*. Walnut Creek, CA: Altamira Press.

Whitehouse, H. (2005), 'Cognitive historiography: when science meets art'. *Historical Reflections* 31(2), 307–18.

Whitehouse, H. (2008), 'Modes of religiosity'. *Bulletin of the Council of Societies for the Study of Religion* 37 (4), 108–12.

Whitehouse, H. and J. Laidlaw (2004), *Ritual and Memory: Toward a Comparative Anthropology of Religion*. Walnut Creek, CA: AltaMira.

Whitehouse, H. and J. A. Lanman (2014), 'The ties that bind us: ritual, fusion, and identification'. *Current Anthropology* 55 (6), 674–95.

Whitehouse, H. and L. H. Martin (2004), *Theorizing Religions Past: Archaeology, History, and Cognition*. Walnut Creek, CA: AltaMira.

Whitehouse, H. and R. N. McCauley (2005). *Mind and Religion: Psychological and Cognitive Foundations of Religiosity*. Walnut Creek, CA: AltaMira.

Williams, J. M., N. C. Ellis, C. Tyers, H. Healy, G. Rose and A. K. MacLeod (1996), 'The specificity of autobiographical memory and imageability of the future'. *Memory and Cognition* 24 (1), 116–25.

Wiltermuth, S. S. and C. Heath (2009), 'Synchrony and cooperation'. *Psychological Science* 20, 1–5.

Xiao, C., W. Mou and T. P. McNamara (2009), 'Use of self-to-object and object-to-object spatial relations in locomotion'. *Journal of Experimental Psychology: Learning, Memory, and Cognition* 35 (5), 1137–47.

Xygalatas, D. (2006), 'Introduction to the cognitive study of religion'. In H. Whitehouse, *Modes of Religiosity. A Cognitive Theory of Religious Transmission*. Trans. D. Xygalatas (in Greek). Thessaloniki: Vanias, pp. 9–87.

Xygalatas, D., U. Schjoedt, J. Bulbulia, I. Konvalinka, E. M. Jegindø, P. Reddish, A. W. Geertz and A. Roepstoff (2013), 'Autobiographical memory in a fire-walking ritual'. *Journal of Cognition and Culture* 13, 1–16.

Yamamoto, N. and A. L. Shelton (2005), 'Visual and proprioceptive representations in spatial memory'. *Memory and Cognition* 33 (1), 140–50.

Yee, E., E. G. Chrysikou and S. L. Thompson-Schill (2013), 'The cognitive neuroscience of semantic memory'. In K. Ochsner and S. Kosslyn (eds), *The Oxford Handbook of Cognitive Neuroscience*. Vol. 1. Oxford: Oxford University Press, pp. 353–74.

Index

allocentric mapping 77–8, 79, 82, 95, 102–3
Ambrosiaster 42
apprehension of symbols 8–9, 11, 46–7
Apuleius 39–40
Asclepius cult 54–5
authority figures 144–5
    absence of 145–6, 151–2

Barsalou, L.W. 23, 26–7
Beck, R. 9, 10, 11, 28, 38–51 *passim*, 61–2, 89–113 *passim*, 125–39 *passim*, 148–9
Bremmer, J.N. 38
Bruner, J. 35
bull-killing *see* tauroctony
Burkert, W. 148–9

Capua mithraeum 43–4
'cattle-theft' initiation 42–3, 57, 62
causality 21
Cautes and Cautopates (torchbearers) 109–12, 134, 136
Celsus 65
Cicero: 'Dream of Scipio' 51, 90
Clauss, M. 59, 63–4, 149
cognitive approach
    Mithraism 11–12, 165–70
    religious phenomena 3–8
conceptual metaphors/conceptual blending
    conflation theory 33–4
    see also space and time perceptions; tauroctony
container, universe as 92–4, 96–7
creeds/sacred texts, absence of 150–1
cult meal 62–4

Damasio, A. 32–3
Deacon, T. 115, 117, 119, 129
Dirven, L. 9, 10–11, 28
Dura mithraeum 47–8, 56, 63

dysphoric experiences 146–7, 153–4, 156, 164

egocentric perspective 73–4, 75–7
    and allocentric mapping 77–8, 79, 82, 95, 102–3
embodied perception *see* space and time perceptions
epidemiology of representations 154–8
episodic memory 73, 86–7, 146, 147–8, 153–4
equinoxes/solstices 94–5, 99, 101, 104, 106–7, 108, 110–12

Father 40, 46, 47–8, 49, 52–3, 55, 59, 62
Fauconnier, G. and Turner, M. 34, 80–1, 86–7, 96–8
feasting and fellowship 62–4
Felicissimus Mithraeum 48–50, 56–62
Firmicus Maternus 27, 28, 42–3, 57, 62
Franklin, N., and Tversky, T. 78–9

Geertz, A. 4
Geertz, C. 13, 17, 25
Genkin, M. 159, 160, 163
Gordon, R.L. 7, 10, 12, 40, 41, 43–4, 55–7, 58, 59, 60, 101, 110, 111
grade hierarchy 23–5
    interpretation of signs 116–17, 138
    progress up 55–62
    self identity 46–62, 65, 152
    shared secrecy 160–2

Harland, P. 63
Homeric Hymns 128

iconic interpretation: tauroctony 120–5
images 8–9, 148–9
    and assumptions 19–20, 22, 25–6
    image-schemas 75, 118–20, 122–5, 137–8, 155

indexical relationships 118–19, 120, 127, 128–9, 139
initiation *see* rituals

Johnson, C. 33–4
Johnson, M. 34–6, 64, 67
journey metaphor
　progress up grade hierarchy 55–62
　purposeful activities and life 64–6
　souls' journey 105–9, 111–13

Kearney, M. 18–22, 23
kin-detection mechanisms 147
Köln vessel 103, 104
Konjic mithraeum 62–3

ladder concept 65, 107–8, 109
Lakoff, G. and Johnson, M. 33, 34, 50, 64, 66, 76, 84, 85–6, 87, 88, 90
Lion 40, 47, 52–3, 55, 59–61
'lived experience' of initiation 41–6
'lived objects'/'lived subjects' 73–4
'lived religion' 10–11

Mainz Vessel 45–6, 54, 61–2, 103
Martin, L.H. 4–5, 6–7, 10, 27–8, 40, 41, 44, 149, 152
memory
　episodic 73, 86–7, 146, 147–8, 153–4
　long-term and short-term 73
　organization of 72–3, 75
　semantic 73, 85, 144, 147–8, 156
　and time 83, 84–5, 86–7, 104–5
mental representations 19–20, 156
Merkelbach, R. 41, 44, 129
Merleau-Ponty, M. 70–1, 75–6, 77, 83
Michon, J.A. 83
minimal group characteristics 142–3, 163
Mithras cult, definition of 1–2
modes theory of religiosity 144–50
　and epidemiology of representations 154–8
　imaginistic 150–4
moving observer metaphor of time 85–7, 108
moving time metaphor 87, 88, 94–5, 108
mysteries and secrecy 158–64
mythology, absence of 150–1

Narayanan, S. 33–4
narratives 27–8, 32–6, 67, 86, 153–4
neural perspective
　embodied perception 71–2, 77
　narrative construction of self 32–6
Nock, A.D. 148
Numenius 106–7
Nymphus 40, 44, 49, 52–3, 57

Origen 65, 107

Panagiotidou, O. 54–5
Peirce, C.S. 116–17, 137
Persian grade 40, 47, 52–3, 55, 60–1
Persian origins 3, 89, 123–4
Petronius 39
Philolaus 91–2
planets
　and grades 48–9, 51–4, 55–6, 57, 60–2, 65
　motion of 91–5
Plato 94
Plutarch 8–9, 40–1, 136
Pöppel, E. 83, 84, 85
Porphyry
　On Abstinence 41, 55, 59
　On the Cave 3, 11, 24, 39, 40, 60, 61, 65, 89–91, 96–7, 98, 101, 106, 111–12, 115, 125, 127, 151
Proclus 106–7
Ptolemic cosmology 91–5, 126–7
purposeful activities and life 64–6
Pythagoras 91–2

Raja, R. and Rüpke, J. 10
Raven 40, 47, 48, 49, 52–3, 55, 56–7, 59
raven-headed servitor 56, 62–3
Rigney, D. 158, 161
rituals/initiation 25–7, 28, 102–5
　'cattle-theft' 42–3, 57, 62
　'lived experience' of 41–6
　narrative of 67
　secrecy 158–9, 161–2, 164
　and social cohesion 143–50, 152, 153–4
Soldier 58–9
souls' journey 105–9, 112–13
Roman Empire and cults 1–3
Rüpke, J. 11
Rutgers, A.J. 129

Santa Prisca mithraeum 48, 56, 63
secrecy 158–64
self identity 31–2
  cult meal 62–4
  grade hierarchy 46–62, 65, 152
  journey metaphor 55–62, 64–6
  'lived experience' of initiation 41–6
  narrative construction of 32–6
  narrative of initiation and initiates' life-stories 67
  in society and cult 36–41
self-essence 147
self-perception 20–1
semantic memory 73, 85, 144, 147–8, 156
sensory perception
  visual system 74, 76, 120–2
  and world view 18–20
Sette Sfere mithraeum 100–1, 102, 107–8, 110–11
sign interpretations 116–17, 137, 138, 139
Simmel, G. 158, 159, 160, 162, 163
social identity/social cohesion 141–2
  feasting and fellowship 62–4
  and group characteristics 142–3
  and rituals 143–50, 152, 153–4
  secrecy and mysteries 158–64
Soldier 40, 47, 52–3, 58–9
solstices/equinoxes 94–5, 99, 101, 104, 106–7, 108, 110–12
souls' journey 105–9, 111–13
space and time perceptions 21, 24
  Cautes and Cautopates 109–12
  mithraea/cave 89–91
  Mithraic universe 95–105
  Ptolemaic cosmology 91–5, 126
  souls' journey 105–9, 112–13
  space: embodied perception 70–82
    body-schema and short-term egocentric maps 75–7
    conceptual blending and 'material anchors' of spatial orientation 80–2
    conceptual metaphor of universe 78–80
    egocentric point of view 73–4
    image-schemas 75
    memory organization 72–3, 75
    neural underpinnings 71–2, 77
    short-term egocentric and long-term allocentric maps 77–8, 79, 82

time: metaphorical perception 83–8
  and memory 83, 84–5, 86–7, 104–5
  primary and complex metaphors 85–8
Sperber, D. 116, 155–6, 157
star-chart 133–7
'star talk' 131–3
sun, passage of 94–5, 98–103, 108, 110–12
Sun-Runner 40, 47, 48, 49, 52, 61–2
symbola 24, 27–8
symbols/symbolic systems 10–11, 17, 25–7
  apprehension of 8–9, 11, 46–7
  see also tauroctony

Tajfel, H. 142, 143
tauroctony 98–9, 115
  iconography: first level interpretation 120–5
  indexical and symbolic interpretation 125–31
  initiate's process of interpretation 116–20
  as map/star-chart 133–7
  plausibility of meanings in interpretation 137–9
  shared secrecy 161–2
  and 'star talk' as view of heavens 131–3
  and torchbearers 110–11, 134, 136
Tertullian 26, 58
time *see* space and time perceptions
Turcan, R. 49
Turner, J.C. 142, 143
'turning points' 35, 41–2

'up' and 'down' metaphors 109–10, 112
'up' and 'higher' metaphors and grade hierarchy 49–62

Vermaseren, M. J. 37, 43
visual representation *see* images; symbols/symbolic systems; tauroctony
visual system 74, 76, 120–2
Vulci mithraeum 99–100, 103

Whitehouse, H. 6, 12, 146, 149, 154–5
  and Lanman, J.A. 143, 144–5, 146–8, 149–50, 153, 154–5

women 40–1, 55
world view 17–18
    Kearney model 18–22, 23
    Mithraic 23–9

zodiac 93–5, 99–103, 104, 106–8, 110–12
Zoroaster 24, 89, 90, 96, 151

www.ingramcontent.com/pod-product-compliance
Lightning Source LLC
Chambersburg PA
CBHW062216300426
44115CB00012BA/2086